从"雷人"到"达人"：100个网络热词汉译英

The Chinese-English Translation of 100 Internet Hot Words

王逢鑫　著

Written by Wang Fengxin

北京大学出版社
PEKING UNIVERSITY PRESS

图书在版编目(CIP)数据

从"雷人"到"达人"：100个网络热词汉译英/王逢鑫著.—北京：北京大学出版社，2012.8

(英语好学系列)

ISBN 978-7-301-20982-0

Ⅰ.①从… Ⅱ.①王… Ⅲ.①英语－词汇－自学参考资料 Ⅳ.①H313

中国版本图书馆CIP数据核字(2012)第163129号

书　　名：从"雷人"到"达人"：100个网络热词汉译英

著作责任者：王逢鑫　著

责 任 编 辑：孙　莹

标 准 书 号：ISBN 978-7-301-20982-0/H·3105

出 版 发 行：北京大学出版社

地　　址：北京市海淀区成府路205号　100871

网　　址：http://www.pup.cn　电子信箱：zbing@pup.pku.edu.cn

电　　话：邮购部62752015　发行部62750672　编辑部62754382

出版部62754962

印　刷　者：北京宏伟双华印刷有限公司

经　销　者：新华书店

880毫米×1230毫米　A5　8.875印张　310千字

2012年8月第1版　2012年8月第1次印刷

定　　价：26.00元

作者简介

王逢鑫，1939年生于山东省青岛市。1957年考入北京大学西方语言文学系英国语言文学专业，攻读英国语言文学。1962年毕业后留校任教，任北京大学外国语学院英语语言文学系教授、博士生导师。1973年，赴英国埃塞克斯大学短期进修。1981年至1983年，在英国爱丁堡大学中文系教授中国文学、语言和文化。曾三次在巴黎联合国教育、科学和文化组织工作，1979年担任同声传译，1990年担任笔译，1999年担任审校。1992年赴加拿大从事加拿大研究。学术领域涉及：语言学（应用语言学、语义学、词汇学、词典学、句法学、语言测试等）、英美文学（诗歌、小说、散文等）、跨文化研究（美国研究、英国研究、加拿大研究等）、及翻译（口译与笔译）理论与实践，在这些领域均有著述。毕生从事教育事业和中外文化交流。主要著作有：

1）《英语意念语法》，北京：北京大学出版社，1989
《英语意念语法（修订版）》，北京：外文出版社，1999
《王逢鑫文法语义篇》，台北：台湾经典传讯，2004
《王逢鑫文法形式篇》，台北：台湾经典传讯，2004

2）《英语情态表达法》，香港：香港商务印书馆，1990；台北：台湾商务印书馆，1991; 北京：商务印书馆国际有限公司，1996

3）《活用英语动词》，香港：香港商务印书馆，1990；台北：台湾商务印书馆，1991；北京：商务印书馆国际有限公司，1996

4）《英汉意念分类词典》，北京：北京大学出版社，1991
《常春藤TOEFL分类式字汇》，台北：台湾常春藤解析英语杂志社，1991
《英语词汇分类联想学习法》，北京：外文出版社，2000

5）《汉英口译教程》，北京：北京大学出版社，1992

6）《英语词汇的魅力》，北京：北京大学出版社，1995
《英语词汇的魅力（修订版）》，北京：外文出版社，2003
《繁星组合英文学习法》，台北：台湾经典传讯，1999
《王逢鑫词汇繁星篇（日常用语）》，台北：台湾经典传讯，2004
《王逢鑫词汇组合篇（自然万象）》，台北：台湾经典传讯，2004

7）《英语构词的玄妙》，北京：北京大学出版社，1997
《英语构词的玄妙（修订版）》，北京：外文出版社，2003

8）《汉英饮食文化词典》，北京：外文出版社，1998
9）《英语同义表达法》，北京：外文出版社，1999
《王逢鑫进阶文法同义表达（词汇&句法）》，台北：台湾经典传讯，2004
《王逢鑫进阶文法同义表达（逻辑&特例）》，台北：台湾经典传讯，2004
10）《英语模糊语法》，北京：外文出版社，2001
11）《英汉比较语义学》，北京：外文出版社，2001
12）《汉英旅游文化词典》，北京：北京大学出版社，2001
13）《高级汉英口译教程》，北京：外文出版社，2004
14）《英语文化》，北京：北京大学出版社，2004
15）《中国人最易犯的汉译英错误》，北京：中国书籍出版社，2008
16）《100个热门话题汉译英》，北京：北京大学出版社，2009

前　言

这是我继《中国人最易犯的汉译英错误》（北京：中国书籍出版社，2008）和《100个热门话题汉译英》（北京：北京大学出版社，2009）之后，第三本关于汉英翻译的结集。一百篇文章绝大部分在《环球时报》上刊登过，时间是从2009年4月至2011年1月。在这两年里，我们的祖国又经历了许许多多不平凡的事件，其中的关键词在这本书里都有记载。

搞翻译理论的人们在探讨到底有没有“不可译性”（untranslatability），争论不休。搞理论实践的人们不理会这样的讨论，因为在他们眼里从源语（source language）出发，什么都得翻译到目的语（target language）中去。原文终将必须全部变为译文，不存在“不可译的”问题。但是关键在于怎样翻译。“不可译的”东西，大都是中国特有的事物和思维方式，在外语里找不到对应的表达方法。省力的解决方案是音译。过去，有些汉语词汇就是由官话（Mandarin Chinese）或粤语（Cantonese）直接音译而进入英语词汇的，例如原产自中国的水果荔枝（litche/lychee）和龙眼（longan），农作物高粱（kaoliang），食物炒面（chow mein）和馄饨（won ton），补品人参（ginseng）和酒类茅台（Maotai）。英美人只睡床，没有炕，于是英语有了kang（炕）这个单词。英国本是航海国家，素有各式各样的船只，但是没有舢板，于是sampan（舢板）在1620年进入了英语词库。台风是发生在西太平洋和南海的飓风，英语本来有hurricanc（飓风）一词，在1771年纳入typhoon（台风），丰富了英语词汇。英国人虽发明过许许多多的游戏玩法，但是没有麻将，于是在1920年引入了mahjong（麻将）这个词。英美人从不磕头，在1804年将叩头音译为 kowtow。英国人研究中国古代哲学，在1671年吸收了yin yang（阴阳）这个中国独有的概念。近60年，也有一些汉语词汇通过音译进入英语词库。最有趣的例子就是“武术”。本来英语有martial art这个对应词。20世纪70年代李小龙的功夫片风靡欧美，kung fu（功夫）一词广为流传。越来越多的西方人学习武术，kung fu 取代了martial art一词。更近的例子是“气功”。英语本来用 breathing exercises的译法，理解为“呼吸锻炼”。实际上气功锻炼包括呼吸、体势、意念三类手段。breathing exercises不能反映气功的真谛。现在干脆采用qigong表示“气功”。

音译虽然省力，但是不能滥用。英语本是英美人的母语，一个外来词能否进入英语，是他们说了算的。每种语言都有自己的构词法，是以其历史、文化、国情和语言特点等因素为构词理据的。强势语言大多具有排他性，采纳借词是十分保守、十分慎重的。能用自己固有的语义相近的词汇，就决不用外语词汇。往往是“旧瓶装新酒”，给现成的词赋予新义。实在找不到对应词时，才会吸收外来的音译词。一个借词能否长盛不衰，要看它代表的事物或概念能否长期存在。否则虽然会收入词典，但是昙花一现，没有什么生命力。例如“航天员”或“宇航员”，英语中有astronaut和cosmonaut两个对应词。前者用于指美国航天员，后者用于指俄罗斯航天员。由“太空”音译而衍生的taikonaut 一词，用于指中国航天员，已被英美词典收录，而且被英美主流媒体使用过。但是由汉语音译进入英语的词汇很少，可以说是凤毛麟角。近一时期，我国网络流行“给力”一词，有的网民随即杜撰出ungeliable，表示“不给力的”的意思。大家觉得好玩，其实是中国人自娱自乐的游戏。ungeliable 的前缀un-和后缀-able 看似符合英语构词法，但是其根词 geli（给力）不是英语。即使穿靴戴帽，这个词也不是英语，不会被英美人接受和理解。不久前，新闻出版总署发出通知，要求禁止汉语出版物随意夹带使用英文单词或字母缩写等外国语言文字，禁止生造非中非外、含义不清的词语等。ungeliable只能在网上流行一阵，却不能进入出版物，估计最终会被人忘记。

网络热词，有些是外来语。如果要翻译成英语，比较好办，回译（back translation）既可。另有大量网络热词，来自口语、方言、俏皮话或典故。例如本书中的雷人、状元、呛声、蜗居、蚁族、瑞雪兆丰年、扫黄、打黑、围脖、丢面子、出点子、馊点子、撞车、撞墙、撞锁、撞衫、靠色、走光、吃醋、泡汤、给力、达人等等。如果要翻译成英语，当然不能音译，一般也不可直译，因为这些词大都有比喻意义或者歧义，甚至多义。最好的办法是意译。正确理解汉语的意思，正确理解在具体语境中的特殊含义，然后准确找出英语的对应词。

有人问我汉译英的难题是什么。我想难题不少。其中一个难题是套话。这是中文写作和讲话的“八股”，特别表现在讲话中。像“高举红旗”、“奋勇前进”、“为……而奋斗”，诸如此类，随处可见。这些套话直译不难，问题是外国人莫名其妙，听不懂是什么意思。人家不熟悉或不习惯这样的文体。译者想忠实于原文，只能直译，但是难以让英美人明白。关键还是改变文风，少写和少说，或者不写和不说这样的套话，我们翻译时就好办了。以我多年的观察来看，我们的文风已经改变了不少。但是还需继续努力改进。

以上是我多年从事汉英翻译的一些心得体会，敬请读者批评指正。

王逢鑫

2011年元旦于北京海淀区蓝旗营小区

目　录

1 雷人

汉语关键词：雷人、触电、雷倒、被雷倒、被雷到

英语关键词：shock, get a shock, get shocked, be shocked, shocker, shocking, thunderstruck, be thunderstruck, thunderous, thundering

句子：这位魔术师的表演雷倒了大厅里所有的观众。

误译：The performance of the magician thundered all the audience in the hall.

正译：（1）The performance of the magician thunderstruck all the audience in the hall.

（2）The performance of the magician shocked all the audience in the hall.

解释：

to thunder 的意思是 to shout, complain, etc. very loudly and angrily，即“像打雷一样大声怒喝”，没有“令人震惊”的意思。

“雷倒”或“雷人”作为动词，意思是“像雷击一样令人震惊”，是表达情感的使动词。有人将“雷倒”译为 to surprise, to astonish, to astound, to amaze, to upset 等表示“使惊讶”或“使不安”的情感性动词。笔者以为都不能足以表达出“像雷击一样”的感觉。“雷倒”除了直译为 thunderstruck 以外，还不妨译为 to shock。原来 to get a shock 和 to get shocked 有 to get an electric shock 的意思，即“触电”。例如：

1. 不要碰这根电线，否则你会触电的。
   Don’t touch that wire or you’ll get a shock.
2. 当我打开电灯开关时触电了。
   I got a shock when turning on my light switch.
3. 为什么当你触摸一个金属物体时会有时候触电？
   Why do you sometimes get shocked when you touch a metal object?

“雷击”与“触电”在表达“令人震惊”的情感时，有异曲同工之妙，例如：

4. 他的恐怖故事雷倒了屋里所有的人。
   （1）His horrifying story thunderstruck all the people in the room.
   （2）His horrifying story shocked all the people in the room.

“雷人”作为名词，意思是“令人震惊的人”。英语可以译为 shocker。例如：

5. 我从没想到会遇到像这位喜剧演员一样的雷人。
   I never expected that I would meet such a shocker as this comedian.

“被雷倒”或“被雷到”的意思是“像被雷击中一样感到震惊”。英语可以译为 to be thunderstruck, to be shocked, to get shocked, to get a shock。例如：

6. 我们被他晋升的消息雷倒了。
   We were thunderstruck by the news of his promotion.
7. 观众被这位名模的怪异发型雷倒了。
   The spectators were shocked by the famous model for her fantastic hairstyle.
8. 当这个年轻人的父母告诉他是领养的时候，他被雷倒了。
   The young man got shocked when his parents told him he was adopted.
9. 当我注意到她的天赋时，我被雷倒了。
   I got a shock when I noticed her talent.

“雷人的”，意思是“令人震惊的”。英语可以译为 thunderous, thundering, shocking。例如：

10. 从报纸上，我读到一些关于这位名人的雷人新闻。
    From the newspaper, I read some thunderous news about the celebrity.
11. 我在网上冲浪，看到一些雷人新闻。
    I surfed the web and came across some thundering news.
12. 这家网站发布了一些关于这个电影明星的雷人新闻。
    The website issued some shocking news about the film star.
13. 这是我的几位同事可能不喜欢我传给别人的一条雷人语录。
    This is a shocking quotation that some of my colleagues might not like me to pass on.
14. 有办法定位和监视网上活动的家长，可能不知道怎样回应他们孩子的网站的雷人语录。
    Parents who manage to locate and monitor online activity may wonder how to respond to a shocking quotation on their child' s site.
15. 这条广告太雷人了，许多广播电台都已拒绝播送它！
    This advertisement is so shocking that many broadcasting stations have refused to air it!
16. 我碰巧看到一条显然是对准青年人的最雷人的广告，推销酒类消费。
    I happened to see a most shocking advertisement clearly aimed at young people, promoting alcohol consumption.
17. 我们都长时间地仔细注视她的雷人发型。
    We all took a good long look at her shocking hairdo.
18. 这个青年男子进到商店寻找雷人服装。
    The young man went into the store in search of a shocking costume.
19. 我正在琢磨如果这个年轻女孩被迫穿上这身雷人服装会有怎样的感觉。
    I'm wondering how the young girl would feel if forced to wear this

shocking garment.

20. 这个女人身穿雷人服装以与她的雷人发型相匹配，而这种发型是根本不适宜于她进入的教堂的。
The woman wore shocking clothes to match her shocking hairstyle, which was not at all suitable for the church she was in.
21. 他在一个网站创建了一个包含雷人歌曲的新专辑。
He created a new album containing shocking songs at a website.
22. 你听到过的最雷人的歌曲是什么?
What's the most shocking song you've ever heard?
23. 观众在观看这个雷人的舞蹈表演时变得激动起来。
The audience became excited at watching the thunderous dance performance.
24. 最近，在我们的小区里接二连三发生雷人事件。
Recently, there has occurred one shocking event after another in our residential area.
25. 本年度最雷人的故事之一是有个男子怀孕了。
One of the most shocking stories of the year is that a man was pregnant.

2 实名制

汉语关键词： 真名、实名、实名制、假名、化名、笔名、外号、绰号、爱称、昵称、匿名

英语关键词： real name, real-name system, genuine name, true name, actual name, false name, assumed name, pseudonym, alias, pen name, nickname, pet name, anonymous

句子： 如果你想在银行开户，你必须使用实名。

误译： If you want to open a personal account in the bank, you must use your authentic name.

正译： If you want to open a personal account in the bank, you must use your real name.

解释：

authentic 的意思是known to be real and genuine and not a copy，关键之处在于“是原件，不是复制品”。authentic不能用来修饰name。在authentic name brands 中，authentic 修饰name brands，其意义为“货真价实的”。例如：

1. 由于我们的产品是百分之百货真价实的人名品牌，我们决不卖假劣伪冒商品。
As our products are 100% authentic name brands, we won't sell knockoffs or imitations.

2. 在当今世界，有许多人买假的提包，而不是货真价实的人名品牌。
In today's world, there are plenty of people buying handbags that are fake, not authentic name brands.

"实名"或"真名"，英语可以译为 real name, genuine name, true name, actual name。例如：

3. 他在文章后面签署了自己的真名。
He signed the article with his real name.
4. 请在登记表中填写实名，以便我们为您提供服务。
Please sign your real name on the registration form so that we can provide service for you.
5. 对于购买火车票是否要留下真名并出示证件，目前仍有争议。
It is still debatable whether one should leave one's real name and show one's identification when buying train tickets.
6. 他的真名不详，而人们提及他的唯一名字叫"老狼"。
His genuine name is unknown, as the only name he is referred to by is "Old Wolf".
7. 当有人问起他的真名时，他坚持说叫约翰·史密斯。
When asked his genuine name, he insisted it was John Smith.
8. 无人知道他的真名和他的住处。
Nobody knows what his true name is and where he lives.
9. 没有用他的真名，他用约翰·史密斯这个名字将文章送至报社。
Instead of using his true name, he sent the article to the newspaper under the name of John Smith.
10. 他的朋友们都叫他"约约"，可是他的真名叫约翰。
His friends call him Jo-Jo, but his actual name is John.

"实名制"，英语可以译为 real-name system。例如：

11. 我国实行个人存款实名制。
In our country, we adopt real-name system for personal bank account.
12. 有人建议在买火车票时实行实名制。
Some people suggest that we should implement real-name system for train tickets.
13. 有的国家已推行互联网实名制。
In some countries, they have promoted Internet real-name system.

“假名”或“化名”，英语可以译为 false name, assumed name, pseudonym, alias。例如：

14. 一名男子给了警方一个假名，没有意识到他提供的名字是一个被通缉罪犯的名字。
A man gave police a false name, not realizing that the name he provided belonged to a wanted criminal.
15. 他用化名在一个非洲国家做生意。
He conducts business in an African country under an assumed name.
16. 这名侦探用化名登记住进这家旅馆。
The detective checked into the hotel under an alias.
17. 那个叫米克·克拉克的罪犯使用好几个化名
The criminal Mick Clark uses several aliases.
18. 这小偷的真名叫约翰·史密斯，化名叫爱德华·杰克。
The thief's real name was John Smith, alias Edward Ball.

“笔名”，英语可以译为 pen name。例如：

19. 一些作家使用笔名或假名，而不使用真名。
Some writers use pen names or pseudonyms instead of their real names.
20. 他用笔名出版了第一部小说。
He published his first novel under a pen name.

“外号”或“绰号”，英语可以译为 nickname。例如：

21. 他的外号叫“左撇子”，因为他是左利手。
His nickname was Lefty because he was left-handed.
22. 他讨厌人家叫他的外号。
He resents being called by his nickname.

“爱称”或“昵称”，英语可以译为 pet name。例如：

23. 为了表示亲昵，人们爱用昵称。
To show endearment, people tend to use pet names.
24. 我的男朋友决不让我当众用爱称叫他。
My boyfriend won't let me call him by his pet name in public.

“匿名”，英语可以译为 anonymous。例如：

25. 他收到一封匿名信，以死威胁他。
He received an anonymous letter, threatening him with dire death.
26. 一个匿名电话，威胁说在附近的一个超市有炸弹爆炸，引起了恐慌。
An anonymous telephone call threatening a bomb blast in a nearby supermarket sparked panic.

3

创业板

汉语关键词：创业、创业资金、创业板市场、创业板、中国创业板、二板市场、创业精神

英语关键词：start an undertaking, do pioneering work, establish an enterprise, start up a business, set up a company, venture capital, starting capital, growth enterprise market, second-board market, ChiNext stock market, pioneering spirit, enterprising spirit, entrepreneurship

句子：中国创业板是中小企业的重要融资渠道。

误译：The ChiNext stock market is an important financing channel for medium-sized and small enterprises.

正译：The ChiNext stock market is an important financing channel for small and medium-sized enterprises.

解释：

汉语表示“中小”概念时，语序是从大到小排列。而英语则相反。汉语说“中小企业”，英语却说 small and medium-sized enterprises，可能跟读音有关，把长的字词放在后边。“大中小企业”，是 big, small and medium-sized enterprises。英语表示地址时，是从小向大排列。例如：中国北京市北京大学外国语学院英语系，译成英语是 English Department, School of Foreign Languages, Peking university, Beijing, China。

“创业”的第一个意思是“创立基业”、“创办事业”或“开创事业”。英语可以译为 to start an undertaking, to do pioneering work。例如：

1. 俗话说：创业难，守业更难。
   As a common saying goes, it is difficult to start an undertaking and it is even more difficult to maintain the undertaking.
2. 人寿保险是家庭的保障，也是创业守成之道。
   Life insurance is the guarantee of a family, and also a way to start and maintain an undertaking.
3. 我们都非常敬佩他的艰苦创业精神。
   We all have a great admiration for his spirit of working hard to start an undertaking
4. 我们为他的艰辛创业的事迹所感动。
   We were all moved by his deeds to start an undertaking through hard work.
5. 他的一生是一部创业史。

His life is a history of doing pioneering work.

6. 企业要进一步发展，就必须进行二次创业。
   To make further development, an enterprise must start a new undertaking.

“创业”的第二个意思是“创办企业或公司”。英语可以译为 to establish an enterprise, to start up a business, to set up a company。例如：

7. 他表现出极大勇气而放弃了一份安定工作并自己创业，。
   He showed a lot of pluck to leave a safe job and established his own enterprise.
8. 这个学生从大学一毕业就自己创业了。
   As soon as the student graduated from the university, he started up his own business.
9. 你20岁就创业了，真是了不起！
   It's great of you to set up a company at the age of twenty!
10. 90%以上的受访者称，他们想毕业后先找份工作，干个两三年后再考虑自己创业。
    More than 90 percent of the interviewees said they would rather first take up a job upon graduation and then consider starting up their own business two or three years later.

“创业资金”，英语可以译为 venture capital, starting capital。例如：

11. 创业资金极大地推动了那个地区的经济发展。
    Venture capital has greatly promoted the economic development in that area.
12. 当你签租约时，你需要多少创业资金？
    How much starting capital do you need when you sign the lease?

“创业板市场”或“创业板”，也称“二板市场”。英语可以译为 growth enterprise market, second-board market。“中国创业板”，英语译为 the ChiNext stock market。例如：

13. 中国创业板旨在为中小企业融资。
    The ChiNext stock market is designed to attract financing for small to medium sized enterprises.
14. 创业板股份涉及很高的投资风险。
    Growth enterprise market stocks involve a high investment risk.
15. 不同于主板市场，二板市场的目标是为中小型高科技新兴企业提供融资途径和成长空间。
    Being different from the main-board market, the second-board market is aimed at providing small and medium-sized newly-emerging high-tech

enterprises with financing channels and developmental space.

16. 这位专家对中国即将启动创业板持乐观态度。

    The expert takes an optimistic attitude towards the forthcoming launch of the growth enterprise market in China.

“创业精神”，英语可以译为 pioneering spirit, enterprising spirit, entrepreneurship。例如：

17. 给我印象最深的，不是他所取得的显著成就，而是他的创业精神。

    What has impressed me most is not the notable success he has achieved but his pioneering spirit.

18. 中国人民非常敬佩美国人民的创业精神、和他们在民族发展中所取得的骄人成绩。

    The Chinese people greatly admire the American people for their enterprising spirit and the proud achievement they have made in their national development.

19. 创新和创业精神应该并驾齐驱。

    Innovation and entrepreneurship should go hand in hand.

4 潜伏

汉语关键词： 潜伏、潜伏的、潜伏期

英语关键词： hide, be latent, lurk，stay in hiding, latent, lurking, insidious, incubation period, latent period

句子： 这部电影描述了我党地下工作者如何潜伏在敌人内部获取机密情报。

误译： The film depicts how the underground workers from our Party concealed in the interior of the enemy to obtain secret information.

正译： The film depicts how the underground workers from our Party hid in the interior of the enemy to obtain secret information.

解释：

to conceal 是及物动词，与“隐藏东西”、“隐瞒事实”或“掩饰情感”有关，但是不涉及“人的躲藏或潜藏”。to hide 与 to conceal 是同义词，既可以当及物动词用，又可以当不及物动词用。还可以表示“人的躲藏或潜藏”。

“潜伏”的第一个意思是“潜藏”、“暗藏”或“隐藏”。英语可以译为 to hide, to be latent, to lurk。例如：

1. 通过一系列实验，这位科学家发现了一些病毒是如何潜伏在人体内而不产生症状的。
Through a series of experiments, the scientist discovered how some viruses could hide inside the body without producing symptoms.
2. 这艘核潜艇潜伏在海底，伺隙出击。
The nuclear submarine hid at the bottom of the sea, waiting for an opportunity to launch an attack.
3. 这种病毒已在体内潜伏了很多年。
The virus has been latent in the body for many years.
4. 有些癌症能在人体内潜伏一段时间，而不需要立即治疗。
Some cancers can be latent in the body for some time, without requiring immediate treatment.
5. 有条鳄鱼就潜伏在水表层下面。
A crocodile was lurking just below the surface.
6. 这只狮子一动不动地潜伏在高高的草丛中，耐心等待机会抓小鹿。
The lion lurked in the tall grass of the meadow, waiting for a chance to catch the young deer.
7. 夜晚，这些街道潜伏着危险。
At night, danger lurks in these streets.
8. 这位经济学家指出在如此虚假繁荣的背后潜伏着金融危机。
The economist points out that a big financial crisis lurks behind such false prosperity.

“潜伏的”，英语可以译为 latent, lurking, insidious。例如：

9. 这个国际组织由于领导软弱而现在处于潜伏的危机。
The international organization is now in a latent crisis due to weak leadership.
10. 我头脑里依然存在某种潜伏的疑惑。
There still remains some lurking suspicion in my mind.
11. 我们的头脑里存在某种潜伏的怀疑，这使我们想知道是否有人做了不公正的事。
There is some lurking doubt in our minds, which makes us wonder whether an injustice has been done.
12. 这种潜伏的疾病会造成广泛而无法衡量的经济损失。
This insidious disease produces extensive and unmeasured economic losses.
13. 这些专家考察了过度使用杀虫剂对我们的环境的潜伏恶果。
The experts examined the insidious effects of the overuse of insecticide on our environment.

“潜伏期”，指“从病毒或细菌侵入人体到疾病开始显露的一段时间”。英语可以译为 incubation period, latent period。例如：

14. 这种病的潜伏期一般为2至7天，但是可能长达10天。
The incubation period of the disease typically ranges from 2—7 days, but can last up to 10 days.
15. 受感染者经过7至10年时间发展成为艾滋病病人，而这段时间叫做"潜伏期"。
It takes 7 to 10 years for an infected person to become an AIDS patient, and this period is called "incubation period".
16. 肺癌的潜伏期有多长？
How long is the latent period of lung cancer?

"潜伏"的第二个意思是"受命潜藏执行秘密任务"。英语可以译为 to lurk, to stay in hiding。例如：

17. 解放前夕，一些国民党特工人员在这座城市潜伏下来。
On the eve of liberation, some KMT secret agents stayed in hiding in this city.
18. 这名特务在一个政府部门潜伏了很久。
The spy stayed in hiding for a long time in a governmental department.
19. 警方获悉几名恐怖分子正潜伏在这个小区的一所公寓里。
Police learned that several terrorists were lurking in an apartment in this residential area.

5 刺激

汉语关键词： 刺激、物质刺激

英语关键词： stimulate, irritate, stimulation, irritation, provoke, upset, incentive

句子： 政府已推出一系列刺激经济的政策，提振了我们的信心。

误译： The government has pushed out a series of policies to provoke economy, enhancing our confidence.

正译： The government has pushed out a series of policies to stimulate economy, enhancing our confidence.

解释：

"刺激经济"的"刺激"有"激活"、"激励"或"推动"的意思，是个褒义词。而 to provoke 的意思是 to stimulate sb to do sth by making him angry，即"激怒"或"招惹"，是贬义的"刺激"，后面要跟人。英语中没有 to provoke economy 这样的搭配。"刺激经济"可以译为 to stimulate economy。

“刺激”的第一个意思是“内、外因作用于人或动物的感觉器官”。动词可以译为 to stimulate, to irritate；名词可以译为 stimulation, irritation。例如：

1. 他喝浓咖啡来刺激神经。
   1) He drinks strong coffee to stimulate his nerves.
   2) He drinks strong coffee to irritate his nerves.
2. 这张人体图表明在皮肤或肌肉上通过针灸刺激的穴位。
   The chart of the human body shows the point on the skin or muscle being stimulated through acupuncture.
3. 这些农药残留物质会刺激皮肤。
   These residues of insecticide can stimulate the skin.
4. 他的眼睛长期受到风沙、烟尘和化学物质刺激。
   His eyes have long been stimulated by sand storms, smoke and chemical materials.
5. 定期适度锻炼会有助于刺激你的食欲。
   Regular moderate exercise may help stimulate your appetite.
6. 这些饮料能引起胃酸增多，并刺激胃。
   These drinks can cause increased stomach acid and irritate the stomach.
7. 这位医生通过刺激疗法医治病人。
   1) The doctor treated the patient through stimulation therapy.
   2) The doctor treated the patient through irritation therapy.

“刺激”的第二个意思是“招惹”。英语可以译为 to provoke。例如：

8. 他失恋了，别刺激他。
   Don’t provoke him, for he is unlucky in love.
9. 虽然他想方设法刺激我，但是我却未被他的奚落感觉受到伤害。
   Although he tried to provoke me, I did not feel hurt by his taunts.
10. 我们不到必须的时候，决不会刺激他。
    We won’t provoke him any more than necessary.

“刺激”的第三个意思是“使人难受”。英语可以译为 to upset。例如：

11. 听到不幸的消息，他受到极大刺激。
    He was badly upset by the sad news.
12. 收到一个匿名电话，她受到刺激。
    She was upset by an anonymous telephone call.
13. 看到邻居买彩票中奖，给他很大刺激。
    He was very much upset by his neighbour who had won a lottery prize.
14. 女朋友吹了，使他受到极大刺激。

He was greatly upset, for he had been jilted by his girl friend.

15. 多年的收藏毁于一旦，对他刺激很厉害。

    He was horribly upset at the overnight loss of his many years' collection.

16. 这话对他刺激很厉害。

    1) He felt terribly upset at the remark.

    2) The remark stung him to the quick.

"刺激"的第四个意思是"激励人或推动事物，使起积极的变化"。英语可以译为 to stimulate。例如：

17. 这位经济学家认为高利润能刺激生产。

    The economist holds that high profit can stimulate production.

18. 这些新建铁路刺激了这个地区的经济发展。

    These newly built railways have stimulated economic development in this area.

19. 中国政府有望将很快发布更多的刺激消费的政策。

    The Chinese government is expected to issue more policies to stimulate consumption very soon.

20. 受政府刺激汽车消费政策的推动，中国的汽车销售量在3月份增长了5%。

    Driven by the government policies to stimulate car consumption, China's automobile sales rose 5 percent in March.

21. 购买者在衰退时对刺激国内消费做出了一点贡献。

    The buyers made a little contribution to stimulate domestic consumption amid the recession.

22. 中国刺激内需的政策使我们相信中国的经济增长复苏将很快到来。

    China's policy to stimulate domestic demand has made us believe the country's economic growth recovery would come soon.

23. 中央政府已采取广泛的步骤来刺激国内经济。

    The central government has adopted a broad range of steps to stimulate the national economy.

24. 成功能刺激人们充分运用他们的能力。

    Success can stimulate people to make full use of their capabilities.

"刺激"的第五个意思是"激励的手段"，即"物质刺激"。英语可以译为 incentive。例如：

25. 他父亲许诺买辆自行车，对他更加努力学习是个刺激。

    His father's promise of a bicycle was an incentive to his harder study.

26. 他一直深信物质刺激是提高生产力的一个关键因素。

    He has always believed that incentive is a key factor to raise productivity.

27. 他认为在大多数职业中，金钱仍然是主要刺激。
He thinks money is still a major incentive in most professions.
28. 一味追求物质刺激，会把人们引向歧途。
The mere pursuit of incentives will lead people astray.

6

阅兵式

汉语关键词： 检阅、检阅军队、阅兵、检阅台、阅兵台、阅兵典礼、阅兵式、海上阅兵式

英语关键词： review, inspect, inspection, review troops, inspect troops, fleet parade, fleet review, reviewing stand, military dress parade, dress parade, military parade, ceremonial parade, military review, look over

句子： 今天，数十艘中国舰艇和来自14个国家的21艘军舰参加了在青岛举行的海上阅兵式。

误译： Today, dozens of Chinese naval ships and 21 naval vessels from 14 countries participated in the dress parade on the sea at Qingdao.

正译： 1) Today, dozens of Chinese naval ships and 21 foreign naval vessels from 14 countries participated in the fleet parade at Qingdao.
2) Today, dozens of Chinese naval ships and 21 naval vessels from 14 foreign countries participated in the fleet parade at Qingdao.
3) Today, dozens of Chinese naval ships and 21 naval vessels from 14 other countries participated in the fleet review at Qingdao.

解释：

汉语的“14个国家”，指中国以外的14个国家，在上下文里不会引起误解。但是直接译为14 countries，会被理解为包括中国在内的14个国家。最好说14 foreign countries或 14 other countries，这样可以避免歧义。又，dress parade 的意思是 a parade in full uniform for review，指受阅者穿全套军服或制服接受检阅，是在陆地上的检阅仪式。fleet parade或 fleet review指舰船列队接受检阅，是海上阅兵式。例如：

1. 中国核潜艇在庆祝中国海军建军60周年的海上阅兵式亮了相。
China displayed its nuclear-powered submarines during a fleet parade to celebrate the 60th anniversary of the founding of the People's Liberation Army Navy.

"检阅"的第一个意思是"高级首长亲临军队或群众队伍面前，举行仪式，检验视察"。动词可以译为 to review, to inspect；名词可以译为 review, inspection。例如：

2. 这位元帅将检阅战斗部队。
   The marshal will review the fighting forces.
3. 来访的女王在总统的陪同下检阅了仪仗队。
   The visiting Queen reviewed a guard of honor in the company of the President.
4. 这位外国总统抵达时，检阅了三军仪仗队。
   On his arrival, the foreign President inspected the guard of honour from the three armed forces.
5. 士兵们排好队接受检阅。
   The soldiers were drawn up for the inspection.
6. 全体船员在甲板上集合，以备检阅。
   The ship's company assembled on the deck for inspection.

"检阅军队"和"阅兵"，英语可以译为 to review troops, to inspect troops。例如：

7. 来访的总统在飞机场的一个欢迎仪式上检阅了军队。
   The visiting President reviewed troops during a welcoming ceremony at the airport.
8. 当俄罗斯总统与中国主席胡锦涛在人民大会堂举行的正式欢迎仪式上检阅军队时，他们并肩前进。
   The Russian President walked with Chinese President Hu Jintao side by side, as they inspected troops during an official welcoming ceremony at the Great Hall of the People.

"检阅台"或"阅兵台"，英语可以译为 reviewing stand。例如：

9. 士兵们迈着坚定的步伐走过检阅台。
   The soldiers passed by the reviewing stand with firm steps.

"阅兵典礼"或"阅兵式"，英语可以译为 military dress parade, dress parade, military parade, ceremonial parade, military review。例如：

10. 中国有望举行庆祝建国60周年的盛大活动，包括10月1日在天安门的阅兵式。
    China is expected to hold grand celebration activities for the 60th founding anniversary, including a military dress parade in Tian'anmen Square on October 1.

11. 在即将到来的国庆节，中央军委主席胡锦涛将检阅盛大的阅兵式。
On the coming National Day, a massive dress parade is to be reviewed by Hu Jintao, Chairman of the Central Military Commission.
12. 为庆祝中华人民共和国建国60周年，中国将于10月1日在天安门举行阅兵式。
China will stage a military parade in Tian'anmen Square on October 1 to celebrate the 60th anniversary of the People's Republic of China.
13. 阅兵式开始时，指挥官下达行进令。
At the beginning of the ceremonial parade, the commander gave the order to march on.
14. 总司令在阅兵式上接受敬礼。
The commander-in-chief took the salute at the military review.

“阅兵场”，英语可以译为 parade ground。例如：

15. 当仪仗队在阅兵场上行进时，一个军乐队正在演奏，几百人正在观看。
When the guard of honour was marching on the parade ground, a military band was playing and hundreds of people were watching.

“检阅”的第二个意思是“回顾”。动词和名词分别译为 to review 和 review。例如：

16. 我们通过这个展览会检阅了我校近期的科研成果。
Through this exhibition, we reviewed the achievements recently made in scientific research at our university.
17. 这个展览会是对我校近期科研成果的一次检阅。
This exhibition is a review of the achievements recently made in scientific research at our university.

“检阅”的第三个意思是“翻检阅读”。动词可以译为 to review, to look over；名词可以译为 review。例如：

18. 为了研究这个问题，他检阅了国内外有关资料。
To study this issue, he looked over relevant domestic and foreign references.
19. 这些文件已经归档，以备检阅。
These documents have been filed for review.

7 感染

汉语关键词：感染、感染力

英语关键词：infect, infection, be infected by, be infected with, catch the infection of, affect, be infectious to sb, appeal

句子：到目前为止，全世界已有数百人感染了甲型H1N1流感。

误译：So far, hundreds of people have been infected through A H1N1 flu all over the world.

正译：1) So far, hundreds of people have been infected with A H1N1 flu all over the world.

2) So far, hundreds of people have been infected by A H1N1 flu all over the world.

解释：

"受到感染"，应译为to be infected with, to be infected by。介词with 或 by 后面的名词表示"造成感染的原因"。而介词through后面的名词表示"感染的方式"。例如：

1. 这位禽流感病人是通过与患病儿子亲密接触而受到感染的。
The bird flu patient was infected through close contact with his son who had been ill.

"感染"的第一个意思是"病原体侵入机体，在体内生长繁殖引起病变"。动词可以译为to infect；名词可以译为 infection。例如：

2. 狗咬的伤口严重感染了。
The wound from the dog bite has become badly infected.
3. 这位医生警告他的病人，让他们不要吃受沙门菌感染的鸡蛋。
The doctor warned his patients not to eat eggs infected with salmonella.
4. 他裸露的伤口很快因受感染而发炎了。
His open wound soon became inflamed by infection.
5. 如果有人受到轻度感染而不用抗生素，可以吃某些特殊种类食物来帮助抵抗感染。
If someone has a light infection and doesn't use antibiotics, they may eat some particular kinds of food to help fight the infection.
6. 他腿上有个装置，帮助消除感染，并愈合伤口。
He has a device on his leg that has helped take the infection out and close

the wound.

7. 这篇文章讨论如何预防禽流感的感染。
   This essay deals with how to prevent infection by bird flu.
8. 随着在美国和加拿大出现新的感染病例，对全球猪流感流行病的恐惧不断增长。
   Fears of a global swine flu pandemic grew continuously with new infections in the United States and Canada.
9. 这个病人受到全身感染，影响到他身体的许多部位。
   The patient has a generalized infection affecting many parts of his body.
10. 结果表明没有发生全身感染，但是在5个病例中发生了局部感染。
    The results showed that no systematic infection happened, but local infection occurred in five cases.
11. 弄清细菌感染与病毒感染的区别是非常重要的。
    It is very important to know the differences between bacterial infections and viral infections.

“感染”的第二个意思是“受到传染”。英语可以译为 to be infected with, to catch the infection of。例如：

12. 他身体不好，容易感染流行性感冒。
    He is liable to be infected with flu because of his poor health.
13. 你必须小心，不要感染猪流感。
    You must be careful not to be infected with swine flu.
14. 他不幸通过输血而感染艾滋病病毒。
    He was unfortunately infected with HIV through blood transfusion.
15. 每年全世界超过三百万人感染疟疾。
    Each year more than three million people become infected with malaria all over the world.
16. 美国将筛查来自受到感染地区的访问者。
    The United States will screen visitors arriving from infected areas.
17. 那些从事与动物脂肪相关职业的人们，最容易感染这种疾病。
    Those who are engaged in occupations connected with animal fats, are most liable to catch the infection of the disease.

“感染”的第三个意思是“通过言语行动引起别人产生相同的思想情感”。英语可以译为 to infect, to affect, to be infectious to sb；“受到感染”，可以译为 to catch the infection of。例如：

18. 这位教师以她对音乐的热情感染了她的学生们。
    The teacher infected her students with her enthusiasm for music.
19. 新年庆祝活动的欢乐气氛感染了在场的每一个人。

The joyful atmosphere of the New Year's celebration affected everybody present.

20. 这位演讲者以爱国热情深深地感染了听众。
The orator deeply affected the audience with his patriotic enthusiasm.
21. 他的欢乐情绪感染了大家。
His joy was infectious to all the people.
22. 青年人容易受到文学，尤其是诗歌的感染。
Young people tend to catch the infection of literature, especially of poetry.

“感染力”的意思是“能引起别人产生相同的思想情感的力量”，英语可以译为 appeal。例如：

23. 一位评论家指出这部电影具有很强的艺术感染力。
A critic points out that the film has a high artistic appeal.
24. 尽管有民族差异，某些可笑的情景还是具有普遍的感染力。
In spite of national differences, certain funny situations have a universal appeal.

8 流行病

汉语关键词： 流行、流行病、流行歌曲、流行音乐、流行色、国际色

英语关键词： pandemic, epidemic, epidemic disease, bad social practice, evil social practice, social malpractice, social ill, prevalent, fashionable, in fashion, in vogue, popular song, pop song, popular music, pop music, fashion colour, trend colour, trendy colour, international colour

句子： 讲排场，摆阔气，是这个地区的流行病。

误译： Waste and extravagance is an epidemic disease in this area.

正译： Waste and extravagance is an evil social practice in this area.

解释：

epidemic disease 的意思是 a large number of cases of a particular disease happening at the same time in a particular community，指的是“人与人之间的传染病”，不是“社会弊病”。

“流行病”的第一个意思是“能在较短时间内广泛蔓延的传染病”。英语可以译为 pandemic, epidemic, epidemic disease。例如：

1. 1918年所谓的西班牙流感成为有记载以来最致命的流感流行病。
The so-called Spanish flu in 1918 became the most deadly influenza pandemic ever recorded.

2. 这位世界卫生组织专家指出这场流行性流感仍然对世界健康状况构成长久的威胁。
The WHO expert points out that the pandemic flu remains a constant threat to the health status of the world.
3. 由于洪水停滞不退、卫生状况恶劣和饮用水不干净，人们害怕在这个不发达国家爆发流行病。
There is a fear of outbreak of an epidemic in this under-developed country because of floodwater stagnation, poor sanitation and impure drinking water.
4. 流行病经常与不良卫生状况紧密相关。
An epidemic disease is often in close connection with bad sanitary conditions.
传染性流行病有关的词汇有：
流行病 epidemics, epidemic disease
地方病 pandemics, pandemic disease
世界流行病 endemics, endemic disease
传染病 infectious disease
接触性传染病 contagion，contagious disease

"流行病"的第二个意思是比喻"广泛流传的社会弊病"。英语可以译为 bad social practice, evil social practice, social malpractice, social ill。例如：

5. 我发现上班迟到在我们单位已经成为一种流行病。
I find that being late for office has become a bad social practice in our unit.
6. 传播名人八卦新闻已经成为一种网络盛行的流行病。
Spreading celebrity gossip news has become a social malpractice prevailing on the Internet.
7. 在许多地方，插队或夹塞儿是一种需要解决的流行病。
In many places, jumping the queue or cutting in line is a social ill that needs to be addressed.

"流行"的第一个意思是"广泛传布"。英语可以译为 prevalent。例如：

8. 吸烟在年轻女子中间越来越流行。
Smoking is becoming increasingly prevalent among younger women.
9. 事实上，这种流行观点不过是许多解释中的一种而已，不一定是正确的。
In fact, this prevalent view is only one of the many explanations, which is not necessarily correct.

10. 这个流行一时的说法已经过时了。
    This once prevalent way of saying has become out of mode.

“流行”的第二个意思是“时尚而盛行”。英语可以译为 fashionable, in fashion, in vogue。例如：

11. 现在又在流行留长发了。
    It is becoming fashionable to have long hair again.
12. 牛仔裤在青年人和中年人中间依然十分流行。
    Jeans are still in fashion among the young people and middle-aged adults.
13. 她发现在这个国家长裙子又开始流行起来，而短裙子不再流行。
    She finds that long skirts have begun to come into fashion again while short skirts are no longer in vogue in this country.

“流行歌曲”的第一个意思是“在一定时期内受到普遍欢迎，广泛传唱的歌曲”。英语可以译为 popular song。例如：

14. 这个老人在年轻时就开始喜欢流行歌曲。
    The old man began to love popular songs when he was young.

“流行歌曲”的第二个意思指“通俗歌曲”。英语可以译为 pop song。例如：

15. 这位流行歌手正计划发布一张新的流行歌曲专辑。
    The pop singer is planning to release a new album of pop songs.
16. 一些老年人爱唱古典歌曲和民歌，而不爱唱流行歌曲。
    Some old people are fond of classic songs and folk songs, instead of pop songs.

“流行音乐”，英语可以译为 popular music, pop music。例如：

17. 这位作曲家的作品对大多数流行音乐爱好者具有吸引力。
    The composers' works are appealing to most lovers of popular music.
18. 他说他创作流行音乐，没有章法。
    He says he composes pop music with no rules.

“流行色”的意思是“在一定时期和地区被人们普遍喜爱的色彩，多指服装颜色”。英语可以译为 fashion colour, trend colour, trendy colour。但是注意 popular colour 的意思是“受人欢迎的颜色”，而 international colour 的意思是“象征……的国际色”。例如：

19. 绿色是今年夏季服装流行色。
    Green is the fashion colour in clothing for this summer.
20. 浅蓝色是当今幼童的流行色。
    Light blue is the trend colour among the young children nowadays.

21. 白色是本季度少女家具的流行色。
White is the trendy color for young girls' furniture this season.
22. 什么是世界范围内汽车的最受人欢迎的颜色?
What is the most popular colour for cars worldwide?
23. 红色是象征“危险”和“停止”的国际色。
Red is the international color for danger and stop.
24. 紫色是象征“家庭暴力”的国际色。
Purple is the international color symbolic of domestic violence.
25. 白色是象征“投降”的国际色。
White is the international color of surrender.

9 恢复疲劳

汉语关键词: 恢复、恢复疲劳

英语关键词: restore, resume, reestablish, renew, get back into, be back to normal, return to normal, regain, recuperate, retake, recapture, reinstate, rehabilitate, recover from fatigue

句子: 这个运动员休息了两天就恢复疲劳了。

误译: After two days' rest, the sportsman recovered fatigue.

正译: After two days' rest, the sportsman recovered from fatigue.

解释:

“恢复疲劳”的意思是“从疲劳中恢复过来”,即“消除疲劳”。从形式上讲,“疲劳”是“恢复”的宾语。但是从逻辑上讲,“恢复”的不是“疲劳”,而是“正常状态”。英语不能说 to recover fatigue,而要说 to recover from fatigue。例如:

1. 你需要重新考虑你的生活方式,努力尽快恢复疲劳。
You need to reconsider your lifestyle and do something to recover from fatigue as soon as possible.
2. 医生说这种药能够帮助肌肉恢复疲劳。
The doctor says that this medicine can help muscles recover from fatigue.

“恢复”的第一个意思是“变成原来的样子”。英语可以译为 to restore, to resume, to reestablish, to renew, to get back into。例如:

3. 经过几次谈判,两国决定恢复中断了10年的外交关系。
1) After a few negotiations, the two countries decided to resume

diplomatic relations that had been suspended for 10 years.

2) After a few talks, the two countries decided to restore diplomatic ties that had been broken off for a decade.

3) After a few negotiations, the two countries decided to reestablish diplomatic relations that had been suspended for 10 years.

4) After a few talks, the two countries decided to renew diplomatic ties that had been broken off for a decade.

4. 1977年8月恢复高考，有27.3万人成为新时期第一批大学生。

In August 1977, the college entrance examination was resumed, with two hundred seventy-three thousand people becoming the first batch of university students in the New Period.

5. 在重建以后，当地人民使这座遭受地震的城镇恢复了昔日的繁荣景象。

After its reconstruction, the local people restored the prosperity of the earthquake-hit town to what it was in the past.

6. 博物馆专家们精心地把这幅古画恢复原状。

The museum experts carefully restored the ancient painting to its original state.

7. 踏青的游人离去之后，小山村恢复了往常的平静。

After the traveling visitors went away, the small mountainous village restored its usual quiet.

8. 产后30天她开始锻炼身体，逐渐恢复了苗条的身材。

Thirty days after delivery she began to do exercise and gradually got back into good shape.

“恢复”的第二个意思是“变为正常的状态”。英语可以译为 to be back to normal, to return to normal, to restore, to regain, to recuperate。例如：

9. 自从两国总统高峰会谈以来，两国关系已恢复正常。

The relation between the two countries has been restored to normal since the summit talk between the Presidents of the two countries.

10. 这个地方的交通秩序已恢复正常。

1) Transport services are back to normal in this place.

2) Transport services have returned to normal in this place.

11. 在医生和护士的精心护理下，这位病人正在逐渐恢复健康。

1) Being nursed carefully by the doctors and nurses, the patient is gradually restoring his health.

2) Being nursed carefully by the doctors and nurses, the patient is gradually recuperating.

12. 这个昏迷了几天的病人终于恢复了知觉。
    1) The patient who had been in a coma for several days finally recovered his consciousness.
    2) The patient who had been in a coma for several days finally regained his consciousness.

“恢复”的第三个意思是“收回失去的东西”。英语可以译为 to recover, to retake, to recapture, to resume, to reinstate, to restore, to rehabilitate。例如：

13. 他们最终赶走了侵略者，恢复了失地。
    1) They finally drove away the invaders and restored their lost territory.
    2) They finally drove away the invaders and retook their lost land.
    3) They finally drove away the invaders and recaptured their lost land.
14. 今天，这里的股票在最后一个交易小时恢复了失地。
    Stocks recovered lost territory in the final hour of trading here today.
15. 他们本来能够恢复失地，但是他们太慢而未能行动。
    They could have recovered lost territory, but they were too slow to act.
16. 该公司已决定恢复张先生原来的职务。
    The company has decided to restore Mr Zhang to his previous post.
17. 文革一结束，这位官员就恢复了原来的职务。
    Soon after the Cultural Revolution, the official was reinstated in his former office.
18. 由于他是无罪的，司法部门最终给他恢复了名誉。
    1) As he was innocent, the judiciary finally restored his reputation.
    2) As he was innocent, the judiciary finally rehabilitated his reputation.
19. 这个软件可以帮助恢复丢失的数据。
    The software can help to restore the lost data.
20. 中国政府已恢复对香港行使主权10多年了。
    Chinese Government has resumed the exercise of sovereignty over Hong Kong for more than 10 years.

10 问责制

汉语关键词： 问责、被问责、问责制、追究责任

英语关键词： hold sb accountable for sth, hold sb answerable for sth, call sb to account, be held accountable for sth, be held answerable for sth, be called to account, ascertain responsibility, ascertain where the responsibility lies, accountability system, accountability

句子： 我们必须建立和实行领导干部问责制。

误译： We must set up and carry out a leadership responsibility system.

正译： We must set up and carry out a leadership accountability system.

解释：

responsibility system 是"责任制"，指"明确规定责任范围的管理制度"。而"问责制"是 accountability system，指"对一切行为和后果追究责任的制度"。

"问责"的意思是"追究责任"，英语可以译为 to hold sb accountable for sth, to hold sb answerable for sth, to call sb to account。"被问责"，可以译为 to be held accountable for sth, to be held answerable for sth, to be called to account。英语 accountable 的意思是 responsible for your actions and expected to explain them when you are asked，即"对自己的行为负有责任，并有说明义务"。例如：

1. 部门领导就丢失机密文件一事问责这名职员。
   The leader of the section held the staff member accountable for the loss of a confidential document.
2. 县政府就这所学校教室坍塌一事问责教育局长。
   The county government held the head of the educational bureau answerable for the collapse of the school classrooms.
3. 地方政府对问责了这些失职官员。
   The local government called to account those wrongdoing officials.
4. 这名官员因隐瞒重大食品安全事故而被问责。
   The official was held accountable for covering up a major food safety incident.
5. 看守长因这名犯人的非自然死亡而被问责。
   The chief jailer was held answerable for the unnatural death of the prisoner.
6. 这位经理就一些现金丢失一事而被问责。
   The manager was called to account over some missing cash.

"追究责任"可以译为 to ascertain responsibility, to ascertain where the responsibility lies。例如：

7. 这样的数据可以用来对非法活动追究责任。
   Such data could be used to ascertain responsibility for unlawful activity.
8. 我们将根据相关法律对违反合同一事追究刑事责任。
   We shall ascertain criminal responsibility for breaking the agreement

according to related laws.

9. 美国应该召回其有害而有毒的金融产品，并追究刑事责任，而不是往其金融体制里拼命输入现金。
The United States should recall its harmful and toxic financial products and ascertain where the responsibility lies instead of pumping money into its financial system.

"问责制",英语译为accountability system 或 accountability。例如：

10. 官员问责制是一种对政府及其官员的行为和后果追究责任的制度。
Officials' accountability is a system in which the government and its officials are held accountable for their actions and consequences.

11. 行政问责制是一种惩罚制度，旨在就其职权范围内一些重大失职、生产事故或安全事故而问责各级政府、相关机构或下属行政机关的领导人员。
Administrative accountability is a system of punishment that is aimed at holding chiefs of governments at various levels, relevant departments or subordinate administrative organs accountable for major wrongdoings or production and safety accidents with their jurisdiction.

12. 行政问责制是中国政府在将自身建成责任政府过程中所采取的重要步骤。
Administrative accountability is an important step made by the Chinese government in building itself into a responsible one.

13. 由于有效地应用行政问责制，近年来一些重要政府官员由于失职或引起财产或人民生命重大损失的事故而辞职。
Because of the effective application of the administrative accountability, a number of key government officials have resigned for malpractices or accidents that caused major losses of property or peoples' lives in recent years.

14. 目前，我国的问责制还有一些不完善的地方亟待改进。
At present, there are still some imperfections that need to be improved in the accountability system of our country.

15. 我们的政府需要问责制和监督制度，而不是靠打电话指挥。
Our government needs an accountability and supervision system instead of relying on phone calls.

16. 中央政府已经决定建立问责制，将官员的事业与其业绩挂钩。
The central government has decided to set up an accountability system that ties up officials' career with their performance.

17. 市政府加强了问责制，严肃处理了有关责任人员。
The municipal government has strengthened the accountability and seriously dealt with those related responsible personnel.

18. 问责制是民主政治的一个重要组成部分，也是构建责任政府的必由之路。
The accountability system is an important part of democracy, and it is also the only way to the construction of a responsible government.

11 高考

汉语关键词： 高考、大学入学考试、考场、考卷、试卷、试纸、考题、试题、考试成绩

英语关键词： prepare an exam, prepare for an exam, university entrance examination, university entrance exam, college entrance examination, college entrance exam, National Matriculation Examination, examination hall, examination room, examination paper, examination question paper, exam paper, test paper, examination question, exam question, examination result, exam result

句子： 几百万高中毕业生正在努力用功准备高考。

误译： Millions of high-schools graduates are working hard to prepare the National Matriculation Examination.

正译： Millions of high-schools graduates are working hard to prepare for the National Matriculation Examination.

解释：

to prepare an exam 的意思是“组织者为考试做准备”，如“出考题”。在这里 to prepare 是及物动词。而 to prepare for an exam 才表示“考生为考试做准备”，如“复习功课”。在这里 to prepare 是不及物动词，后面需加介词 for。例如：

1. 每位教员都将为他的学生准备考题。
Each instructor will prepare an exam for his students.
2. 这位教师准备了考题，包括涉及这一章所有相关资料的问题，还有一套答案。
The teacher prepared an exam that included questions on all relevant material from the chapter, along with an answer key.
3. 学生准备考试花费时间和精力。
It takes time and energy for the students to prepare for the examination.

“大学入学考试”，英语可以译为 university entrance examination, university entrance exam, college entrance examination, college entrance exam。例如：

4. 在我国，课堂教学主要是面向大学入学考试的。
   In our country, classroom instructions are mainly oriented towards the university entrance examination.
5. 大学入学考试对学生来说，是真正的挑战。
   The university entrance exam is a real challenge to the students.
6. 在许多国家，高中毕业生要经过激烈竞争才能通过全国性大学入学考试。
   There is a fierce competition among the high-school graduates in many countries to pass the nationwide college entrance examination.
7. 一名学生被发现在大学入学考试中作弊。
   A student was found cheating in the college entrance exam.

“高考”，即“全国普通高等学校招生入学考试”。英语可以译为 National Matriculation Examination。例如：

8. 当我们录取新生时，高考被用作选择学生的一个标准。
   When we rccruit new students, the national matriculation examination is used as a criterion for student selection.
9. 6月7日和8日，我国各地将举行高考。
   On June 7 and 8, the National Matriculation Examination will be held in various places of our country.

“考场”，英语可以译为 examination hall, examination room。例如：

10. 进入考场之前请先核对座位号码。
    Please check your seat number before entering the examination hall.
11. 我很好地回答了每一个问题，怀着轻松的心情离开了考场。
    I gave a good reply to every question and left the examination room with a light heart.

“考卷”或“试卷”，英语可以译为 examination paper, examination question paper, exam paper, test paper。例如：

12. 我在答题之前先仔细看了一遍考卷。
    I carefully went over the examination paper before answering the questions.
13. 为了节约的缘故，试卷将利用每张纸的两面印。
    For reasons of economy, examination question papers will be printed using both sides of each page.

14. 由于试卷泄露了，这次考试取消了。
The examination was cancelled because the exam paper had leaked.
15. 直到监考人员告诉你打开试卷时，你再打开试卷。
Do not open this test paper until you are told to do so by the supervisor.

注意 test paper 还有"试纸"的意思。例如：

16. 我们的化学老师让我们把试纸浸入液体中。
Our chemistry teacher asked us to immerse the test paper in the liquid.

"考题"或"试题"，英语可以译为 examination question, exam question。例如：

17. 这个学生正确地回答了所有的试题。
The student answered all the examination questions correctly.
18. 老师正在他在课堂上所教内容的基础上出考题。
The teacher is writing exam questions on the basis of what he has taught in class.

"考试成绩"，英语可以译为 examination result, exam result。例如：

19. 如果你遇到关于网上发布研究生考试成绩的任何问题，请与我们联系。
Please contact us if you encounter any problems regarding the Online Release of Examination Results for Undergraduate Students.
20. 当我收到考试成绩时，我感到那样放心。
When I received my exam result, I felt so relieved.

12 选报志愿

汉语关键词： 志愿、选报志愿、申请、报考

英语关键词： apply for, choose and register for the university and the major, choice of and registration for the university and the major, enter oneself for an examination, register for an examination, aspire, aspiration, wish, ideal, volunteer

句子： 这些高中毕业生正在老师的指导下选报志愿。

误译： These high-school graduates are applying for the university and the major under the guidance of their teacher.

正译：These high-school graduates are choosing and registering for the university and the major under the guidance of their teacher.

解释：

“选报志愿”的意思是“选择和报考期望上的大学和专业”，这是具有中国特色的考试制度决定的，关键是要经过入学考试。英语很难找到对应的词语。to apply for 的意思是 to make a formal request, usually in writing, for sth such as a job, a place, at college, university, etc.，即“申请，通常为书面申请”。我国大学本科生和硕士生可以根据学业成绩申请读国外一些大学的硕士或博士学位，而不需入学考试。“选报志愿”可以译为 to choose and register for the university and the major, the choice of and registration for the university and the major。例如：

1. 他正计划申请就读一所美国大学的研究生院。
   He is planning to apply for a graduate school in an American university.
2. 考生选报志愿时有多个学校可供选择，其中第一志愿最重要。
   When an applicant chooses and registers for the university and the major, there are several universities he may make a choice of, among which the first option is most important.
3. 优先选报一所好大学，还是一个好专业，已引起热烈讨论。
   Whether we should choose and register for a good university or a good major as a priority has provoked a heated discussion.
4. 家长们在为孩子选报学校时应该非常小心，以避免上当受骗。
   When choosing and registering for the school for their children, parents should be very careful to avoid being cheated.
5. 选报一所好大学和一个好专业能够最好地支持和满足一个学生的职业目标。
   The choice of and registration for a good university and a good major can best support and meet a student's career goal.
6. 学生们应该选报最能实现他们智力兴趣的专业。
   Students should choose the major that best fulfills their intellectual interests.

“报考”的意思是“报名投考”。英语可以译为 to enter oneself for an examination, to register for an examination。例如：

7. 我妹妹打算报考师范学院。
   My sister intended to enter herself for the examination for the teachers' college.

8. 有一千多名大学毕业生前来报考公务员。
Over a thousand college graduates came to register for the civil service examination.
9. 如果你想报考研究生，你不会受年龄与婚姻状况的限制。
If you want to register for the entrance examination for a graduate school, you won't be restricted by your age and marital status.
10. 他想出国深造的强烈欲望使他报考了美国研究生入学考试资格考试。
His strong desire to have a further study abroad made him register for the GRE examination.

“志愿”的第一个意思是“志向和愿望”。英语动词可以译为 to aspire, to wish。名词可以译为 aspiration, wish, ideal。例如：

11. 这个男孩的志愿是当名警察。
1) The boy aspires to be a policeman.
2) The boy's aspiration is to become a policeman.
3) The boy wishes to be a policeman.
4) The boy's wish is to become a policeman.
12. 这个女学生在小时候就立下志愿当一名像居里夫人那样的科学家。
When she was young, the girl student harboured an aspiration to be a scientist like Marie Currie.
13. 当这个学生收到北京大学录取通知书时，他发现他已实现了自己的志愿。
When he received the admission notice from Peking University, the student found he had realized his wish.
14. 玛丽的志愿是将来当一名律师，而罗斯的志愿是当一名医学专家。
Mary's ideal is to be a lawyer in the future while Rose's is to be a specialist in medicine.

“志愿”的第二个意思是“自愿”。英语可以译为 to volunteer。例如：

15. 这位大学生志愿到西部山区去工作。
The college student volunteered to go to work in the mountainous area of Western China.
16. 现在许多大学生志愿参军。
Now many college students volunteer to join the army.

13

舞弊

汉语关键词：舞弊、高考舞弊、徇私舞弊、营私舞弊、选举舞弊

英语关键词：wrong, wrongdoing, cheat, cheating, serve one’s selfish interests by engaging in irregularities, resort to fraudulent practices for personal gain, do malpractice for personal benefit, engage in malpractices for selfish ends, commit illegalities for personal gain, malpractice, fraudulent practice, fraud, electoral fraud, election fraud, vote fraud, election rigging, vote rigging, electoral corruption

句子：我们必须严肃处理这些高考舞弊事件。

误译：We must seriously handle these wrong events in the national entrance examination.

正译：1) Wc must seriously handle these wrongdoing events in the national entrance examination.

2) We must seriously handle these cheating events in the national entrance examination.

解释：

wrong 的意思是 not morally right or honest，因此 wrong event 强调的是“不道德的事件”。而“舞弊”指的是违法的事情。wrongdoing 的意思是 illegal or dishonest，因此 wrongdoing event 既指“非法”，又指“不道德”的事件，可以表示“舞弊事件”。

“舞弊”的第一个意思是“通过欺骗方式做违法的事情，例如在考试、选举和会计活动中”。英语可以译为 to cheat。例如：

1. 任何被发现在考试中舞弊者将被立即逐出考场。
   Anyone caught cheating in the exam will be kicked out of the examination hall immediately.
2. 那些考试舞弊的学生如果不受到惩罚，长大后会变成犯罪的官员或商人。
   Those students who cheat in the examination might grow up to be a criminal official or businessman if not punished.
3. 这位总统候选人被揭露在选举中舞弊。
   The presidential candidate was exposed of cheating in the election.
4. 这个政客坚持说他没有与总统密谋在选举中舞弊。
   The politician insisted that he did not conspire with the president to cheat in the election.

5. 如果你在会计活动中舞弊，你会受到惩罚并处以罚款。
If you cheat in accounting, you'd be punished and fined.
6. 这个犯罪嫌疑人被指控在高考前向学生家长出售包括接收器、耳机、充电器和电池等舞弊工具，并获得暴利。
The suspect was charged with selling cheating devices, including receivers, earpieces, chargers and batteries, to parents of students before the national entrance exam and made a large profit.
7. 他在临高考之前出售舞弊工具而被抓捕。
He was caught selling cheating devices to students just before the national matriculation exam.
8. 据报道在一些考点发现了舞弊骗局。
Cheating scams were reported to have been uncovered in some exam venues.
9. 近年来舞弊现象增长，破坏了公正原则。
The cheating phenomenon has increased in recent years, violating the fairness principle.

“徇私舞弊”或“营私舞弊”，英语的译法很多，有 to serve one's selfish interests by engaging in irregularities, to resort to fraudulent practices for personal gain, to do malpractice for personal benefit, to engage in malpractices for selfish ends, to commit illegalities for personal gain。例如：

10. 这个官员被指控进行徇私舞弊之类的非法行动。
The official was accused of having taken such illegal acts as serving his selfish interests engaging in irregularities.
11. 公务员不可疏忽职守，滥用权力或徇私舞弊。
1) Civil servants must not neglect their duty, abuse their power, or resort to fraudulent practices for their personal gains.
2) Civil servants must not neglect their duty, abuse their power, or do malpractice for their personal benefit.
3) Civil servants must not neglect their duty, abuse their power, or engage in malpractices for selfish ends.
12. 这个行政人员因徇私舞弊而被捕。
The administrator was arrested for committing illegalities for his personal gain.

“舞弊”的第二个意思是“通过欺骗方式违法的事实或行为”。英语可以译为 malpractice, fraudulent practice, fraud。例如：

13. 这名收税员以涉嫌舞弊而正在受审。
He is currently standing trial for alleged malpractices.

14. 这名会计帮助造假帐，现在因会计舞弊而遇到麻烦。
The accountant helped to cook the books and is now in trouble for fraudulent practice in accountancy.
15. 市政府认真保护揭发浪费、舞弊及贪污的人。
The municipal government is serous about protecting those people who blow the whistle on waste, fraud and corruption.

世界上天天有选举，而舞弊也时有发生。因此英语表达“选举舞弊”的方法非常多，有 electoral fraud, election fraud, vote fraud, election rigging, vote rigging, electoral corruption。例如：

16. 六个人因与选举舞弊相关的罪名而锒铛入狱。
Six men have been jailed for charges relating to electoral fraud.
17. 这位历史学家写了一本书，论述选举舞弊的历史。
The historian wrote a book, dealing with the history of election fraud.
18. 这位专家指出选举舞弊也可能在立法机构内发生。
The expert points out that vote fraud can also take place in legislatures.
19. 选举舞弊在那座城市引起了一场政治骚乱。
The election rigging provoked a political turmoil in that city.
20. 该政党的一位前领导人警告说在这个非洲国家即将到来的选举中有可能选举舞弊猖獗。
A former leader of the political party warned of the possibility for rampant vote rigging in the upcoming election in the African country.
21. 选举舞弊和选举中其他形式的不公平竞争正在增长。
Electoral corruption and other forms of unfair competition in the election are on the rise.

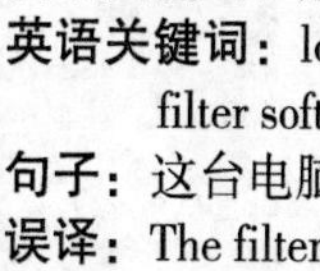

14 过滤

汉语关键词：过滤、过淋、过滤器、过滤网、过滤嘴、过滤软件、安装、卸载
英语关键词：load, install, unload, uninstall, remove, filter, filtrate, filter tip, strain, filter software, filtering software
句子：这台电脑预装的过滤软件是可以卸载的。
误译：The filter software programme preinstalled on the computer is uninstallable.
正译：1. The filter software programme preloaded on the computer can be unloaded.

2. The filter software programme preloaded on the computer can be uninstalled.
3. The filter software programme preloaded on the computer can be removed.
4. The preinstalled filter software programme on the computer is unloadable.
5. The preinstalled filter software programme on the computer is removable.

解释：

"安装"是 to load, to install；"可以安装的"是 loadable, installable。"卸载"是 to unload, to uninstall, to remove；"可以卸载的"是 unloadable, removable。英语前缀 un- 有两个意思，一是表示否定概念，即 not，例如 unable（不能）；二是表示相反过程，例如 unlock（开锁），undo（解开），unfold（展开）。但是，uninstallable 的意思是 un + installable（不可安装的），而不是 uninstall + able（可以卸载的）。例如：

1. 这种过滤软件可以由计算机用户关掉或卸载。
   This filter software can be switched off and uninstalled by computer users.

"过滤"或"过淋"的第一个意思是"用滤纸、滤布或其他多孔材料将流体或气体中所含的固体颗粒或有害成分分离出去"。英语可以译为 to filter, to filtrate。例如：

2. 所有的饮用水均须过滤。
   All drinking water must be filtered.
3. 这台空气过滤器用来过滤房间里的空气。
   The air filter is used to filtrate air in the room.
4. 过滤器装置可以有效地过滤杂质。
   A filter device can effectively filtrate impurity.

"过滤器"或"过滤网"，英语可以译为 filter。例如：

5. 在燃料进入发动机之前，过滤器先把燃料过滤。
   The filter cleans the fuel before it enters the engine.
6. 加装过滤器以改善水的味道和气味。
   The filters are added to improve the taste and smell of the water.
7. 过滤网可以截住空气中的尘埃。
   A filter can trap dust from the air.
8. 这种颗粒过滤网能够拦截颗粒物质。
   The pellet filter intercepts the particulate matter.
9. 空调过滤网应该每周消毒或更换。
   Air conditioner filters should be disinfected or replaced every week.

"过滤嘴"，英语可以译为 filter tip, filter。例如：

10. 他一直抽过滤嘴香烟，而从不抽不带过滤嘴的香烟。

He always smokes filter-tipped cigarettes, and never smokes cigarettes without filters.

"过滤"的第二个意思是"用滤网、细筛子或纱布等分离出茶水、咖啡或煎过的中药里的渣子"。英语可以译为 to strain, to filter, to filtrate。例如：

11. 她用过滤网把茶过滤到一个预热的茶壶里。
She strained tea through a strainer into a preheated teapot.
12. 她小心翼翼地用细筛子去掉咖啡渣子，然后用杯子端上来。
She strained the coffee carefully through a fine sieve to remove the grounds and then served in cups.
13. 用不了多少时间就可以把咖啡过滤好。
It won't take long to filter the coffee.
14. 他用一块纱布过淋了煎好的中药。
1) He strained the decocted medicinal herbs with a piece of gauze.
2) He filtrated the decocted medicinal herbs with a piece of gauze.

"过滤"的第三个意思是"通过技术手段分离出不良信息或内容，限制其在网络的传播"。英语可以译为 to filter。例如：

15. 这个软件旨在过滤互联网的色情内容。
The software is designed to filter pornography on the Internet.
16. 由于我们没有专门知识决定哪个网站是下流淫秽的，哪个是可以接受的，所以我们不能过滤网站。
As we do not have the expertise to decide which website is indecent and obscene, and which ones are acceptable, we are not in a proper position to filter websites.

"过滤软件"，英语可以译为 filter software, filtering software。例如：

17. 互联网过滤软件旨在保护青年人不受色情和其他不健康内容传播的戕害。
The Internet filter software is targeted at protecting youths from the spread of pornography and other unhealthy content.
18. 有些网民认为要求个人电脑安装过滤软件可能会侵犯用户隐私。
Some netizens think that the requirement for personal computers to be loaded with filtering software may violate the users' privacy.

15

分数线

汉语关键词： 分数、分数线、录取分数线、学分、学分制

英语关键词： scoreline, bottom score for enrollment, bottom mark for enrollment, score, mark, point, grade, fraction, fractional number, credit system, credit

句子： 他的高考成绩超过了该大学录取分数线。

误译： The score he got in the national entrance exam exceeded the scoreline set for enrollment at this university.

正译： 1) The score he got in the national entrance exam exceeded the bottom score set for enrollment at this university.

2) The score he got in the national entrance exam exceeded the bottom mark set for enrollment at this university.

解释：

“分数线”，即“录取分数线”，不能字对字地译为 scoreline，因为它有不同的意思。scoreline 的第一个意思是 the final score or result in a game or competition，即“体育比赛的最终比分”。score line 的第二个意思是 a line made by a cut in a surface, done with a sharp tool，即“用尖锐工具在平面上刻出的一道划痕”。“分数线”实际上指符合录取标准的最低分数。英语可以译为 bottom score for enrollment, bottom mark for enrollment。例如：

1. 这场足球赛的结果是一个2-1的最终比分。
   The result of the football game was a 2-1 scoreline.
2. 客队表现得不像最终比分显示的那样糟糕。
   The guest team did not play as badly as the scoreline suggests.
3. 这个刻痕操作造成了一道划线。
   The scoring operation resulted in a scoreline.
4. 去年，我省理工类本科分数线在600分以上。
   Last year, the bottom mark for the enrollment of science and technology undergraduates in our province was over 600 scores.

“分数”的第一个意思是“考试或比赛时表示成绩的数字”。英语可以译为 score, mark, point, grade。例如：

5. 你可以通过输入你的身份证号码和准考证号码在线查询你的分数。
   You can inquire your score on line by inputting your ID number and admission ticket number.

6. 在高考中，这个学生得了不算太坏的514分。
   In the college entrance exam, the student got a not-so-bad score of 514.
7. 她在高考中仅得到可怜的335分，包括数学19分的垃圾分数。
   She got a poor score of only 335 in the national matriculation exam, including a junk 19 points in mathematics.
8. 老师给了我的论文一个好分数。
   The teacher gave me a good mark for my paper.
9. 他的数学分数在班上是名列前茅的
   His mark in math is second to none in the class.
10. 按照平均分数，我在同班同学中名列第二。
    I ranked the second among my classmates in terms of average marks.
11. 从数字上看，他的分数并不给人深刻印象，但是他的成绩却排在全班前20%以内。
    Numerically, his marks are not impressive, but his achievements rank in the upper 20 percent of the class.
12. 他这学期所修各门课程的平均分数是92分。
    The average score of all the courses he has taken this term is 92 points.
13. 因为我的论文交晚了，老师扣了分数。
    The teacher took off points because my paper was late.
14. 裁判员们给了决赛双方相等的分数。
    The judges awarded both finalists equal points.
15. 由于他的论文缺乏精确和质量，他得到了一个不及格的分数。
    As his paper lacked both accuracy and quality, he received a failing grade.

“分数”的第二个意思是数学专门名词，英语可以译为 fraction, fractional number。例如：

16. 当计算面积时，我们通常将普通分数变为小数。
    When figuring dimensions, we usually change common fractions to decimals.
17. 连续数据可以用分数表示，也可以用整数表示。
    Continuous data can be expressed in either fractional numbers or whole numbers.
18. 四分之一是一个真分数。
    One forth is a proper fraction.

“学分”，英语可以译为 credit。例如：

19. 这名学生选了一门4个学分的课程。
    The student selected a course for four credits.

20. 你需要再修3个学分才能毕业。
    You need three more credits to graduate
21. 他修了三门学分课程，包括英国文学史。
    He took three credit courses, including the History of English Literature.

“学分制”，英语可以译为 credit system。例如：

22. 职业教育和培训的学分制可以给人们对他们的个人学习以更大的控制力。
    The credit system for vocational education and training may give people greater control over their individual learning.

16 状元

汉语关键词： 文科学生、理科学生、文科班、理科班、状元、中状元、高考状元、文科状元、理科状元

英语关键词： liberal arts student, science student, liberal arts-oriented class, science-oriented class, Number One Scholar in the palace examination, Champion Scholar in the palace examination, student who came top in the college entrance examination, come out first in the highest imperial examination, liberal arts-oriented student who came top in the college entrance examination, science-oriented student who came top in the college entrance examination, master

句子： 今年北京文科状元是位女生。

误译： The liberal arts student who came top in the college entrance examination at Beijing this year is a girl student.

正译： The liberal arts-oriented student who came top in the college entrance examination at Beijing this year is a girl student.

解释：

liberal arts student 是“文科学生”，science student 是“理科学生”，指在大学学习的学生。“准备学习文科的学生”，可以译为 liberal arts-aimed student 或 liberal arts-oriented student；“准备学习理科的学生”，可以译为 science-aimed student 或 science-oriented student。“文科班”，可以译为 liberal arts-oriented class；“理科班”，可以译为 science-oriented class。例如：

1. 来自这个理科班的大多数学生已被重点大学录取。
Most of the students from this science-oriented class have been recruited into key universities.
2. 许多文科班的学生也对自然科学非常感兴趣。
Many students from liberal arts-oriented classes are also greatly interested in natural science.

“状元”的第一个意思是指“科举考试的殿试一甲第一名”。英语可以译为Number One Scholar in the palace examination, Champion Scholar in the palace examination。“中状元”，可以译为to come out first in the highest imperial examination。例如：

3. 皇帝把这名新科状元招为驸马。
1) The emperor married a princess to the Number One Scholar newly selected in the palace examination.
2) The emperor adopted the Champion Scholar newly selected in the palace examination as his son-in-law.
4. 这个故事讲述了古时候一位书生如何苦读十年而最终中了状元。
The story tells how a scholar in ancient times studied hard for ten years and finally came out first in the highest imperial examination.

“状元”的第二个意思是指“高考取得第一名的人”。英语可以译为student who came top in the college entrance examination。例如：

5. 这位专家说有些高考状元只是比同龄人更加适应应试教育。
The expert said that some of the students who came top in the college entrance examination are just more adaptable to the exam-oriented education than their peers.
6. 这位理科状元进入大学后得到一笔奖学金。
Entering the university, the science-oriented student who had come top in the college entrance examination received a scholarship.
7. 根据一项调查，大约40%的高考状元在大学毕业后选择到国外大学留学。
According to a survey, about 40 percent of the students who had come first in the college entrance examinations chose to have their postgraduate studies at overseas universities upon their graduation.

“状元”的第三个意思是比喻“在某一行业中成绩最突出的人”。英语可以译为master。例如：

8. 行行出状元。
1) In every art it is good to have a master.

2) Every profession produces its own best.
3) Every profession produces its own topmost master.
4) Every profession produces its own leading authority.
5) Every trade has its own master.
6) There are masters in every walk of life.

9. 当地政府授予这个青年人"养猪状元"称号。
The local government conferred the title of "the Best Pig-Keeper" on the young man.

17 录取

汉语关键词： 录取、被录取、考取、录取通知书、上大学

英语关键词： recruit, admit, enroll, accept, recruited, be admitted, be enrolled, be accepted, matriculate, admission notice, admission letter, admission offer, enrollment notice, enrollment certificate, notice of acceptance, letter of acceptance, go to university, enter university, get into university

句子： 我急切想知道是否被北京大学录取了。

误译： I am anxious to know if I am admitted by Peking University.

正译： I am anxious to know if I am admitted to Peking University.

解释：

to admit sb to sth 的意思是 to allow sb to become a member of a club, a school, or an organization，即"允许某人成为某单位的一名成员"。这里要用介词 to，而不可用 by。

"录取"的第一个意思是"通过考试选择和接受合格的人"，英语可以译为 to recruit, to admit, to enroll, to accept。例如：

1. 这个政府部门正在从大学毕业生中间录取公务员。
This governmental department is recruiting civil servants from university graduates.
2. 本公司将从应聘人员中择优录取。
Our company will admit the best applicants among the competitors.
3. 学校当局决定破格录取这个残疾男孩为大学生。
The school authorities decided to enroll the handicapped boy as a student of the university as an exceptional treatment.
4. 今年，我们大学将录取两千名新生。

This year, our university will enroll 2,000 new students.

5. 这所大学的招生办公室拒绝录取他为学生。
   The admissions office of the university refused to accept him as a student.

"被录取"或"考取"，英语可以译为 to be recruited, to be admitted, to be enrolled, to be accepted, to matriculate。to matriculate 的意思是 to officially become a student at a university, 即"考入大学"。例如：

6. 去年，我弟弟被清华大学录取为研究生。
   Last year my brother was recruited as a postgraduate student by Tsinghua University.
7. 请告诉我是否被录取了？
   Would you kindly let me know if I am admitted?
8. 2000年，我考取南京大学，在那里主修物理4年。
   In 2000, I was admitted to Nanjing University where I studied for four years with a major in physics.
9. 确实，名牌大学毕业生在人才市场上受欢迎，所以许多学生会不遗余力上好的大学。
   It is true that graduates from prestigious universities are popular in talent markets, so, many students would spare no efforts to get enrolled in good universities.
10. 我接到通知已被北京师范大学录取。
    I was informed that I had been accepted by Beijing Normal University.
11. 他在2008年考入大学，主修化学。
    He matriculated in 2008, majoring in chemistry.

"录取通知书"，英语可以译为 admission notice, admission letter, admission offer, enrollment notice, enrollment certificate, notice of acceptance, letter of acceptance。例如：

12. 警方在本月初逮捕了两名伪造和贩卖假大学录取通知书的人。
    At the beginning of this month, the police arrested two people who had made and sold fake university admission notice.
13. 这个学生高考落榜，没有收到任何学院或大学的录取通知书。
    The student failed in the national entrance examination and did not receive any admission letter from a college or university.
14. 我依然没有收到任何录取通知书。
    I still haven't got any admission offer.
15. 我已拿到了复旦大学的录取通知书了。
    I have got the enrollment notice from Fudan University.

16. 据报道警方已拘留了8名伪造和贩卖假大学录取通知书的人。
It is reported that police has detained eight people for falsifying and selling fake university enrolment certificates.
17. 收到哈佛大学的录取通知书，让我高兴极了。
It gives me so much happiness to receive a notice of acceptance from Harvard University.
18. 学校表示，将在星期二发出录取通知书。
The school said it would mail out letters of acceptance on Tuesday.

“上大学”，英语可以译为 to go to university, to enter university, to get into university。例如：

19. 今年有1千零20万学生参加高考，大约60%由于扩招而能上大学。
More than 10.2 million students sat for the national entrance exam this year and about 60 percent could go to university thanks to the expansion of China's higher education system.
20. 如果学生们不能上顶尖的大学或主修受欢迎的专业，他们在毕业后找工作时将面临巨大困难。
If the students do not get into top universities or study popular majors, they will face big difficulties finding jobs after graduation.
21. 一年一度的高考被许多学生视为一生一次上大学的机会。
The annual National Matriculation Examination is regarded by many students as a once-in-a-lifetime opportunity to get into university.
22. 那一年有950万考生参加了高考，但是只有567万人考上大学。
That year, more than 9.5 million candidates competed in the national entrance examination, but only 5.67 million were able to enter college.
23. 对许多学生来说，上一所好大学意味着毕业后站在一个有前途职业生涯的门槛上。
To many students, entering a good university means standing on the threshold of a promising career after graduation.

“录取”的第二个意思是“讯问记录”，英语可以译为 to interrogate and record。例如：

24. 警察录取了犯罪嫌疑人的口供。
The policeman interrogated the suspect and recorded his confession.

18 极端

汉语关键词：极端、极端天气

英语关键词：extreme, extreme weather, dire, abject, ultra-, extremely, exceedingly

句子：今年极端天气发生得比往年频繁。

误译：Extreme weather has occurred more frequent this year than previous years.

正译：1) Extreme weather has occurred more often this year than previous years.

2) Extreme weather has occurred more frequently this year than previous years.

3) Extreme weather has been more frequent this year than previous years.

解释：

frequent 是形容词，不能修饰动词。需要用表示时间频度的副词 often 或 frequently 修饰动词 to occur。

“极端”的第一个意思是“事物顺着某个发展方向达到的顶点”，是个名词。英语可以译为 extreme。例如：

1. 正如谚语所说，走极端是危险的。
   As a proverb goes, extremes are dangerous.
2. 爱和恨是两个极端。
   Love and hate are two extremes.
3. 喜和悲是两个极端。
   Joy and grief are extremes.
4. 他在极端政治观点之间摇摆不定。
   He oscillates between political extremes.
5. 当人们采用一种新思想时，他们容易走极端。
   People tend to go to extremes when they adopt a new ideology.
6. 我们要全面地看问题，不要走极端。
   We must look at an issue in an overall way, and mustn't run to an extreme.
7. 他犹犹豫豫，拿不定主意，常常从一个极端走到另一个极端。
   He is hesitant and unable to make a decision, often going from one extreme to the other.
8. 股民在买卖股票时应该避免走极端。
   Stock investors should avoid the extremes when they buy and sell stocks.
9. 在这个观点上，这位哲学家小心翼翼不把他的理论推向极端。
   On this point, the philosopher is careful not to push his theory to an extreme.
10. 她过去一直很害羞，现在却走向了另一个极端。
   1) She used to be very shy, but now she has gone to the other extreme.

2) She used to be very shy, but now she has gone to the opposite extreme.
3) She used to be very shy, but now she has run into the opposite extreme.
4) She used to be very shy, but now she has changed from one extreme kind of behaviour to another.

11. 自由市场无政府主义者们通过反对一切税收而将这种想法引向极端。
Free-market anarchists take the idea to an extreme by opposing all taxation.
12. 在丛林中，他们为了生存而被迫采取了极端行动。
In the jungle, they were driven to extremes in order to survive.

“极端”的第二个意思是“偏激”、“绝对”或“彻头彻尾”，是个形容词。英语可以译为 extreme, dire, abject, ultra-。例如：

13. 他的政治观点相当极端。
His political views are rather extreme.
14. 自学能力对一个学生极端重要。
Self-taught ability is of extreme importance to a student.
15. 世界上有千百万人生活在极端贫困之中。
1) Millions of people live in extreme poverty in the world.
2) Millions of people live in dire poverty in the world.
3) Millions of people live in abject poverty in the world.
16. 只有这样我们才能在党内真正发扬民主，同时避免极端民主。
Only in this way can we really extend democracy within the Party and at the same time avoid ultra-democracy.
17. 这颗炸弹是一名右翼极端分子放置的。
The bomb was planted by a right-wing extremist.
18. 我同极端分子没有来往。
I have had no truck with extremists.
19. 我与极端主义格格不入。
I have had no truck with extremism.
20. 我从来没有赞同过政治极端主义。
I have never associated myself with political extremism.

“极端”的第三个意思是表示程度极深，相当于“极其”或“非常”，是个副词。英语可以译为 extremely, exceedingly。例如：

21. 他发现找工作极端困难。
1) He found it extremely difficult to get a job.
2) He found it exceedingly difficult to get a job.
22. 她因肥胖而感到极端苦恼。
She feels exceedingly annoyed for being obese.
23. 希特勒极端仇视犹太人。

1) Hitler had extreme hatred for the Jews.
2) Hitler was extremely hostile towards the Jews.

24. 这位经济分析师认为试图救助楼市是极端愚蠢的行为。
The economic analyst holds that trying to save the real estate market is an exceedingly foolish act.

25. 不吃早饭被许多人认为是极端错误的减肥方法。
Eating no breakfast is considered by many as an exceedingly wrong way of slimming.

“极端”的第四个意思是“极其不正常”，是个形容词。英语可以译为 extreme。例如：

26. 全球变暖可能导致更加频繁的极端天气。
Global warming may lead to more frequent extreme weather.

27. 由于大气的不稳定性，在未来极端天气将更加频繁。
Extreme weather will be more frequent in the future due to the instability of the atmosphere.

28. 我国许多地方最近经历了极端天气状况，包括热浪、暴风雨和洪水。
Many places of our country have recently experienced extreme weather conditions including heat waves, storms and floods.

29. 在我国，诸如干旱、暴风雨和洪水之类的极端天气事件已变得愈加频繁，愈加严重。
Extreme-weather events such as drought, storms and floods have already become more frequent and more severe in our country.

30. 我们准备好应付更加频繁的极端天气。
We are braced for more frequent extreme weather.

31. 这些偏远的山村极易受到极端天气的侵袭。
The remote mountainous villages are highly vulnerable to extreme weather.

32. 沙漠里极端热。
The heat in the desert was extreme.

33. 孩子们只有在极端情况下才可与其父母分离。
Children will be removed from their parents only in extreme circumstances.

34. 在极端情况下，这两个触点可能会焊接在一起。
In extreme instances, the contacts may weld together.

35. 不要做出诸如离开国家之类的极端事情。
Don't go doing anything extreme like leaving the country.

36. 这是我见过的最极端的虐待动物的事例。
It was the most extreme example of cruelty to animals I had ever seen.

19 虚拟

汉语关键词： 虚拟、虚拟货币、虚拟语气

英语关键词： invented, fabricated, fictitious, virtual, virtual money, virtual currency, hypothetical, supposed, subjunctive, subjunctive mood, imitate

句子： 虚拟货币不能兑换成像美元或人民币之类的现实货币。

误译： Subjunctive money cannot be exchanged into real money like US dollars or Renminbi.

正译： Virtual money cannot be exchanged into real money like US dollars or Renminbi.

解释：

有的学生学了虚拟语气，知道其英语为 the subjunctive mood，就错误地以为凡是“虚拟”二字，英语就一定译成 subjunctive。其实，subjunctive 的意思是 the form or mood of a verb that expresses wishes, possibility or uncertainty，一般仅用在英语语法之中。subjunctive mood 是个语法术语。例如：

1. 许多中国学生发现虚拟语气很难掌握。
   Many Chinese students find that the subjunctive is very difficult to master.
2. 这个动词表现为虚拟语气。
   The verb is in the subjunctive.

“虚拟”的第一个意思是“虚构的或凭想象编造的”。英语可以译为 invented, fabricated, fictitious。例如：

3. 这部小说里有些情节是虚拟的。
   In this novel, some plots are invented.
4. 这整个事件是虚拟的。
   The whole incident is fabricated.
5. 这部武打影片的情节是虚拟的。
   The plots of this martial arts film are fictitious.
6. 这是作家创造的一个虚拟人物。
   This is a fictitious figure created by the writer.

“虚拟”的第二个意思是“假设的，或不符合事实的”。英语可以译为 hypothetical, supposed, subjunctive。例如：

7. 在虚拟条件下，这个计划是可行的。
   Under hypothetical conditions, the plan is feasible.

8. 这个虚拟案例的存在是令人质疑的。
   The existence of the supposed case is questionable.
9. 这个学生发现英语的虚拟语气很难学。
   The student found it difficult to learn the subjunctive mood of English.

"虚拟"的第三个意思是"模拟"，是个动词。英语可以译为 to imitate。例如：

10. 戏曲表演常以扬鞭虚拟骑马。
    In the performance of traditional Chinese opera, an actor often imitates riding a horse by swinging the whip.

"虚拟"的第四个意思是"与由高科技术实现的仿实物或伪实物的技术相关的"。英语可以译为 virtual。例如：

11. 该期刊的目标是在虚拟现实领域传播研究成果，引起讨论。
    The aim of the journal is to disseminate research and provoke discussion in the area of virtual reality.
12. 虚拟世界不同于现实生活。
    The virtual world is different from real life.
13. 在虚拟世界，规则是完全不同的。
    In the virtual world, the rules are entirely different.
14. 在中国，成功的网上视频游戏玩家已从虚拟世界赚取现实货币。
    Successful online video game players in China have made real money from the virtual world.
15. 虚拟技术的原则可以应用于不同领域，像虚拟通讯、虚拟药物、以及许多其他方面。
    The principles of virtual technology can be applied to different fields, like virtual communications, virtual medicines and many more.
16. 虚拟经济的出现是发展中的市场经济的必然。
    The appearance of virtual economy is the necessity of developing market economy.
17. 网上购物是一种购物方式，即从名叫网上商店的虚拟商店通过点击鼠标选择商品来购买东西。
    Shopping online is the way of shopping, that is, buying goods from a virtual store which is called an online store, by selecting the items with mouse clips.
18. 顾客可以直接从虚拟商店设计和定做服装。
    Customers can design and order apparel directly from the virtual shop.
19. 禁止人们用虚拟货币购买实体商品。
    People are forbidden to use virtual currency to buy real goods.

20. 中国将从虚拟货币利润征收20%的个人所得税。
    China will put a personal income tax of 20 percent on profit from virtual money.
21. 应阻止虚拟卖家在现实世界逐利。
    Virtual sellers should be prohibited from flipping for a profit in the real world.
22. 这个青年人意识到参与虚拟股市的一些积极与消极方面。
    The young man became aware of some of the positive and negative aspects of participating in the virtual stock market.

20 滑坡

汉语关键词： 滑坡、山体滑坡、塌方

英语关键词： landslide, landslip, go downslope, slide downslope, decline, slump, downslide

句子： 这个装置的目的是使汽车在滑坡时安全而省油。

误译： The device is aimed at making a car safe and petrol-saving when it is landsliding.

正译： The device is aimed at making a car safe and petrol-saving when it is running downslope.

解释：

landslide 一般当名词用，意思是 a mass of earth, rock, etc. that falls down the slope of a mountain，即"山体滑坡"，指自然现象，不是指汽车滑坡。

"滑坡"的第一个意思是指"地表斜坡上大量的土石在重力作用下整体下滑的自然现象"。英语可以译为 landslide, landslip。例如：

1. 滑坡会对建筑物、公路、铁路、农田和森林造成很大破坏。
   Landslide can cause great damages to buildings, highways, railways, farmlands and forests.
2. 每年，季雨都会在这个地区导致滑坡和骤发洪水。
   Every year, seasonal downpours cause landslides and flash floods in this area.
3. 昨晚，这条公路附近发生一起特大山体滑坡事故。
   Last night, a massive landslide occurred in the vicinity of the highway.
4. 在这个地区，特大山体滑坡阻断了公路。
   In this region, massive landslides blocked the highway.

5. 暴雨过后，滑坡掩埋了好几幢房屋。
After the rainstorm, a landslide buried several houses.
6. 这次滑坡填死了动物常常来饮水的水坑。
The landslide earthed up the pool where the animals usually drank.
7. 损坏是由地震引起的滑坡造成的。
The damage resulted from the landslide initiated by the earthquake.
8. 在这个地方，上周的洪水和滑坡造成120多人死亡。
In this place, floods and landslides over the last week killed more than 120 people.
9. 上周，这些旧房子被滑坡毁坏了。
The old houses were destroyed by a landslip last week.

有时，landslide 也可以当动词用，意思是“滑坡”或“塌方”。例如：

10. 忽然，一个非常高大的、一面陡直的煤矿废土石堆的牢固部分开始塌方。
Suddenly, a substantial part of a very large, steep-sided colliery spoil heap began to landslide.

“滑坡”的第二个意思是指“汽车下坡行驶或顺坡下滑”。英语可以译为 to run downslope, to slide downslope。例如：

11. 孩子们在玩小汽车滑坡的游戏。
The children were playing with a toy car running downslope.
12. 今天早晨，这里发生了汽车滑坡事故。
This morning, here occurred an accident in which a car slided downslope.
13. 由于结冰的道路很滑，汽车容易滑坡。
As the icy road is slippery, cars tend to slide downslope.

“滑坡”的第三个意思是比喻“经济或成绩急剧下降”。英语动词可以译为 to decline, to slump, to landslide, to go downslope；名词可以译为 decline, slump, landslide, downslide。例如：

14. 由于管理不善，这个地区旅游业开始滑坡。
Because of poor management, tourism industry began to decline in this area.
15. 由于缺乏有效的监督，这个工厂的产品质量出现滑坡。
Due to the lack of an effective supervision, the quality of the products has declined in this factory.
16. 受经济危机的影响，这个拉美国家的汽车生产和销售都已大幅滑坡。
Affected by the economic crisis, car production and sale have declined by a big margin in this Latin American country.

17. 这名大学生由于不刻苦努力，他的学习成绩迅速滑坡。
As the college student didn’t study hard, his academic performance declined rapidly.
18. 在全球经济衰退的背景下，中国的进出口今年已明显滑坡。
In the context of global economic recession, China’s import and export have conspicuously slumped this year.
19. 当发生金融危机时，经济开始滑坡，人们开始削减开支，停止消费。
When the financial crisis occurred, the economy began to landslide and people began cutting costs and stopped spending.
20. 由于在学生中缺少体育积极分子和善于表演的人才，这个大学在体育和文化活动方面开始滑坡。
Due to the lack of sports activists and cultural performers among the students, the university started to go downslope in both sports and cultural activities.
21. 本市工业生产短期出现的滑坡现象已被制止住了。
The decline of the industrial production, which had lasted for a short period of time, has already been checked.
22. 当前的经济滑坡预示着一次大的危机的即将到来。
The current economic slump foretells the imminent coming of a major crisis.
23. 全球经济滑坡已严重影响这个国家的旅游业。
The global economic landslide has seriously affected the tourism industry in this country.
24. 由于自然灾害，这个地区的经济严重滑坡。
1) As a result of natural disasters, there has been a massive decline in economy in this area.
2) As a result of natural disasters, there has been a massive landslide in economy in this area.
25. 在许多国家人们越来越关注经济是否会走向滑坡。
There is a growing concern among the people in many countries about whether the economy would head for a downslide.
26. 地方政府已采取一系列有效措施来阻止经济滑坡，并防止社会动荡。
The local government has taken a series of effective measures to stop an economic downslide and prevent social unrest.

21 日全食

汉语关键词： 日食、日全食、日偏食、日全环食、日环食

英语关键词： solar eclipse, sun eclipse, eclipse of the sun, full solar eclipse, full sun eclipse, full eclipse of the sun, total solar eclipse, total sun eclipse, total eclipse of the sun, solar full eclipse, solar total eclipse, sun's full eclipse, sun's total eclipse, partial solar eclipse, partial sun eclipse, partial eclipse of the sun, solar partial eclipse, sun's partial eclipse

句子： 7月22日，将出现21世纪最长时间的日全食。

误译： On July 22, there will be the longest sun full eclipse of the 21st century.

正译： On July 22, there will be the longest full sun eclipse of the 21st century.

解释：

将“日全食”字对字地译为 sun full eclipse，不合乎英语习惯。作为中心词的名词前面有一个以上修饰词时，包括形容词和名词，谁排列在先，谁排列在后；或者说哪个修饰词离中心词最近，哪个次之，是个复杂的问题。不容易找到普遍规律。在这里，sun eclipse（名词修饰名词）的关系更加密切，不可分开。译为 full sun eclipse，比较好。

“日食”可以译为 solar eclipse, sun eclipse 或 eclipse of the sun。例如：

1. 日食是当月球经过地球和太阳中间时人们一时全部或部分看不见太阳的现象。
   A solar eclipse is an occasion when the moon passes between the earth and the sun so that you cannot see all or part of the sun for a time.
2. 发生日食时，有些动物很恐惧。
   Some animals are frightened during an eclipse of the sun.
3. 天文学家能够精确计算出什么时候会发生日食或月食。
   Astronomers can precisely calculate when there will be eclipses of the sun or the moon.
4. 这些儿童通过特殊的镜片观看日食。
   These children viewed the sun eclipse through special lenses.
5. 对那些足够幸运而能目睹日食的人来说，最好不要用肉眼或通过望远镜直接观看太阳。
   For those who are lucky enough to witness the eclipse of the sun, it is advisable not to look directly at the sun with the naked eye or through a telescope.

6. 观察日食的最重要事情是天空无云。
The most important thing for watching the solar eclipse is that there are no clouds in the sky.

“日全食”的译法很多，包括 full solar eclipse, full sun eclipse, full eclipse of the sun，或 total solar eclipse, total sun eclipse, total eclipse of the sun。此外，在Google上也可以查到solar full eclipse, solar total eclipse 以及the sun's full eclipse, the sun's total eclipse的说法，但是用的较少。例如：

7. 日全食是日食的一种类型。此时月亮在太阳前面经过并完全遮住太阳，这是一种非常奇妙的景观。
A total eclipse of the sun is one type of solar eclipse. When the moon passes in front of the sun and blocks it completely, this is an amazing sight.
8. 他有幸观测了本世纪的第一次日全食。
He is lucky to have observed the first full solar eclipse of the century.
9. 在俄罗斯，到2061年才会出现下一次日全食。
The next full solar eclipse in Russia will not take place until 2061.
10. 全世界的观众将能够在7月22日通过电视、互联网和移动电话观看本世纪时间最长的日全食。
Worldwide audience will be able to watch the longest total solar eclipse of this century through TV, Internet and mobile phones on July 22.
11. 当发生日全食时，温度和湿度可能急剧下降，风向可能改变，风速可能加快，而且在白昼时天可能忽然变暗。
When full solar eclipse takes place, temperature and humidity may fall sharply, wind direction may change, wind speed may go faster and it may darken suddenly during the daytime.
12. 来自世界各地的天文学家可望来到这里观测日全食。
Astronomers from all over the world are expected here to take observations of the sun's total eclipse.

“日偏食”可以译为 partial solar eclipse, partial sun eclipse或partial eclipse of the sun。也有少数人译为solar partial eclipse, the sun's partial eclipse。例如：

13. 在其他城市，像北京和香港，将看到大约75%的日偏食。
Other cities, like Beijing and Hong Kong, will see partial solar eclipses of about 75 percent.
14. 已向希望在本月底观测日偏食的人们发布了安全警告。
Safety warnings have been issued to anyone hoping to catch a glimpse of the sun's partial eclipse at the end of this month.

15. 2008年2月7日，从新西兰全境都可以看到日偏食。
    A partial eclipse of the sun was visible from all parts of New Zealand on February 7th, 2008.

"日环食"可以译为 annular solar eclipse, annular eclipse of the sun。"日全环食"可以译为 total annular solar eclipse, full annular solar eclipse。例如：

16. 据报导明天将有日环食。
    It is reported that there will be an annular eclipse of the sun tomorrow.
17. 2005年10月3日星期一，在西班牙、葡萄牙、非洲和印度洋发生了日环食。
    An annular solar eclipse occurred on Monday, 3 October, 2005, in Spain, Portugal, Africa, and the Indian Ocean.

22 小金库

汉语关键词： 金库、小金库、国库、宝库

英语关键词： state treasury, national treasury, exchequer, coffers, bank vault, vault, unauthorized departmental coffers, hidden coffers, hidden reserves, off-book accounts, secret assets, treasure house, treasure trove

句子： 政府三令五申任何单位不得私设小金库。

误译： The government has repeatedly issued orders that no unit is allowed to set up a private little treasury.

正译： The government has repeatedly issued orders that no unit is allowed to set up hidden reserves.

解释：

treasury 有两个意思，一是泛指 a place where valuable things are stored，即"宝库"或"金库"；二是专指 the government department that controls public money，即"财政部"。而"小金库"指的是"未在本单位财务会计部门列收列支或未纳入预算管理、私存私放的各种资金"，不是指存放钱的小型金库，译为 little treasury 是不合适的。

"金库"的第一个意思是"经管国家预算资金收支的机构"，即"国库"。英语可以译为 state treasury, national treasury, exchequer。例如：

1. 罚款一律上缴国库，任何单位或个人不得截留。

1) All penalties collected shall be handed over to the National Treasury, and may not be withheld by any unit or individual.
2) All penalties shall be turned over to the State Treasury, and no unit or individual may retain them.

2. 这个官员渎职，结果使国库遭受重大损失。
The misfeasance of the official resulted in a considerable loss to the exchequer.

“金库”的第二个意思是“金融机构或企业存放日常备用现金的地方”。英语可以译为 treasury, coffers。例如：

3. 那个较小的房间被用作金库。
The smaller room was used as a treasury.
4. 在这个石油输出国，油价的飙升使得国家金库充裕并刺激了经济的发展。
In this oil-exporting country, an oil boom filled up its state coffers and fanned its economic growth.
5. 这个国家的金库总是充盈。
The coffers of the nation are always full.
6. 在这个不发达国家，政府的金库几乎空了。
In this under-developed country, the government's coffers were almost empty.
7. 这个贼从国家金库里偷钱。
The thief stole money from the nation's coffers.

“金库”的第三个意思是“银行存放贵重物品的地方”。英语可以译为 bank vault, vault。例如：

8. 这位贵妇人的大部分首饰都存放在银行金库里。
Most of the rich lady's jewellery is stored in bank vaults.
9. 这些绘画中的最宝贵的部分存放在一家瑞士银行的金库里。
The most valuable of those paintings are stored in the vault of a Swiss bank.

“小金库”的第一个意思是指“在单位财务以外另立账目、私自存放和支配的公款”。英语可以译为 unauthorized departmental coffers, hidden coffers, hidden reserves, off-book accounts。例如：

10. 那些私设小金库的部门领导人将被撤职，并必须对他们的行动承担全部责任。
Those department leaders who set up unauthorized departmental coffers will be relieved of their duties and have to take full responsibility for their actions.

11. 中国最近做出新的努力治理被称为小金库的违法账目。
China has recently made a new effort to stamp out illicit accounts known as hidden coffers.
12. 有些部门正大量私设小金库。
Some departments are secretly running a large number of hidden reserves.
13. 涉及小金库的案件将受到严厉查处。
Cases involving off-books accounts will be investigated and dealt with severely.

“小金库”的第二个意思是指“家庭成员中个人私自保存和支配的钱财”，即“私房钱”。英语可以译为 secret assets。例如：

14. 大多数妻子相信她们的丈夫没有小金库，而她们紧紧掌管着家庭钱财。
Most wives believe their husbands have no secret assets and they have a grip on their family purse strings.

“宝库”的第一个意思是“储藏珍贵物品的地方”。英语可以译为 treasure house, treasury。例如：

15. 由于这个皇宫的宝库是对公众开放的，所以参观者可以看到王室储藏的所有珍宝。
As the treasure house in the palace is open to public, the visitors can see all the treasures stored by the royal family.

“宝库”的第二个意思是比喻“集中珍贵东西的处所”。英语可以译为 treasure house, treasury, treasure trove。例如：

16. 这个画廊是一个中世纪艺术宝库。
1) The gallery is a treasure house of medieval art.
2) The gallery is a treasure trove of medieval art.
17. 这本书是一个有用信息的宝库。
This book is a treasury of useful information.
18. 图书馆是一个知识宝库。
The library is a treasure house of knowledge.
19. 实践是开启知识宝库的钥匙。
Practice is the key to the treasure house of knowledge.
20. 读书是开启思想宝库的钥匙。
Reading is the key to the treasure house of ideas.
21. 海洋是矿物和食物的宝库。
The ocean is a treasure house of minerals and foods

23 演习

汉语关键词：演习、军事演习

英语关键词：manoeuvre, exercise, drill, military manoeuvre, military exercise

句子：最近，中俄两国举行了联合反恐军事演习。

误译：China and Russia have recently conducted a united anti-terror military exercise.

正译：1) China and Russia have recently conducted a joint anti-terror military exercise.

2) China and Russia have recently held a joint anti-terrorist military exercise.

解释：

联合军事演习是两个或多个国家为了一个共同目的联合起来一起举行的军事演习。参与国家相互配合，相互协调，但是各自保持独立性。united 具有 united as one 或 united into one 的含义，即“成为一体”。英语没有 united military exercise 的搭配。但是英语可以说 joint military exercise，因为 joint 的意思是 involving two or more people together，只是涉及到双方或多个方面，而没有强调“成为一体”。

“演习”的第一个意思是“用于军事目的按照预定方案进行的实地练习”。英语可以译为 manoeuvre, exercise, drill。例如：

1. 边境上曾有过大规模的军事演习。
   There have been large-scale military manoeuvres on the frontier.
2. 陆军正在沙漠中进行军事演习。
   The army is on manoeuvres in the desert.
3. 在这次军事演习中，对方被我军歼灭了。
   In the military exercise, the opposition was annihilated by our army.
4. 据报道伊朗在波斯湾举行了一次海军演习。
   It was reported that Iran conducted a navy manoeuvre in Persian Gulf.
5. 陆军在多种地形和全天候条件下举行了一次接近实战的演习。
   The army conducted a close-to-real-war exercise in multiple fields and under all weather conditions.
6. 士兵们在沙漠里举行了一次实弹演习。
   1) The soldiers held a live-ammunition manoeuvre in the desert.
   2) The soldiers held a manoeuvre with live ammunition in the desert.
7. 安全部队举行了决定性的战术演习，以解救数百名被恐怖分子劫持的人质。
   The security forces launched a decisive tactical manoeuvre to free hundreds of hostages held by the terrorists.

8. 这支部队在一个废弃的村子里举行了巷战演习。
The troops staged a street-fighting exercise in an abandoned village.
9. 昨天，本市居民在防空演习中疏散。
Local residents evacuated during an air-defence drill in this city yesterday.
10. 这两国空军最近举行了双边防空演习。
The air forces of the two countries have recently conducted a bilateral air-defence exercise.
11. 昨天上午，我市举行了防空演习。
Yesterday morning, an anti-air-raid drill was staged in our city.
12. 防空演习已被取消了。
The antiaircraft manoeuvres have been scrubbed out.

“演习”的第二个意思是“以防止灾害或事故为目的按照预定方案进行的实地练习”。英语可以译为 drill, exercise。例如：

13. 消防队员在防火演习中试图用水射流扑灭火焰。
The fire-fighters tried to put out the flames with water jets during a fire-fighting exercise.
14. 船员们举行了防火演习和弃船演习。
The crew went through a fire-fighting drill and a drill to abandon ship.
15. 消防演习是火灾时演练疏散一座建筑物人员的方法。
A fire drill is a method of practicing the evacuation of a building in case of a fire.
16. 每年，日本举行大规模防地震演习。
Every year, Japan holds massive anti-earthquake drills.
17. 这些警察在一次防洪演习中扛沙袋加固堤坝。
The policemen carried sandbags to reinforce a bank during an anti-flood drill
18. 这艘货船的船员举行了一场海上救生演习。
The crew of the cargo ship conducted a life-saving drill at sea.
19. 游轮在离港前必须举行一次救生艇演习。
Cruise ships are required to hold a life boat drill prior to departure.
20. 船员中的每位成员每个月必须参加至少一次弃船演习和一次防火演习。
Each member of the crew shall participate in at least one abandon drill and one fire drill every month.
21. 公司组织了一次疏散演习，使全体员工熟悉疏散计划并检验其有效性。
The company conducted an evacuation drill to acquaint their staff members with the evacuation plan and to test its effectiveness.
22. 上周五，这个超市举行了一次紧急疏散演习，作为员工培训。
The supermarket conducted an emergency evacuation drill for staff training last Friday.

23. 几支医疗队参加了在地震灾区举行的救援演习。
Several medical teams participated in the rescue drill in the earthquake-hit area.

24 个体户

汉语关键词：个体、个体户、个体工商户、个体经济
英语关键词：individual, self-employed business, self-employed economy
句子：流动商贩有望登记成个体户。
误译：1) Pedlars are expected to be registered as individual household.
2) Pedlars are expected to be registered as individual entrepreneur.
正译：Pedlars are expected to be registered as self-employed business.
解释：

“个体户”的全称为“个体工商户”，意思是“以家庭或个人为单位，拥有一定资金，独立经营自负盈亏的经济实体”。在这里，“个体”强调的是“个体（包括个人和家庭）所有和经营，而不是集体或国家所有或经营”。将“个体户”字对字译为 individual household 不合适。individual 的意思是 connected with one person rather than as part of a group, 强调的是“与个人相关，而不是群体中的部分”。household 的意思是 all the people living together in a house，指“同住一个屋檐下的全体成员”，强调的是“社会单元”。individual household 的意思是“单个的一户人家”。“个体户”最好译为 self-employed business，既包括 self-employed person，也包括 self-employed household。self-employed 的意思是 working for oneself, and not employed by others，即“自己雇佣自己”。此外，“个体工商户”是个广泛的概念，包括资金雄厚、独立经营的大商户，也包括小本生意、微利经营的小商贩。entrepreneur 的意思是 person who makes money by starting or running businesses, especially when this involves taking financial risks，尤指涉及财务风险的企业家，不能代表所有的个体工商户。有人将“个体户”译为 individual engaged in small-scale business, household engaged in small-scale business, small-scale privately-owned business, individually-owned business, small private business，译法五花八门，不如译为 self-employed business。例如：

1. 中国有一千多万人干个体户。
China has more than ten million people engaged in self-employed

businesses.

2. 这个百货商场的一些柜台转让给几个个体户了。

   1) Some counters of this department store have been transferred to a few self-employed businesses.

   2) Some counters of this department store have been made over to a few self-employed businesses.

“个体”的第一个意思是“单个的人或生物，与集体或群体相区别”。英语可以译为 individual。例如：

3. 任何群体都是由个体组成的。

   Any group is made up of individuals.

4. 个体离不开群体。

   An individual can't isolate itself from a group.

5. 个体行为是由一系列变量和因素形成的。

   Individual behaviour is shaped by a range of variables and factors.

6. 个体意识是一个个体的意识。

   Individual consciousness is the consciousness of one individual.

7. 财产个体所有制存在于所有的社会，甚至最古老的社会。

   Individual ownership of property has existed in all societies, even the most ancient.

8. 个体农业的发展在国与国、地区与地区、及农户与农户之间是极其不同的。

   The development of individual farming varies strongly between countries, regions and households.

“个体”的第二个意思是“个体户”。英语可以译为 self-employed business。例如：

9. 他干了几年个体，挣了一点钱。

   He ran a self-employed business for years and earned a little money.

10. 她下岗以后，向银行贷款开始干了个体。

    After she was laid off, she made a loan from the bank and started to run a self-employed business.

11. 他作为个体劳动者受雇佣在一个建筑工地干活。

    He was employed on a building site as a self-employed labourer.

12. 这个大学毕业生决定自己创业，正在申请个体经营执照。

    This university graduate has decided to start up his own business and he is now applying for a licence for self-employed business.

“个体经济”，可以译为 self-employed economy。例如：

13. 个体经济目前在中国经济中起着独特的作用。
    Self-employed economy currently plays a unique role in national economy in China.
14. 在个体经济中，生产方式归个人所有，经营基于所有者自身的劳动。
    In the self-employed economy, the means of production is owned by the individual and the business is based on the labour of the owners themselves.

25 酒后驾车

汉语关键词： 酒后驾车、醉酒驾驶

英语关键词： drink and drive, drive after drinking, drive under the influence of alcohol, drive under influence, DUI, drunk driving, drunken driving, intoxicated driving, drive while drunk, drive while intoxicated, DWI

句子： 警察警告司机们不要酒后驾车。

误译： Police warns the drivers not to drive after drinking wine.

正译： Police warns the drivers not to drive after drinking.

解释：

在汉语中，“饮酒”或“喝酒”是个动宾结构，但是英语不需要译成 drinking wine 这样的动宾结构，而在一定语境里译为 drinking 就可以了。同样地，汉语说“读书”，英语只要译成 reading 就可以，而不必说 reading books。例如，“我喜欢读书”译为 I am fond of reading 就可以了，而不必译为 I am fond of reading books。

“酒后驾车”指“在酒精影响下驾车”，我国法律规定“驾驶员每百毫升血液或呼吸中，酒精含量大于 20 毫克而小于 80 毫克为酒后驾车”。英语名词可以译为 drinking and driving, driving after drinking, driving under the influence of alcohol, driving under influence，或缩略为 DUI；动词可以译为 to drink and drive, to drive after drinking, to drive under the influence of alcohol, to drive under influence。例如：

1. 警察因这名司机酒后驾车而拘留了他。
   The policeman detained the driver for drinking and driving.
2. 警方指控那位司机酒后驾车。
   Police charged the driver with driving after drinking.

3. 警方开始在主要餐馆和娱乐场所地点实行24小时巡查以防止酒后驾车。
   Police began to patrol major restaurants and entertainment venues on a 24-hour basis to prevent driving after drinking.
4. 对那些酒后驾车，而且每百毫升血液中酒精含量大于20毫克而小于80毫克的人，他们的驾驶证将被扣留3个月。
   For those who drive after drinking and have a blood-alcohol content between 20 mg and 80 mg per 100 ml, their license will be suspended for three months.
5. 在我国，警方最近开始了为期两个月的整治酒后驾车的工作。
   In our country, police have recently begun a two-month crackdown on driving under the influence of alcohol.
6. 警察正在测试一个出租汽车司机，确定他是否酒后驾车。
   The policeman was testing a taxi driver to determine whether he was driving under the influence of alcohol.
7. 这名男子因酒后驾车和粗心驾驶而被捕，并被送往监狱。
   The man was arrested for driving under the influence and negligent driving and taken to jail.
8. 唯一可以阻止酒后驾车的方法是给违法者更加严厉的处罚。
   The only way to prevent driving under the influence is to mete out stiffer penalties to violators.
9. 这名男子因被怀疑酒后驾车而被拘留。
   The man was detained by the police for suspicion of DUI.

“醉酒驾驶”指“在醉酒状态下驾车”，我国法律规定“驾驶员每百毫升血液或呼吸中，酒精含量大于或等于80毫克为醉酒驾驶”。英语名词可以译为drunk driving, drunken driving, intoxicated driving, 或缩略为 DWI；动词可以译为to drive while drunk, to drive while intoxicated。例如：

10. 醉酒驾车容易导致交通事故。
    Drunk driving can easily cause traffic accidents.
11. 这个事故是这个司机经常醉酒驾驶的必然后果。
    The accident is the inevitable consequence of the driver’s habitual drunken driving.
12. 他被控告醉酒驾驶而不得不出庭受审。
    He has to appear in court on a charge of drunken driving.
13. 警方逮捕了一名一夜间两次开两辆不同汽车醉酒驾驶的妇女。
    Police arrested a woman twice in one night in two different cars for driving while drunk.
14. 每百毫升血液或呼吸中，酒精含量等于或大于80毫克的醉驾司机将被拘留15天，他们的驾驶证将被扣留6个月。

Drunk drivers whose alcohol content is 80 mg per 100 ml or above will be detained for 15 days and their licenses will be suspended for six months.

15. 如果一名醉驾司机在一年内被抓两次，其驾驶证将被吊销2至5年。

    If a drunk driver is caught twice within a year, his or her license will be revoked for two to five years.

16. 他因醉酒驾驶被罚款500元。

    He was fined 500 yuan for driving when intoxicated.

17. 这名男子因被怀疑醉酒驾车而被拘留。

    The man was taken into custody on suspicion of DWI.

26 反腐倡廉

汉语关键词： 腐败、腐败现象、腐烂、腐朽、反腐倡廉

英语关键词： decay, rot，decaying, decayed, rotting, rotten, putrid, corrupt, corruption, decadent, musty, combat corruption and build a clean government

句子： 一个国家的兴起与腐败现象如同水火一样是不相容的。

误译： The rise of a nation is as incompatible with corruption phenomenon as fire is with water.

正译： The rise of a nation is as incompatible with corruption as fire is with water.

解释：

将"腐败现象"字对字直译为corruption phenomenon，有些累赘。译为 corruption 就够了。

"腐败"的第一个意思是"腐朽变质"，即"腐烂"。英语动词可以译为to decay, to rot；名词可以译为decay, rot；形容词可以译为decaying, decayed, rotting, rotten, putrid。例如：

1. 后院的树木好像在腐烂。

   The trees in the back yard seem to be decaying.

2. 这个窗框已经完全腐烂。

   The window frame has rotted away completely.

3. 木材涂上油漆，可以防止腐烂。

   When wood is painted, it can be prevented from decay.

4. 这木材决不能受潮，因为那样很快会腐烂。

   The wood must not get damp as rot can quickly result.

5. 这个地方的土壤主要由腐烂的树叶组成。
The soil in this place is mainly composed of decaying leaves.
6. 在腐烂食物中能发现蛆。
Maggots can be found in decaying food.
7. 食物废弃物，包括食物加工废弃物、过期食物和变性食物、以及腐烂食物，都保存了许多有用的营养物质。
Food wastes, including food-processing wastes, out-of-date and denatured food, and decayed food retain many useful nutrients.
8. 家庭主妇正试图清理装满腐败食物的冰箱。
The housewife was trying to clean a refrigerator filled with rotting food.
9. 这些水果正开始腐烂。
The fruit is starting to go rotten.
10. 这些腐败食物标签表明已远远超过销售截止日期。
These rotten food labels are well past their sell-by date.
11. 千万不要吃腐败的食物，因为它能引起严重中毒。
You can never eat putrid food, as it may cause intense poisoning.

“腐败”的第二个意思是“思想陈旧或行为堕落”，即“腐朽”。英语可以译为 corrupt, decadent, musty。例如：

12. 这个新任命的官员很快就变腐败了。
The newly appointed official soon became corrupt.
13. 这个腐败官员在被认定犯受贿和贪污罪后被判处无期徒刑。
The corrupt official was sentenced to life in prison after he was convicted of bribery and corruption.
14. 网民们再次证明他们会千方百计揭露腐败的政府官员。
Internet users once again proved they would leave no stone unturned to expose corrupt government officials.
15. 在我国，反对腐败思想与文化，及反对没落生活方式的斗争将是长期存在的。
In our country, the struggle against the corrosion of decadent ideology, culture and moribund style of life will be long lasting.
16. 我们决不向消极腐败思想做任何让步。
We will never make any concession to the negative and musty ideology.

“腐败”的第三个意思是“制度、组织、机构或措施混乱与黑暗”。英语形容词可以译为 rotten, corrupt；名词可以译为 corruption。例如：

17. 这个组织已腐败透顶。
The organization is rotten to the core.
18. 腐败会从根本上扼杀一个民族、一个国家的生机与活力。

Corruption will completely strangle the vigour and vitality of a nation or a country.

19. 中国共产党的性质和宗旨，决定了党同腐败现象如同水火一样是不相容的。
 The nature and aims of the Communist Party of China determines that it is as incompatible with corruption as fire is with water.
20. 只有全社会对于腐败现象持“零容忍度”，才能从根本上消除和减少腐败的发生。
 Only when the whole of society is zero-tolerant towards corruption, can we eliminate or reduce its occurrence.
21. 将“零容忍度”作为政府预防腐败的一个基本理念，帮助民众从生活小事做起，从身边出发，采取“不支持腐败、不宽容腐败，拒绝与腐败合作”的鲜明立场。
 We must take “zero-tolerance” as an underlying principle in the government’s effort to prevent corruption, and help the people to adopt the clear-cut stand of “not supporting corruption, not tolerating corruption, and refusing to collude with corruption” by starting from small issues arising from everyday life around them.
22. 古往今来，没有任何一个国家能够在官员腐败现象猖獗的情况下成为强国或者保持强国的地位。
 Today as well as throughout history, no nation has become or remained strong and powerful with rampant corruption of its officials.
23. 政府已采取严厉措施打击一切形式的政治腐败。
 The government has taken strict measures against all forms of political corruption.
24. 近年来，学术腐败一直是中国学术界的一个热门话题。
 In recent years, academic corruption has been a hot topic in the Chinese academic community.
25. 如果学术腐败在中国得不到制止，科学和技术发展在这个国家将会被延误。
 If academic corruption can’t be curbed in China, scientific and technological development will be delayed in the country.
26. 教授们将自己的名字署在他们没有做出任何贡献的论文上，是一种学术腐败。
 It is a form of corruption for professors to have their names put to papers, to which they have contributed nothing.
27. 这是世界上许多国家反腐的重要经验。
 This is an important lesson in anti-corruption drawn from many countries in the world.

“反腐倡廉”，英语可以译为 to combat corruption and build a clean government。例如：

28. 反腐倡廉是顺利进行改革开放和现代化建设的一项重要保证。
To combat corruption and build a clean government is an important guarantee for the smooth reform, opening-up and modernization drive.

27

职业病

汉语关键词：职业病、工伤

英语关键词：occupational disease, occupation disease, occupational illness, work illness, work-related illness, employment disease, industrial disease, occupational injury, work injury, work-related injury, on-the-job injury, employment injury

句子：据报道，一位农民工接受了开胸验肺手术以弄清他的职业病病情。

误译：It is reported that a rural migrant worker received an open-chest surgery to find out the truth about his professional illness.

正译：It is reported that a rural migrant worker received an open-chest surgery to find out the truth about his occupational illness.

解释：

professional 的意思是 connected with a job that needs special training or skill, especially one that needs a high level of education，指与需要专门培训或专门技能的职业相联系的，即“专业的”，涉及范围较小。这个词不能用来修饰疾病。occupational 的意思是 connected with a person's job，指与一个人的职业相关的，即“职业的”，涉及范围较大。这个词可以用来修饰疾病。

“职业病”的意思是指“劳动者在生产劳动及其他职业活动中，接触职业危害因素所引起的疾病”。英语可以译为 occupational disease, occupation disease, occupational illness, work illness, work-related illness, employment disease, industrial disease。例如：

1. 皮肤病是工厂工人中的常见职业病。
Skin disorders are common occupational diseases among factory workers.
2. 警方已控制了引发职业病的事故现场。
Police have kept the occupational-disease-inductive accident site under

control.

3. 这个煤矿主强迫煤矿工人不采取任何职业病防护措施就工作。
The coalmine owner forced the coal-miners to work without taking any occupational-disease-prevention measures.
4. 职业病检查结果应向工会通报。
The result of the occupational disease checkup should be announced to the trade union.
5. 职业病危害，意思是指对从事职业活动的劳动者可能导致职业病的各种危害。
Occupational disease harm refers to all kinds of harms which could result in the occupational diseases to the labourers who undertake the occupational activities.
6. 用人单位应当按照适用规定，安排职业病病人进行治疗、康复和定期检查。
The Employer should have the occupational-disease victims treated, rehabilitated and regularly examined in accordance with applicable regulations.
7. 今年晚些时候，将要实施一种新的职业病（例如尘肺病）诊断标准。
A new diagnosis standard of occupational diseases, such as dust-related lung disease, will be implemented later this year.
8. 由于管理不善，这个工厂患职业病的风险急剧增长。
Due to poor management, the risk of getting an occupation disease has increased sharply in this factory.
9. 职业病界定为由暴露于与职业有关的因素引起的，而不是由工伤引起的任何异常身体状况或疾病。
An occupational illness is defined as any abnormal condition or disorder, other than one resulting from an occupational injury, caused by exposure to factors associated with employment.
10. 这些老工人记忆力差、有精神压力、情绪动荡，而且衰老加快，这些是职业病的常见症状。
These aged workers suffered from poor memory, as well as stress, mood swings and accelerated aging, which are common symptoms of occupational illness.
11. 他不能肯定他是否具有对职业病的有效索赔要求。
He is unsure whether he may have a valid compensation claim for a work illness.
12. 背痛、肌肉劳损和关节炎是最常见的职业病。
Back pain, muscular strain and arthritis are the most common work-related illnesses.

13. 万一发生工伤或职业病，根据《国家保险法》第11章支付保险金。
In the case of employment injury or employment disease, benefits are granted in accordance with Chapter 11 in the National Insurance Act.
14. 尘肺病是一种影响长期在煤尘环绕下工作的煤矿工人的职业病。
Black lung disease is an industrial disease that affects coal miners after working for long periods of time around coal dust.

“工伤”，可以译为 occupational injury, work injury, work-related injury, on-the-job injury, employment injury。例如：

15. 在建筑业，工伤的发生率要高一些。
There is a higher rate of occupational injury in the construction industry.
16. 上下班途中因车祸受伤的人们将不属于工伤保险的范围。
People injured in a car accident while traveling to or from work will not be covered by the work injury insurance.
17. 他因工伤而在医院卧床三天。
He was kept in bed at the hospital for three days because of a work-related injury.
18. 由于产品破碎，我受到工伤，一个手指破了。
I had an on-the-job injury due to broken products and my finger was broken.
19. 这个建筑工人由于工伤而不能工作。
The construction worker was unable to work due to an employment injury.

28 呛声

汉语关键词：呛声、呛(读第一声)、呛(读第四声)
英语关键词：provoke, voice strong protests against, irritate, choke, stifle, provocative
句子：达赖喇嘛在台湾所到之处，当地民众对他呛声。
误译：Wherever Dalai Lama went in Taiwan, the local people made choking sounds to him.
正译：Wherever Dalai Lama went in Taiwan, the local people voiced strong protests against him.

解释：

汉英词典将“呛”译为 to choke。它的意思是 to be unable to breathe because the passage to your lungs is blocked or you cannot get enough air，即“抽噎”。若将“呛声”字对字译为 choking sound，就犯了错误。其实 choking sound 的意思是“因呼吸困难而发出的急促喘息声”，与“呛声”毫不相干。“呛声”来自闽南话，即“唱声”，是台湾民众常用语，意思是“大声发出自己的声音，表达自己的意见和想法，以激烈话语公然向对方挑衅抗议”。英语可以译为 to provoke, to voice strong protests against。例如：

1. 半夜时，这个婴儿听上去好像停止了呼吸，接着拼命吸气，后又咳嗽，并发出抽噎声。
   In the middle of the night, the baby sounded as if he stopped breathing then gasped for air then coughed and made this choking sound.
2. 在搜索过程中，这位警官听到从房间角落传来抽噎声。
   During the search, the police officer heard a choking sound coming from the corner of the room.
3. 你怎么敢跟我呛声？
   How dare you provoke me?
4. 数年前，台湾几十万民众集会呛声因贪腐而臭名昭著的前领导人陈水扁。
   A few years ago, hundreds of thousands of people in Taiwan rallied to voice strong protests against the former leader Chen Shui-bian, who was notorious for his corruption.

“呛”（读第四声）的第一个意思是“有刺激性的气体进入呼吸器官而难以忍受”。英语可以译为 to irritate, to choke, to stifle。例如：

5. 厨房里，油烟呛我的嗓子。
   In the kitchen, the oil smoke irritated my throat.
6. 消毒水的气味呛鼻子，我受不了。
   As the smell of the disinfectant irritates my nose, I can’t stand it.
7. 浓烟呛得我几乎喘不过气来。
   The heavy smoke almost choked me.
8. 辣椒的味儿呛得我直咳嗽。
   I choked at the smell of pepper so much that I couldn’t stop coughing.
9. 我被公共厕所的恶臭呛得几乎喘不过气来。
   I nearly choked at the foul smell of the public lavatory.
10. 这个男孩差一点被浓烟呛死。
    The boy almost choked to death in the thick fumes.

11. 当我孤独的时候，我会点上一支香烟，不是因为上瘾，也不是因为赶时髦，而只是想呛自己一下，然后大哭一场。
When I feel lonely, I would like to light a cigarette, neither for addiction, nor for fashion, but just for choking myself and for crying.
12. 劣质油漆的气味呛人，有害于人体健康。
The smell of the inferior paint is choking and harmful to the health of the people.
13. 浓烟弥漫房间，呛得消防队员们喘不上气来。
The heavy smoke filled the room and almost stifled the firemen.
14. 大多数受害者是被烟呛死的。
Most of the victims were stifled by the fumes.

"呛"（读第四声）的第二个意思是比喻"说话生硬尖刻有火气"。英语可以译为 provocative。例如：

15. 为什么你今天说话这么呛？
Why do you speak in such a provocative way today?

"呛"（读第一声）的意思是"因水或食物进入气管引起咳嗽，又突然喷出"。英语可以译为 to choke。例如：

16. 这个孩子吃饭吃呛了。
The child choked over his food.
17. 他喝水呛着了。
He choked for the water went down the wrong way.
18. 当心婴儿在喂奶时会咳嗽，喷溅或呛着。
Be aware that the infant will cough, sputter and choke during feedings.
19. 我游泳时呛了一点儿水。
I choked a bit when I was swimming.
20. 将猫处死的方法很多，不必非用奶油呛死它。
There are more ways of killing a cat than by choking it with cream.
21. 男孩急速冒出水面，大口喘气，被含盐的海水呛着了。
The boy raced to the surface, gasping for air and choking from the salt water.

29 排练

汉语关键词： 排、排练、排演、彩排

英语关键词： rehearse, rehearsing, have a rehearsal, do a rehearsal, hold a rehearsal, run through, have a dry run, do a dry run, practise a dry run, dress rehearsal, have a dress rehearsal, hold a dress rehearsal

句子： 为庆祝建国60周年，演员们正在排练一个歌舞节目。

误译： In celebration of the 60th anniversary of the founding of the People's Republic of China, the actors were exercising a singing and dancing programme.

正译： In celebration of the 60th anniversary of the founding of the People's Republic of China, the actors were rehearsing a singing and dancing programme.

解释：

to exercise 的意思是 to train sb by means of exercises，即"通过练习进行培训"，其宾语是人，没有"排练节目"的含义。to rehearse 的意思是 to practise a play, a piece of music, etc. in preparation for a public performance，即"为准备公演而练习节目"，具有"排练节目"的含义。

"排练"、"排演"或"排"的意思是"戏剧、音乐、舞蹈等文艺形式在上演前，导演指导演员们逐段练习"。英语动词可以译为 to rehearse, to have a rehearsal, to do a rehearsal, to hold a rehearsal, to run through, to have a dry run, to do a dry run, to practise a dry run；名词可以译为 rehearsal, rehearsing。例如：

1. 导演说，"今天，我们将只排练最后一场。"
   The director said, "Today, we'll just be rehearsing the final scene."
2. 我们正观看演员们排练一个话剧。
   We were watching the actors rehearsing a play.
3. 演员们仅给了两个星期排练。
   The actors were given only two weeks to rehearse.
3. 休息之后，我们继续排练合唱节目。
   1) We continued to rehearse the chorus after the break.
   2) We continued rehearsing the chorus after the break.
4. 今天上午，演员们排练得不好。
   This morning, the actors were poorly rehearsed.
5. 这个京剧团最近排了一出名叫《赤壁》的京剧。

This Beijing opera troupe has recently rehearsed a Beijing opera called Red Cliff.

6. 演员们排练了他们的角色。
   The actors rehearsed their parts.
7. 要保证他们排练好他们的角色，这样在播放时才会一切顺利。
   Make sure they have rehearsed their parts so that things will go smoothly on the air.
8. 这两天毕业生们一直忙着排练毕业典礼。
   These two days, the graduates have been busy rehearsing the graduation ceremony.
9. 迈克鞠了一躬，就开始说出他已排练很久的简短问候话语。
   Mike bowed and launched into the brief speech of greeting he had so long rehearsed.
10. 仪仗队正在排练。
    The guard of honour is having a rehearsal.
11. 在星期五上演之前，我们在星期四一起进行了一次排练。
    Before the show on Friday, we did a rehearsal together on Thursday.
12. 新当选总统正在为总统就职典礼做准备，今天进行了一场排练。
    The newly elected president is getting ready for the presidential inauguration, holding a rehearsal today.
13. 我们再排练一遍第3幕，好吗？
    Could we run through Act 3 again, please?
14. 让我们排练吧。
    1) Let's have a dry run.
    2) Let's do a dry run.
15. 在英语讲演比赛之前，我在父母面前排练了几次。
    I did several dry runs in front of my parents before the English speech contest.
16. 今晚我们将排练上演的节目。
    We are going to practise a dry run of the performance tonight.
17. 全体演员在排练中间，休息一下喝咖啡。
    The whole cast broke off for coffee in the middle of rehearsal.
18. 排练时，这个女演员违约没有到场。
    The actress defaulted on the rehearsal.
19. 他们的新版《茶馆》现正在排练之中。
    Their new production of Teahouse is currently in rehearsal.
20. 他加人了一个小剧团，扮演一些配角，排练总是不守时，因而在同事中间不受欢迎。
    He joined a small theatrical company, acted in minor parts, was

invariably unpunctual at rehearsals and was accordingly unpopular with his fellow-actors.

21. 参加演戏的学生中有几个人在排练时忽视学习，但是演出后他们很快就赶上了。
Some of the students in the play neglected their studies during rehearsals, but after the performance they caught up quickly.
22. 我们认为您也许会参加我们的排练。
We think you might like to participate in our rehearsal.
23. 所有的排演都将在学校礼堂举行。
1) All rehearsals will be held in the school auditorium.
2) All rehearsing will take place in the school auditorium.

"彩排"的意思是"文艺演出、节庆活动或大型文体表演正式进行前的化装排练"。英语动词可以译为 to have a dress rehearsal, to hold a dress rehearsal；名词可以译为 dress rehearsal。例如：

24. 我们为演出做好一切准备，并在演出前几天进行了彩排。
We got everything ready for the performance and had a dress rehearsal a few days ahead.
25. 学生们彩排了他们安排好为春节晚会表演的舞蹈。
The students held a dress rehearsal for a dance they were scheduled to perform for the Spring Festival party.
26. 我们被邀请去旁观彩排。
We were invited to sit in on the dress rehearsal.
27. 彩排进行得不好。
The dress rehearsal didn't go well.
28. 顺利的彩排预示着演出成功。
A smooth dress rehearsal augured well for the play.
29. 彩排时，演员们身穿演出时穿的服装。
At a dress rehearsal, the actors wear the clothes they will wear in the performance.
30. 星期四晚上，北京残奥会开幕式带妆彩排在国家体育场举行。
A full dress rehearsal of the opening ceremony of the Beijing Paralympics was held at the National Stadium on Thursday evening.

30 透明度

汉语关键词： 透明、透明度、透明性、不透明、半透明

英语关键词： transparent, transparency, transparence, diaphaneity, openness, opaque, translucent, semi-transparent

句子： 我们必须进一步提高司法工作的透明度。

误译： We must further increase the degree of transparency of judicatory work.

正译： We must further increase the transparency of judicatory work.

解释：

degree of transparency 指可以分级或量化的透明程度，如宝石的透明度可以分为若干级别。司法工作的透明度指其公开性，一般不易设立量化的表示公开程度的标准。因此，使用 degree 一词，就有些多余，可以删去。例如：

1. 这些棕色晶体呈现高级别的透明度和光泽度。
   These brown crystals exhibit a high degree of diaphaneity and luster.
2. 水晶一般都有很高的透明度。这块水晶尤其有很高级别的透明度。
   Crystal in general has a very high transparency. This piece of crystal in particular has a very high degree of transparency.

“透明”的第一个意思指“能够透过光线”。英语可以译为 transparent。例如：

3. 水是无色透明的液体。
   Water is a colourless transparent liquid.
4. 玻璃是一种透明材料。
   Glass is a transparent material.
5. 普通玻璃是透明的。
   Plain glass is transparent.
6. 并非所有玻璃都是透明的。
   Not all glass is transparent.
7. 这个昆虫的翅膀几乎是透明的。
   The insect’s wings are almost transparent.
8. 透明塑料盖即使在打开若干次以后也可以保证包装完全封闭。
   A transparent plastic lid ensures complete sealing of the package even after several openings.

9. 一个透明体没有影子，它也不反射光波。
A transparent body casts no shadow, neither does it reflect light- waves.
10. 这个科学家创造了一种具有钢一样强度的透明薄膜。
The scientist created a transparent film with the strength of steel.

“透明”的第二个意思是比喻“公开，不隐蔽”。英语可以译为transparent。例如：

11. 透明的招标做法使得政府采购更加规范。
The transparent bidding practice makes the government purchasing more regulated.
12. 交易将以完全透明的方式进行。
Transactions will be conducted in a fully transparent manner.
13. 这项支助的费用将以完全透明的方式反映在预算内。
The cost of this support will be reflected in the budget in a fully transparent manner.

“透明度”或“透明性”的第一个意思是“物体能够透过光线的程度”。英语可以译为transparency, transparence, diaphaneity。例如：

14. 硅石具有很高的透明性，可以用来制造玻璃。
Silica has a very high transparency, which can be used to make glass.
15. 净度、透明度和光泽度是评估这块钻石价值的三个决定性因素。
Clarity, transparence and luster are three decisive factors in appraising the value of the diamond.
16. 颜色、透明度、质地和净度是翡翠分级级别的重要因素。
Colour, transparence, texture and clarity are important factors in classifying the degree of emerald.
17. 这个晶体已失去了透明性。
The crystal has lost its diaphaneity.

“透明度”的第二个意思是比喻“事情公开的程度”，即“公开性”。英语可以译为transparency, diaphaneity, openness。例如：

18. 市场的成熟度是靠它的透明度和竞争能力来培育的。
The maturity of a market is nurtured by its transparency and competitiveness.
19. 政府应该提高决策的透明度。
The government should improve the transparency in decision- making.
20. 这个国家银行已采取步骤提高其政策透明度的级别。
The national bank has taken steps to increase the degree of transparency in its policies.

21. 医院应该增强住院患者治疗消费的透明度。
The hospital should enhance the diaphaneity of medical consumption by the in-patients.
22. 这位官员常常谈论透明度，但是很少表现出行动。
The official often talks about openness, but shows little action.
23. 这位亚洲领导人指出他的国家所需要的是更多的透明度和更少的贪腐。
The leader of the Asian country pointed out that what his country needed was more openness, less corruption.
24. 市政府定期发表工作报告，有助于提高政府工作的透明度。
The municipal government regularly issues a work report, which is helpful to enhance the openness of government work.

“不透明”，可以译为 opaque。例如：

25. 这道砖墙是不透明的。
The brick wall is opaque.
26. 不透明玻璃透光较少，而反射或吸收了大部分光。
Opaque glass transmits less light and reflects or absorbs most of it.
27. 他通过不透明镜片观看日食。
He viewed the sun eclipse through opaque lens.
28. 他在灯和眼睛之间摆放了一个不透明体。
He interposed an opaque body between a light and the eye.

“半透明”，可以译为 translucent, semi-transparent。例如：

29. 瓷器总是半透明的，而陶器是不透明的。
Whereas porcelain is always translucent, pottery is opaquc.
30. 厕所窗户和浴室窗户是半透明玻璃制成的。
The lavatory windows and the bathroom windows are made of translucent glass.
31. 这种窗帘布料很轻，而且是半透明的。
The fabric in the curtains was light and semi-transparent.
32. 一道宽带光的光束通过一个半透明反射镜会分成两道相同的光束。
The beam of a broadband light will be split into two identical beams by a semi-transparent mirror.

31 气候

汉语关键词： 天气、气候、政治气候、经济气候、成气候、不成气候

英语关键词： weather, climate, climatic, political climate, economic climate, make achievements, get somewhere, make no achievements, won't get anywhere, will get nowhere, become prevalent, become well received, become popular

句子： 人类正在遭受气候变化带来的危害。

误译： Humankind is suffering from the harm caused by weather change.

正译： Humankind is suffering from the harm caused by climate change.

解释：

weather 的意思是the condition of the atmosphere at a particular place and time, such as the temperature, and if there is wind, rain, sun, etc.，即“天气”，指在一个特定地点和时间的大气状况，天气是一个时刻(point of time)概念，是在不断变化的，没有规律的。而气候是一个时段(period of time)概念，指在一段很长时间内的气象状况，变化不大，有一定规律。英语climate 的意思是the regular pattern of weather conditions of a particular place，指的正是“气候”。例如：

1. “天气”和“气候”的区别在于时间的衡量。“天气”是在一个短时间内的大气状况，而“气候”则是指在相对长的时段内大气是如何“表现”的。
   The difference between weather and climate is a measure of time. Weather is what conditions of the atmosphere are over a short period of time, while climate is how the atmosphere “behaves” over relatively long periods of time.
2. 当我们谈论气候变化时，我们谈论的是长期的每日天气平均值的变化。
   When we talk about climate change, we talk about changes in long-term averages of daily weather.

“气候”的第一个意思是“一定地区里经过观察所得到的概括性的气象状况”。英语可以译为climate(名词)，climatic(形容词)。例如：

3. 这个城市气候干燥寒冷。
   This city has a dry and cold climate.
4. 这个国家的内陆地区是夏季炎热、而冬季寒冷下雪的大陆性气候。
   In the interior of the country, the climate is continental with hot summers

and cold, snowy winters.

5. 这座沿海城市以其温和的海洋性气候、多彩的海滨度假胜地和好客的居民，吸引人们来旅游、休假或安度晚年。
   This coastal city attracts people to come to travel, recess or spend their senectitude with its mild maritime climate, colourful seashore resorts and hospitable habitants.
6. 由于气候的缘故，我更愿意住在昆明。
   I would rather live in Kunming for climate.
7. 全球气候变化对人类生存和发展已产生深刻影响。
   Global climate change has a profound impact on the existence and development of humankind.
8. 气候变化没有国界。
   Climatic change knows no boundary.
9. 发达国家和发展中国家都应该积极采取措施应对气候变化。
   Both the developed and the developing countries should take active measures to deal with climate change.
10. 9月22日，胡锦涛在纽约出席联合国气候变化峰会开幕式并发表重要讲话。
    On September 22, Hu Jintao attended the opening session of the United Nations Climate Change Conference in New York and issued an important speech.

"气候"的第二个意思是比喻"社会动向"、"发展态势"或"社会环境"。英语可以译为climate。例如：

11. 这个亚洲国家的政治气候正在发生重大转变。
    A great change is taking place in the political climate in this Asian country.
12. 在美国，政治气候的变化对总统选举产生巨大的影响。
    In the United States, the change of political climate produces a great influence upon the presidential election.
13. 这幅画与当时的政治气候非常协调。
    The painting was very much in tune with the political climate at the time.
14. 经济气候是一个用于以任何方式、形式和形态描述经济目前状况的名词。
    Economic climate is a term used to describe the current state of the economy in any way, shape or form.
15. 最坏的时候已经过去，经济气候正在逐步回暖。
    The worst is over, and the economic climate is gradually getting warmer.

16. 面临英国企业的经济气候将变得更加有风险和更加艰难。
The economic climate facing UK businesses will become riskier and more difficult.

“成气候”的第一个意思是比喻人“有成就”或“有发展前途”。英语可以译为to make achievements, to get somewhere。“不成气候”或“成不了气候”的意思是比喻人“没有成就”或“没有发展前途”。英语可以译为 to make no achievements, won't get anywhere, will get nowhere。例如：

17. 只要你坚持不懈工作，你在科学研究方面会成大气候的。
So long as you persist in your work, you can make great achievements in scientific research.
18. 如果你们球队的队员齐心合力，是会成气候的。
If all the members of your team take concerted actions, they can get somewhere.
19. 人们普遍承认中国足球队在短期内是难成气候的。
It is generally acknowledged that Chinese football teams can hardly get anywhere in a short period of time.
20. 我国学者对气象经济的研究还不成气候，仍处于初始阶段。
The scholars in our country haven't made any great achievements in the study of meteorological economy, which is still in the initial stage.
21. 你们这样做是不会成气候的。
In doing so, you won't get anywhere.
22. 别瞎折腾了。你们成不了什么气候。
Stop messing about. You will get nowhere.

“成气候”的第二个意思是比喻事物“流行”。英语可以译为to become prevalent, to become well received, to become popular。例如：

23. 我国网上书店已成气候。
In our country, online bookshops have become prevalent.
24. 由于人们普遍重视心理健康，现在心理咨询业渐成气候。
As people generally attach importance to psychological health, psychological counseling business has gradually become well received.
25. 这位专家认为山寨版笔记本难成气候。
This expert holds that knockoff notebook computers can hardly become well received.
26. 据报导，美国网上售车渐成气候。
It is reported that car sale on line has gradually become popular in the United States.

32 当家做主

汉语关键词： 当家做主、当家、当家的、做主、作主

英语关键词： become masters of one's own country, become masters of one's own destiny, take the responsibility, on one's own responsibility, decide, make the decision, have the final say, back up, support, run a household, manage household affairs, keep house, be master of one's own house, rule the roost, main, the best, that one is most adept at, master of a household, mistress of a household, head of a family, husband, abbot

句子： 60年前随着新中国的成立，中国人民开始当家做主。

误译： With the founding of New China 60 years ago, the Chinese people started to be masters.

正译： With the founding of New China 60 years ago, the Chinese people started to be masters of their own country.

解释：

master 的意思是 a person who is able to control sth，即“主人”。但是，to be masters 没有说明做谁的主人。“当家做主”实际上是“做自己国家或自己命运的主人”。

“做主”或“作主”的第一个意思是“做主人”。常说的“当家做主”，就是“当家做主人”。英语可以译为 to become masters of one's own country, to become masters of one's own destiny。例如：

1. 只有在人民当家做主的时候，科学才能真正服务于人民。
   It is only when the people have become masters of their own country that science can really serve the people.
2. 当西藏废除了腐朽、黑暗的封建农奴制的时候，百万农奴挣脱了枷锁，当家做主了。
   When the decadent and dark feudal serfdom was abolished in Tibet, one million serfs were unshackled and became masters of their own destiny.

“做主”的第二个意思是当事人自己“对某件事情负完全责任并做出决定”。如果强调“负责任”，英语可以译为 to take the responsibility 或 on one's own responsibility；如果强调“做决定”，英语可以译为 to decide, to make the decision, to have the final say。例如：

3. 这件事，我来做主。
   I'll take the responsibility for this matter.

4. 每件事都是由他做主干的。
Everything was done on his own responsibility.
5. 我们是否做这个工作，我可做不了主。
I am not in a position to decide whether we'll do this work.
6. 这件事要我们大家共同做主才行。
This is up to all of us to make the decision.
7. 我们女儿的婚姻大事由她自己做主。
Our daughter has the final say in choosing the man she wants to marry.

“做主”的第三个意思是当事人“支持别人”或“为别人撑腰”。英语可以译为 to back up, to support。例如：

8. 当官不为民做主，不如回家卖红薯。
If I didn't back up the common people as an official, I would rather go back home to become a small pedlar selling sweet potatoes.
9. 这件事，你可得给我做主。
For this matter, you should back me up.
10. 有厂长给你做主呢，你就放手干吧！
1) Go ahead boldly with your work, as you have the factory director to back you up.
2) With the factory director supporting you, you can just go ahead boldly with your work.
3) With the support from the factory director, you may just go ahead boldly with your work.

“当家”的第一个意思是“主持家务”或“理家”。英语可以译为 to run a household, to manage household affairs, to keep house, to be master of one's own house。例如：

11. 我年纪轻，当不了家。
I am too young to run a household.
12. 不当家不知柴米贵。
If you don't manage household affairs, you have no idea how expensive rice and firewood are.
13. 当家才知柴米价。
One has to keep house to know the prices of rice and firewood.
14. 她很会当家。
1) She is good at keeping house.
2) She is a good housewife.
3) She is a good homemaker.
15. 他媳妇是当家理财的好手。
His wife is good at keeping house and making financial planning.

16. 当她还十几岁时，就当家了。
When she was still in her teens, she became master of her own house.

“当家”的第二个意思是“领导”。英语可以译为 to rule the roost。例如：

17. 在我们工厂里，是书记当家。
It is the Party secretary who rules the roost in our factory.
18. 村长是一村的当家人。
A village head is a person who rules the roost in the village.

“当家”的第三个意思是“主要的”，用作形容词。英语可以译为 main。例如：

19. 过去北方到了冬天，大白菜就是当家菜。
In the past, Chinese cabbages became the main vegetables in North China in winter.

“当家”的第四个意思是“最拿手的”，用作形容词。英语可以译为 the best, that one is most adept at。例如：

20. 回锅肉是本店的当家菜。
The double-cooked pork slices is the best dish of our restaurant.
21. 女主人用她的当家菜来款待我们。
The hostess treated us to the dish she was most adept at cooking.

“当家的”的第一个意思是“主持家务的人”，用作名词。英语可以译为 master of a household, mistress of a household, head of a family。例如：

22. 老当家的去世以后，他的长子成了当家的。
After the old master of the household passed away, his eldest son became the master.
23. 有什么问题，就问女当家的。
Consult the mistress of the household if you have any problem.
24. 当家的病得很厉害。
The head of the family was seriously ill.

“当家的”的第二个意思是指“丈夫”，用作名词。英语可以译为 husband。例如：

25. 她当家的在县政府工作。
Her husband works in the county government.

“当家的”的第三个意思是“主持寺院的和尚”，用作名词。英语可以译为 abbot (of a temple)。例如：

26. 这个寺院里当家的是一位60来岁的老和尚。
The abbot of the temple is an old monk in his sixties.

33 弱势群体

汉语关键词： 群体、弱势群体

英语关键词： colony, group, mass, disadvantaged group，socially vulnerable group, vulnerable group

句子： 全社会都应重视和关注弱势群体。

误译： The whole society should pay attention to and show concern for the weak group.

正译： The whole society should pay attention to and show concern for the disadvantaged group.

解释：

虽然 the weak 作为集合名词具有 people who are poor, sick or without power 的意思，即“穷人”、“病人”或“没有权力的人”，但是它涵盖不了“弱势群体”的“在政治、经济、文化以及生理健康等方面处于弱势地位的人群的概念”。“弱势群体”，英语可以译为 disadvantaged group，socially vulnerable group 或 vulnerable group。例如：

1. 弱势群体包括流浪儿、残疾人、下岗工人、贫困山区妇女和孤寡老人等。
The disadvantaged group includes waifs, handicapped people, laid-off workers, women in poverty-stricken mountainous areas, lone old people and widowed old people.
2. 目前，我国大约有过亿人口属于弱势群体。
At present, there are over one hundred million people who belong to disadvantaged groups in our country.
3. 未成年人是社会的弱势群体，应该得到更多的保护。
Minors are of socially vulnerable groups that should be given more protection.
4. 弱势群体指在社会地位、经济收入、受教育程度、竞争能力等方面处于弱势地位的社会群体。

Vulnerable groups refer to those social groups, which are disadvantaged in social status, financial income, education and competitiveness.

“群体”的第一个意思是“由许多在生理上发生联系的同种生物个体组成的整体，如动物中的海绵、珊瑚和植物中的某些藻类”。英语可以译为 colony。例如：

5. 这种紫色管海绵群体生活在一个死亡的珊瑚岬上。
   This purple tube sponge colony lives on a dead coralhead.
6. 在浅水域有一个珊瑚群体，它需要阳光。
   A colony of corals can be found in the shallow waters, which requires sunlight.
7. 这位研究人员说他不知道这种病毒是否会导致一个群体崩溃。
   The researcher says that he does not know if this virus may cause a colony to collapse.

“群体”的第二个意思是泛指“由许多本质上有共同点的互相联系的个体组成的整体”，与“个体”是相对的。英语可以译为 group。例如：

8. 一个英雄群体的雕像耸立在市广场中心。
   The statues of a group of heroes stand in the centre of the city square.
9. 他们是一个了不起的英雄群体，从潜伏在每个黑暗角落的敌人那里拯救了我们的城市。
   They are a wonderful group of heroes saving our city from the enemy that lurked around every dark corner.
10. 近年来，我们的城市出现了许多写字楼、购物中心、大型超市、展览馆、体育馆和住宅小区等建筑群体。
    In recent years, there have appeared many groups of construction like office buildings, shopping malls, large supermarkets, exhibition halls, gymnasiums and residential areas in our city.
11. 我认为群体风气会对创新性和团队绩效产生一些影响。
    I think group climate can make some impacts upon creativity and team performance.
12. 据信这名小组成员已违反大家一致同意的群体规范。
    This group member is believed to have violated an agreed-upon group norm.
13. 群体决策能够提高合作解决问题的技能。
    Group decision-making can improve collaborative problem-solving skills.
14. 这位社会学家详细谈论了个人主义与集体主义，或曰个人取向与群体取向之间的区别。

The sociologist talked in detail about the difference between individualism and collectivism, or in other words, between individual orientation and group orientation.

15. 这位学者对股票市场的群体认同进行了系统分析。

The scholar made a systematic analysis of group identification in stock markets.

16. 这门课程内容包括三个部份：个体行为、群体行为和组织系统。

The contents of this course include three parts: individual behaviour, group behaviour and organization system.

17. 群体选择描述的是在生物群体之间，而不是在个体之间运作的自然选择。

Group selection describes natural selection operating between groups of organisms, rather than between individuals.

18. 这种家族意识和家族荣誉感可能是在他们生活中团队精神或群体意识的唯一表现形式。

This sense of family consciousness and family honour is probably the only form of team spirit or group consciousness in their life.

19. 群体凝聚力是使群体成员更紧密团聚在一起的力量。

Group cohesiveness is the force bringing group members closer together.

20. “群体无聊”在网上已成为一个流行语，它以某种方式反映了网络文化，青年人对其他传统娱乐方式感到厌倦后，进而在虚拟世界里消磨时间。

Group boredom has turned into a catchphrase on the Internet, which reflects in a way the cyber culture in which young people kill their time in the virtual world after being bored by other traditional entertainments.

“群体”的第三个意思是“群众”或“民众”，与“官员”或“干部”是相对的。英语可以译为 mass。例如：

21. 根据这位外国记者的理解，群体事件是汉语对大型抗议、骚乱、示威或群众请愿的委婉语。

To the mind of the foreign reporter, mass incident is a Chinese euphemism for a large protest, riot, demonstration, or mass petition.

22. 没有解释这个人为何死亡，是这次群体事件的中心。

The unexplained death of the man was at the centre of the mass incident.

23. 由于一名女性雇员在本县一家旅馆因不明原因死亡，而发生了一次群体事件。

A mass incident occurred due to the death for unknown reasons of a female employee at a hotel in this county.

34 活字典

汉语关键词： 活、活字典

英语关键词： living, live, active, lively, vivid, walking, walking dictionary, walking encyclopaedia

句子： 他学识渊博，被人称为活字典。

误译： Being profound in knowledge, he was called a living dictionary.

正译： Being profound in knowledge, he was called a walking dictionary.

解释：

“活字典”是个比喻说法，形容一个学识渊博的人。living dictionary 的意思是 a dictionary that exists，即“现在人们使用的字典”，不是用来指人。但是 walking dictionary 的意思是 a person who has an impressive knowledge of facts or words，指“学识渊博的人”。

作为形容词，“活”的第一个意思是指“有生命的、存活的或依然活跃的”。英语可以译为 living, live, active。例如：

1. 魔术师从帽子里变出一只活兔子来。
   The magician produced a live rabbit from his hat.
2. 他在河里捉了一条大活鱼。
   He caught a big live fish in the river.

试比较：

3. 他在河里活捉了一条大鱼。
   He caught a big fish alive in the river.
4. 动物园里的老虎爱吃活食。
   The tigers in the zoo like to eat small live animals.
5. 科学家发现在在个沙漠里竟然还有野兔、野鼠之类的活物。
   The scientist found that there were such live animals as wild hares and wild rats in this desert.
6. 这个农家妇女喜欢用活物喂鸡。
   The farming woman likes to feed her chickens with live insects.
7. 我只好死马当活马医。
   I could not but deal with it like treating a dead horse as if it were a live one.
8. 如果停止供氧，那些活标本就会自动死亡。
   If the oxygen supply is cut off, these living specimens will die of themselves.

9. 水杉被誉为植物王国的活化石。
Metasequoia is praised as a living fossil in the botanic kingdom.
10. 活火山随时都可能爆发。
An active volcano can explode at any time.
11. 英国科学家说他们在火星上发现了活冰川。
British scientists said that they had found an active glacier on Mars.
12. 由于地心引力，活冰川的冰总是在向前移动，就像河里的水在不停地流动一样。
Due to gravity, the ice of an active glacier always moves forward like the water in a river.

作为形容词，"活"的第二个意思是"生动的"。英语可以译为lively, vivid。例如：

13. 这个小女孩是欢乐的活化身。
The young girl is a lively phantom of delight.
14. 这个喝醉酒的司机成为醉酒驾车的活标本。
The drunk driver became a lively example of those who drive while intoxicated.
15. 他的英雄事迹是一部反腐斗争的活教材。
His heroic deed is a vivid object lesson in fighting against corruption.
16. 这部小说女主人公是中国农村妇女善良、朴实、热情和真诚品质的活化身。
The heroine of the novel is a vivid embodiment of such characteristics as kindness, simplicity, enthusiasm and honesty of the women in China's rural areas.

作为形容词，"活"的第三个意思是比喻"在某一方面与之相似"。英语可以译为living(形容有生命的), live(形容无生命的)。例如：

17. 人人夸他是个活雷锋。
Everybody praises him as a living Lei Feng.
18. 我不是活雷锋，但我喜欢替别人做好事。
I am not a living Lei Feng, but I enjoy doing good deeds for others.
19. 这首歌的名字叫《东北人都是活雷锋》。
This song is entitled Everybody from Northeast China is a living Lei Feng.
20. 这位救济穷苦百姓的老僧被人们称为活佛。
The old monk who relieved the poor was called a living Buddha.
21. 她在战争中帮助和保护了许多妇女儿童，被人称为活菩萨。
As she helped and protected many women and children in the war, she

was known as a living Goddess of Mercy.

22. 他们过着悠然自得的日子，赛过活神仙。
   They are leading a carefree and content life, just like living immortals.
23. “饭后一支烟，赛过活神仙” 的说法对烟民其实是一种误导。
   The saying that one who smokes a cigarette after dinner is just like a living immortal is in fact misleading to the smokers.
24. 人人骂他是个杀人不眨眼的活阎王。
   Everybody called him a living Ruler of the Hell who killed people without blinking.
25. 他暮气沉沉，简直是个活死人。
   He is the very picture of lethargy, just like a living dead man.
26. 德国法西斯集中营是人间活地狱。
   The German fascist concentration camp was a live hell on earth.
27. 他总是犯错误，成为受批判的活靶子。
   He was always making mistakes, becoming a live target for criticism.

作为形容词，“活” 的第四个意思是“熟悉或精通某一方面知识”。英语可以译为 walking。例如：

28. 我们的英语老师是个活字典，因为他知道许多英语单词。
   Our English teacher is a walking dictionary, for he knows many English words.
29. 人们称他为活字典，因为如果他不炫耀他的大量词汇，他是不会满足的。
   People call him a walking dictionary because he isn’t satisfied unless he’s showing off his huge vocabulary.
30. 这位植物学家被称为中国植物学界的活字典。
   This botanist is regarded as a walking encyclopaedia in China’s botanical circles.
31. 因为他熟知公交车路线，熟知在什么地方乘车和换车，因此人们称他为活地图。
   As he is familiar with the bus routes, and knows well where to take or change the bus, people call him a walking map.

注意，walking map 的原义是 map for walking，指帮助人们在一个地区步行活动的地图或路线图。例如：

32. 居民们和参观者可以利用这个路线图，它提供在哪里购物和吃饭，有什么地方可看的新鲜建议。
   The residents and visitors can use this walking map that provides fresh tips about where to shop, where to dine and what to see.

35

主题

汉语关键词：主题、主题公园、主题游乐园

英语关键词：theme, theme park, theme amusement park, motif, subject

句子：第十一届全运会的主题是“和谐中国，全民全运”。

误译：The subject of the 11th Chinese National Games is “Harmonious China and People’s Games”.

正译：The theme of the 11th Chinese National Games is “Harmonious China and People’s Games”.

解释：

subject 的意思是 a thing or person that is being discussed, described or dealt with，指的是“正在被讨论，描述或处理的事物或人物”，即具体的“话题”或“题材”。而全运会主题指的是“主题口号”，即“用概括的语言表现出来的主旨”，是抽象的思想。英语的theme 有 the main idea in a talk, piece of writing or work of art等意思，是合适的选择。例如：

1. 主题不仅仅是一部文学作品的题材。相反地，主题是一个重大的、反复重现的思想，一部作品的更大的意义，包括对生活或普通人的任何思考或领悟。

   A theme is not simply the subject of the literary work. Instead, the theme is a major and often recurring idea, the larger meaning of a work, including any thoughts or insights about life or people in general.

“主题”的第一个意思是指“用概括的语言表达的主旨”。英语可以译为theme。例如：

2. 来自内地和香港、澳门、台湾的四位歌手，联袂高唱第十一届全运会开幕式主题歌。

   The four singers coming respectively from Mainland China, Hong Kong, Macao and Taiwan gave a joint performance of the theme song for the Opening Ceremony of the 11th Chinese National Games.

3. 2010年上海世博会的主题是“城市，让生活更美好”。

   The theme of the 2010 Shanghai Expo is “Better City, Better Life”.

4. 民族团结是国庆节天安门狂欢之夜的一个重大主题。

   Ethnic unity was a major theme of the grand evening gala in Tian’anmen Square on National Day.

5. 2008年北京奥运会的主题是“同一个世界，同一个梦想”。
The theme of the 2008 Beijing Olympics was “the same world, the same dream”.
6. 自然、爱情、生命，死亡、时间及永恒是这位诗人最喜爱的主题。
Nature, love, life, death, time and eternity are favorite themes of the poet.
7. 这本书的主要主题被反复的题外话搞得模糊不清。
The main theme of the book is obscured by frequent digressions.

“主题公园”，英语可以译为 theme park。例如：

8. 迪斯尼乐园是世界上最爱欢迎的主题公园之一。
Disneyland is one of the world’s most popular theme parks.
9. 这个主题公园是由一家合资企业投资兴建的。
This them park is funded by a joint venture.

“主题游乐园”，英语可以译为 theme amusement park。例如：

10. 北京欢乐谷是一个主题游乐园，每天接待数千名游客。
The Happy Valley in Beijing is a theme amusement park, which entertains thousands of visitors every day.
11. 这个主题游乐园给儿童，也同样给成人提供数小时的娱乐和消遣。
This theme amusement park provides hours of cntertainment and fun for children and adults alike.

“主题”的第二个意思是指“文学、艺术作品中所表现的中心思想，是作品思想内容的核心”。英语可以译为 motif。例如：

12. 这部小说的一个中心主题是一切行动皆有后果，个人不可袖手旁观，仅做生活的观察员。
One central motif of the novel is that all actions have consequences, and that it is impossible for an individual to stand aloof and be a mere observer of life.
13. 这种节奏对旋律的延续，对诗歌主要主题的形成，都是至关紧要的。
This rhythm is important to the continuity of the melody and the shaping of the principal motif of the verse.
14. 本书的主要主题基本上是在第三章确立的。
The principal motif of this book is established primarily in Chapter Three.

“主题”的第三个意思是泛指“谈话、文章、文件、会议等的主要内容”。英语可以译为 subject。例如：

15. 这位专家认为朝核六方会谈要讨论的主题不能改变。
The expert holds that the subject to be discussed in the Six-Party Talks on Pyongyang's nuclear programme cannot be changed.
16. 论文第一章概述了主题。
The first chapter of the thesis gives a general overview of the subject.
17. 老师告诉学生们如何变换谈话的主题和如何回到原先的主题。
The teacher told his students how to change the subject of a conversation and how to return a previous subject.
18. 我们的谈话涉及许多主题。
Our conversation ranged over many subjects.
19. 老师要求这个学生解释他对这篇文章主题的看法。
The teacher asked the student to explain his view on the subject of the essay.

36 亮剑

汉语关键词： 亮、亮剑、亮化、亮牌、亮黄牌、亮红牌、亮底、亮底线、亮分、亮分儿、亮观点、亮丑

英语关键词： shine, get light, flash, light, show, lay bare, lay open, shining sword, show one's sword, lay one's cards on the table, show the yellow card, show the red card, show one's bottom line, disclose one's true plan, disclose one's true view, show the result, show the marks, display the marks, make public one's view, air one's opinion, make public one's error

句子： 你看过电视连续剧《亮剑》吗？

误译： Have you ever watched the TV serial entitled "A Shining Sword"?

正译： Have you ever watched the TV serial entitled "Show Your Sword"?

解释：

shining sword 的意思是"亮闪闪的剑"，指的是一件锐利的兵器。"亮"是个形容词，可以译为 shining。电视连续剧《亮剑》的意思是"向敌人显露出自己的剑"，表现的是一种行动，一种精神。"亮"是个动词，可以译为 to show。例如：

1. 这位剑客不畏强敌，在他们面前敢于亮剑。
Being not afraid of any powerful enemies, the swordsman dared to show his sword in front of them.

作为动词，“亮”的第一个意思是“发光”或“显现出亮光”。英语可以译为 to shine, to get light, to flash。例如：

2. 路灯彻夜亮着。
   Streetlights shone throughout the night.
3. 屋子里亮着灯光。
   There are lights shining in the room.
4. 当我起床时，天开始亮了。
   It was beginning to get light when I got up.
5. 当他最后睡着时，天快亮了。
   It was getting light when he finally fell asleep.
6. 我看见远处手电筒忽然亮了一下。
   I saw an electric torch suddenly flash in the distance.

“亮化”，英语可以译为 to light。例如：

7. 市政府已计划投资2,000万元对全市200栋楼宇进行亮化。
   The city government has planned to make an investment of 20 million yuan in lighting 200 buildings.

作为动词，“亮”的第二个意思是“显示”或“显露”。英语可以译为 to show, to lay bare, to lay open。例如：

8. 在恰当时刻，他会亮牌子。
   At the right moment, he would show his sign.
9. 在这本书里，作者亮了自己的内心思想感情。
   In this book, the author laid bare his innermost thoughts feelings.
10. 她亮出自己的内心思想不感到羞愧，她用平易简朴的语言对人们讲述她的喜与悲。
    She was not ashamed to lay bare her innermost thoughts and she told people about her happiness and sadness in plain and simple language.
11. 这种热带蝙蝠，一亮翅膀足有脸盆大。
    When this kind of tropical bat lays open its wings, it appears as big as a basin.

“亮牌”，英语可以译为 to lay one’s cards on the table。例如：

12. 该你亮牌了，该你告诉你的同事们你是否支持他们的建议。
    It is time for you to lay your cards on the table and tell your colleagues whether you support their suggestion.

“亮黄牌”，英语可以译为 to show the yellow card，其比喻意义为 to give a warning，即“警告”。例如：

13. 对待第一次可记名警告的犯规行为，裁判员可以亮黄牌。
For a first bookable offence, a referee can show the yellow card.
14. 警察给司机亮黄牌，因为他在马路上开车时打手机。
The policeman showed the yellow card to the driver who had used a hand-held mobile phone while driving on the road.

“亮红牌”，英语可以译为 to show the red card。例如：

15. 对待第二次可记名警告的犯规行为，裁判员给球员亮红牌，罚他出场。
For a second bookable offence, the referee showed the player red card and sent him off the field.
16. 酒馆主人对这个喝醉酒的司机亮红牌，并把他请出酒馆。
The pub owner showed the red card to the drunk drinker and sent him off the pub.
17. 环保部门给这个工厂亮了红牌，命令它暂停生产，因为它向河里排放污水。
The environmental protection department showed the red card to the factory, ordering it to suspend production, because it had discharged effluent into the river.

“亮底”的第一个意思是“把底细公开出来”，也可以说成“亮底线”。英语可以译为 to show one's bottom line, to disclose one's true plan, view, etc.。例如：

18. 你早就该给我们亮底了。
You should have shown your bottom line long before.
19. 别瞎猜了。让他亮底吧。
Stop making any wild guess. Let him disclose his true plan.
20. 别对我们卖关子了。你最好马上亮底吧。
Don't leave us in suspense. You'd better disclose your true view at once.

“亮底”的第二个意思是“显示出结局”，英语可以译为 to show the result。例如：

21. 这场比赛还没有亮底呢。
The result of the competition is yet to show.
22. 谁是第一名，评委们马上就要亮底了。
As to who ranks in the first place, the judges will soon show the result.

“亮分”或“亮分儿”，英语可以译为 to show the marks, to display the marks。例如：

23. 裁判们亮出各自打的分儿。
    The umpires showed the marks that they had given.
24. 评委们请亮分。
    Will the judges please display the marks?

“亮观点”，英语可以译为 to make public one's view, to air one's opinion。例如：

25. 几位经济学家就如何应付金融危机各自亮了观点。
    A few economists made public their views respectively about how to cope with the financial crisis.
26. 专家与房奴就房价是否会上涨各自亮了观点。
    Experts and mortgage slaves aired their opinions respectively about whether house prices would rise.

“亮丑”，英语可以译为 to make public one's error。例如：

27. 他严于律己，敢于亮丑。
    He is strict with himself and also daring to make public his own errors.

37 亮相

汉语关键词： 亮相、首次亮相

英语关键词： make one's debut, make one's public appearance, make one's appearance in public, strike a pose on the stage, declare one's position, state one's position

句子： 国庆节，特战兵方阵在天安门广场阅兵中首次亮相。

误译： On National Day, the Special Forces formation made its first debut in the military parade on Tian'anmen Square.

正译： 1) On National Day, the Special Forces formation made its debut in the military parade on Tian'anmen Square.

2) On National Day, the Special Forces formation made its first public performance in the military parade on Tian'anmen Square.

解释：

to make one's debut 的意思是 to make one's first public appearance, 即“第一次在公众面前露面”。debut 已经具有“首次亮相”的含义，前面不必再用 first。例如：

1. 今晚，这个小提琴手将在最后一支出场乐队中首次亮相。
   1) The violinist will make his debut for the last band this evening.
   2) The violinist will make his first public appearance for the last band this evening.
2. 这只大熊猫最近在北京动物园首次亮相。
   1) This giant panda has recently made its debut in Beijing Zoo.
   2) This giant panda has recently made its first public appearance in Beijing Zoo.

"亮相"的第一个意思是"戏曲演员上下场时或表演舞蹈时做出短时的静止姿势"。英语可以译为 to strike a pose on the stage。例如：

3. 这位名角在台上一亮相，就博得观众的喝彩。
   As soon as this famous actor struck a pose on the stage, the audience gave him a loud applause.
4. 当这位舞蹈演员在舞台独自站在聚光灯下时，她靓丽亮相。
   As the dancer stood alone on stage in the spotlight, she struck a beautiful pose.
5. 芭蕾舞演员被她的男舞蹈演员们举起以后，她靓丽亮相，而这时聚光灯正照在她身上。
   After the ballet dancer was picked up by her boy dancers, she struck a beautiful pose, and the spotlight was on her then.

"亮相"的第二个意思是比喻人通过行动"公开露面或表演"，或事物"出现"。英语可以译为 to make one's public appearance。例如：

6. 这位歌星不经过深思熟虑决不亮相。
   This star singer never makes his public appearance without careful consideration.
7. 最近在全国各地网络发言人纷纷亮相。
   Recently, Internet spokespersons have made their successive appearance in various places of our country.
8. 新当选的委员会全体成员在台上集体亮相。
   All the newly elected members of the committee made their collective appearance on the stage.
9. 这个地方官员喜欢到处亮相，题词，做指示。
   This local official is fond of making his public appearance here and there, making inscriptions and giving instructions.
10. 这位影星在国际电影节开幕式上以红衣惊艳亮相。
    This film star made a beautiful appearance in red dress at the opening ceremony of the international film festival.

11. 近来，几位新主持人在电视上陆续亮相。
Recently, a few new TV anchorpersons have made their appearance one after another on television.
12. 来自十多个国家的近三千只狗在这个国际狗展上齐亮相。
More than three thousand dogs coming from over ten countries made their public appearance together at the international dog show.
13. 据报道各地关于地方政府机构改革的方案陆续亮相。
It is reported that proposals on the reform of local government agencies from various places have made their appearance one after another.
14. 这种手机在本地市场首次亮相。
This type of mobile phone has made its first public appearance in the local market.

“亮相”的第三个意思是比喻通过言语“公开表态，亮明观点”。英语可以译为 to declare one's position, to state one's position。例如：

15. 我们的意见都说了，就等你亮相了。
Since we have all aired our opinions, we are waiting for you to declare your position.
16. 这位总统候选人通过公众讲话在这些政治问题上亮相。
The presidential candidate declared his position on these political issues through public speeches.
17. 你应该就这个问题亮相，亮观点。
You should publicly state your position and views on this issue.
18. 在弄清事情原委之前，不要急于亮相。
Don't state your position before you get to the bottom of the matter.

38 钓鱼执法

汉语关键词： 钓、钓鱼、渔业法、钓鱼执法、执法圈套、执法碰瓷、沽名钓誉

英语关键词： fishing law, entrap, entrapment, fish, angle, fish for fame and compliments, angle for fame and compliments, hanker after fame and compliments, crave popular acclaim, court fame and compliments, court popularity, court publicity, seek publicity, strive for reputation

句子： 上海钓鱼执法事件引起国内外媒体的关注。

误译： The incident of the fishing law enforcement in Shanghai has drawn the attention from the media at home and abroad.

正译： The incident of the entrapment in Shanghai has drawn the attention from the media at home and abroad.

解释：

fishing law 的意思是“渔业法”。如果将“钓鱼执法”直译为 fishing law enforcement，会让人误解为 enforcement of fishing law，即“《渔业法》的执行”，与原义大相径庭。例如：

1. 要求制订国际渔业法的呼声越来越高。
   The call for international fishing law has grown louder.
2. 为了保护其沿海水域，这个欧洲国家已通过了一项渔业法。
   To protect its coastal waters, the European country has passed a fishing law.

“钓鱼执法”，又叫“执法圈套”或“执法碰瓷”。英语可以译为 to entrap，其意思是 to trick sb, and encourage them to do sth, especially to commit a crime, so that they can be arrested for it，即“诱捕”。名词为 entrapment，其意思是 the illegal act of tricking sb into committing a crime, so that they can be arrested for it。例如：

3. 钓鱼执法是执法者诱惑、劝说或鼓励一个人去犯罪的行为。
   Entrapment is the act of a law enforcement officer luring, inducing or encouraging a person to commit a crime.
4. 上海市政府调查了对地方交管人员在调查黑车非法营运时诱捕一名货车司机的投诉。
   The Shanghai Municipal Government looked into the complaint of local transport supervisors entrapping a van driver while investigating illegal cab operations.
5. 这名货车司机认为这明显的是钓鱼执法，并感到非常恼怒和受辱，因而他自断一根手指以示抗议。
   The van driver said he believed it was obviously an entrapment and felt so angry and insulted that he cut off his finger as a protest.
6. 星期一，上海市政府确认地方交管人员在调查黑车非法营运时诱捕了一名货车司机。
   On Monday, the Shanghai Municipal Government confirmed that local transport supervisors entrapped a van driver while investigating illegal cab operations.
7. 最近，一些法学界人士就钓鱼执法的合理性进行了热烈讨论。

Recently, some people from the legal circles have had a heated discussion about the rationality of entrapment.

8. 这名男子坚持说他没有犯任何法，而是成为钓鱼执法的受害者。
The man holds that he didn't commit any offence, but became a victim of entrapment.

"钓"的第一个意思是"用钓钩捕鱼或其他水生动物"。英语可以译为 to fish, to angle。例如：

9. 你可以在这条小溪里钓鳟鱼。
You can fish for trout in this stream.
10. 他们在狭长的海湾里钓鲑鱼。
They fished the loch for salmon.
11. 垂钓者用铁丝笼子钓龙虾。
Anglers go fishing for lobsters with wire cages.
12. 他用捕蟹笼子钓螃蟹。
He uses a crab pot to fish for crabs.
13. 咱们在这个周末到海上去钓鱼吧。
1) Let's go fishing on the sea this weekend.
2) Let's go angling on the sea this weekend.
14. 人们禁止在这个池塘钓鱼。
People are not allowed to angle for fish in this pond.

"钓"的第二个意思是比喻"用手段猎取名利"。英语译法很多，包括 to fish for fame and compliments, to angle for fame and compliments, to hanker after fame, to crave popular acclaim, to court fame and compliments, to court popularity, to court publicity, to seek publicity, to strive for reputation 等。例如：

15. 这位老者问为何当今社会沽名钓誉之徒这么多。
The old man asked why there are so many people who are fishing for fame and compliments in the present society.
16. 我怀疑他是只不过是在沽名钓誉。
1) I suspected that he was merely fishing for fame and compliments.
2) I suspected that he was merely angling for fame and compliments.
3) I suspected that he was merely hankering after fame and compliments.
4) I suspected that he was merely craving popular acclaim.
5) I suspected that he was merely courting fame and compliments.
6) I suspected that he was merely courting popularity.
7) I suspected that he was merely courting publicity.
8) I suspected that he was merely seeking publicity.
9) I suspected that he was merely striving for reputation.

39

瑞雪兆丰年

汉语关键词： 瑞雪、兆、兆头、预兆、预示、丰年、丰收、特大丰收

英语关键词： timely snow, auspicious snow, seasonable snow, omen, portent, sign, harbinger, augury, foretell, predict, promise, give promise of, be the harbinger of, forebode, foreshadow, augur, portend, good harvest, bumper harvest

句子： 瑞雪兆丰年。

误译： An auspicious snow foretells a year of bumper harvest.

正译： 1）An auspicious snow foretells a big harvest.

2）A seasonable snow predicts a good yield.

3）A timely snow promises a good harvest.

4）A seasonable snow promises to bless the crops in the coming year.

5）A fall of seasonable snow gives promise of a fruitful year.

6）Snow is the harbinger of an abundant year for harvest.

解释：

harvest 的原义为 the time of year when the crops are gathered in，指“收获季节”，也称 harvest time。后来，harvest 又有 the act of cutting and gathering crops 的意思，即“收割”或“收获”。继而，harvest 又指 crops or the amount of crops, cut and gathered，即“收成”。“丰年”实指“好收成”，译为 good harvest 就可以了。bumper 的意思是 unusually large, producing an unusually large amount，即“特大的”。bumper harvest 指“特大丰收”，是罕见的。70 年代，我国媒体将“我国连续三年获得丰收”，译为 We have had bumper harvest for three successive years in our country。一位与我共事的英国专家对我说，一年获得 bumper harvest，已属不易。三年连续获得 bumper harvest，有些夸张。这句话不妨改为 We have had good harvest for three successive years in our country。例如：

1. 在这个亚洲国家，他们遇到了一个特大丰收年 — 好像是多少年从这片土地上得到最好收成中的一次。

   Here in this Asian country, they've had a bumper year for harvest — one of the best harvests from the land in years, it seems.

“瑞雪”可以译为 timely snow, auspicious snow 或 seasonable snow。例如：

2. 今天早晨，北京普降瑞雪。
   This morning, there was an extensive and timely snowfall in Beijing.
3. 因为雪是足够冷的，能杀死害虫以保证收成，所以冬雪又称“瑞雪”。
   For snow is cold enough to kill destructive insects to ensure a harvest, the winter snow is also called auspicious snow.
4. 昨天，华北地区喜降瑞雪。
   Yesterday, there was a welcome fall of seasonable snow in north China.

英语有下面三个谚语，与汉语“瑞雪兆丰年”的意境相近：

5. A snow year, a rich year.
   瑞雪年，丰收年。
6. A good winter brings a good summer.
   好冬带来好夏。
7. Under water, famine; under snow, bread.
   洪水造饥馑，瑞雪兆丰年。

作为动词，“兆”的意思是“预示”，英语可以译为 to foretell, to predict, to promise, to give promise of, to be the harbinger of, to forebode, to foreshadow, to augur, to portend。作为名词，“兆”的意思是“预兆”或“兆头”。英语可以译为 omen, portent, sign, harbinger, augury。例如：

8. 风湿痛预示着暴风雨的来临。
   Rheumatic pain foretells the coming of a storm.
9. 蚂蚁搬家预示要下雨。
   Ants moving home predict a rainfall.
10. 头顶上空乌云密布，预示要下雨。
    There were dark clouds overhead promising rain.
11. 拂晓时晴空万里，预示着温暖晴朗的天气。
    The day dawned bright and clear, which gave promise of warm, sunny weather.
12. 这个股民认为股市上涨预示着经济复苏，但是事情并不那样简单。
    The stock investor thinks that a rising stock market is a harbinger of economic recovery, but things are not so simple.
13. 密集的云预示着一场暴风雨的来临。

The gathering clouds forebode a coming storm.

14. 乌云预示暴风雨的来临。
    Dark clouds foreshadows a storm.
15. 各团体之间的冲突对和谈的前途不是一个好兆头。
    Conflicts among the various groups do not augur well for the future of the peace talks.
16. 这是一个好兆头。
    1) It is a good omen.
    2) It augurs well.
17. 这是一个坏兆头。
    1) It is a bad omen.
    2) It augurs badly.
18. 这些奇怪的事件预示着什么？
    What do these strange events portend?
19. 打雷是即将来临的暴风雨的预兆。
    Thunder is a sign of an impending storm.
20. 这个事件证明是注定要发生的灾难的预兆。
    The event proved to be a portent of the disaster that was to come.
21. 一些动物的异常行为是即将发生的地震的预兆。
    The abnormal behaviours of some animals are portents of an imminent earthquake.
22. 政变发生前必有预兆。
    There must be signs before a coup takes place.
23. 打雷是即将来临的暴风雨的预兆。
    Thunder is a sign of an impending storm.
24. 这个统计数字只是作为参考标准有用，而不一定是癌症的预兆。
    The statistic is only useful as a guide, and is not necessarily a harbinger of cancer.
25. 作为一个青年，他无法做什么事情来证明关于他的未来的凶兆是否正确。
    As a youth, he could do nothing to justify an evil augury of his future.

40 有偿家教

汉语关键词：家教、家庭教育、自家教育、家庭教师、有偿、无偿

英语关键词：family education, home education, private tutoring, home tutoring, tutoring, private tutor, tutor, paid, compensated, unpaid, uncompensated, free, gratis, non-reimbursable

句子：他的父母请了一位家教来教他英语。

误译：His parents employed a family teacher to teach him English.

正译：His parents employed a private tutor to teach him English.

解释：

英语表示“家庭教师”，不用 family teacher 的说法。tutor 的意思是 a private teacher, especially one who teaches an individual student or a very small group，正好表达了“家庭教师”的意思。

“家教”的第一个意思是“子女在家庭接受的影响和教育”，即“家庭教育”。英语可以译为 family education。例如：

1. 他在很小时候就接受了严格的家教。
   He received strict family education when he was very young.
2. 农村的许多孩子没有机会接受家教，因为他们的父母到城里打工谋生去了。
   Many of the children in the rural areas have no chance to receive family education because their parents have gone to the city to work for a living.
3. 家庭教育、学校教育和社会教育是教育的三大支柱，三者缺一不可。
   Family education, school education and social education are the three big props of education, none of which is dispensable.

注意 home education 不同于 family education。home education 的意思是 the education of children at home, typically by parents but sometimes by tutors，也可以说成 home school, home schooling 或 home learning，即“自家教育”。例如：

4. 自家教育是对学校教育的一种替代方式，或一种以父母为主导进行教育的选择，在其中父母可以自由决定他们子女的教育途径。
   Home education is an alternative to school education or a parent- directed educational option, in which parents have the freedom to determine their child's educational path.

5. 这对父母解释了为什么他们希望他们的孩子接受自家教育。
The parents explained why they wished their child to receive home education.

注意“有家教”和“没有家教”的译法：

6. 这个孩子有家教。
1) The child is well brought up.
2) The child is well-bred.
7. 这个孩子缺乏家教。
1) The child is not properly brought up.
2) The child is ill-bred.

“家教”的第二个意思是“进行单独或小团体辅导”。英语可以译为 private tutoring, home tutoring, tutoring。例如：

8. 一些学生需要能帮助他们做家庭作业的家教服务。
Some students need private tutoring services which can help them with their homework.
9. 在一些国家，父母花许多钱为他们的子女请家教。
In some countries, parents spend a lot of money on private tutoring for their children.
10. 本家教代理公司为我市学生提供一对一家教。
This tutoring agency provides one-on-one home tutoring for students in our city.
11. 在这个地区，禁止教师通过家教或教私自办的班来挣外快。
In this area, teachers are prohibited from making extra money out of tutoring or teaching privately organized classes.

“家教”的第三个意思是“家庭教师”。英语可以译为 private tutor, tutor。例如：

12. 这个中学生的父母给他请了一个大学高材生当家教，帮助他准备高考。
The parents of the schoolboy engaged a top student from a university as his private tutor who would help him prepare for the National Entrance Exam.
13. 自从请了家教以后，他的数学成绩就大大地提高了。
His math grades have greatly improved since he got a tutor.
14. 在她长期生病期间，她父亲给她请了个家教。
Her father hired a tutor for her during her long illness.

“有偿”的意思是“有代价的”或“有报酬的”。英语可以译为 paid, compensated。例如：

15. 教师不应利用工作之便通过有偿家教谋取私利。
Teachers should not take advantage of their work to seek personal gain through paid tutoring.
16. 未经旅游者同意，旅行社不得在旅游合同约定之外提供其他有偿服务。
No travel agency may, without the consent of the tourists, provide any paid service other than those agreed on in the travel contract.
17. 在这个学校里，不准老师在正常工作时间进行有偿家教。
In this school, teachers are not permitted to do compensated tutoring during normal working hours.

“无偿”的意思是“不要回报的”或“没有报酬的”。英语可以译为 unpaid, uncompensated, free, gratis, non-reimbursable。例如：

18. 无偿劳动指的是制造产品或提供服务而没有报酬的劳动。
Unpaid labour refers to the work that produces goods or services but is unremunerated.
19. 我们有义务向贫困地区的人民提供无偿教学援助。
We have an obligation to provide the people in the poverty- stricken areas with uncompensated teaching assistance.
20. 这位律师为弱势群体提供无偿的法律服务。
This lawyer provides free legal service for disadvantaged groups.
21. 这些大学生定期无偿献血。
These college students regularly donate blood gratis.
22. 我知道他的帮助不会是无偿的。
I knew that his help wouldn’t be given gratis.
23. 这位科学家无偿地为国家奉献了他的全部生命。
The scientist has contributed all his life gratis to his country.
24. 中国向非洲的最不发达国家提供了无偿的经济援助。
1) China gave free economic aid to the most under-developed countries in Africa.
2) China gave economic aid gratis to the most under-developed countries in Africa.
3) China rendered economic assistance gratis to the most under-developed countries in Africa.
4) China offered non-reimbursable assistance to the most under-developed countries in Africa.

41 唱高调

汉语关键词： 高调、高调门、高格调、唱高调、低调、低调门

英语关键词： high tune, high tone, high pitch, high-pitched, lofty tone, high-sounding, high profile, mouth high-sounding words, say fine-sounding things, affect a high moral tone, utter high-flown words, low tune, low tone, low pitch, low-pitched, low key, depressing and pessimistic, low profile

句子： 我们要尚务实，戒高调。

误译： We should advocate the realistic spirit and guard against making high tunes.

正译： We should advocate the realistic spirit and guard against making high-sounding talks.

解释：

high tune 指曲调高，是音乐术语。“戒高调”的意思是“不要光说不做的漂亮话”，与音乐无关。high-sounding 的意思是 intended to sound important，能表达“唱高调”的比喻意义。

“高调”的第一个意思是“唱歌或说话比一般频率高的音调”，即“高调门”。英语可以译为 high tune, high tone, high pitch, high-pitched。例如：

1. 这位歌手以她的高调门歌唱使我们惊叹不已。
   The singer marveled us with her high-tune singing.
2. 她小心翼翼不要把调门儿定得太高。
   She was careful not to set the tune too high.
3. 如果我把调门儿定得太高，那确实像驴叫。
   If I set the tone too high, it does sound like ass.
4. 如果你对一个离你较远的人讲话，你得高调门大嗓子说话。
   If you speak to a person who is farther away, you have to speak with a high tone and in a loud voice.
5. 这位歌手能轻松地高调门唱歌，而不伤害嗓子。
   1) The singer can sing high pitches at ease without hurting his voice.
   2) The singer can sing high-pitched at ease without hurting his voice.
6. 这位歌手唱高调门的歌唱得非常好。
   The singer can sing high-pitched songs very well.
7. 学生们齐声高调门唱歌。
   The students sang together at a high pitch.

“高调”的第二个意思是比喻“高昂的论调”，即“高格调”。英语可以译为 lofty tone。例如：

8. 高调做事，你会变得很优秀。
Act with a lofty tone, and you will become excellent.
9. 高格调是与生俱来的，不是教出来的。
A lofty tone is innate, and does not come by teaching.

“高调”的第三个意思是比喻“不切实际或光说不做的”。英语可以译为 high-sounding。例如：

10. 我们都对他的高调宣传报道表示怀疑。
We were all suspicious of his high-sounding publicity stories.
11. 该委员会主席批评了警方采取的高调姿态。
The chairperson of the committee criticized the high-sounding gesture the police had adopted.
12. 该委员会主席批评警方采取了高调态度。
The chairman of this committee criticized the police for taking a high-sounding attitude.

“唱高调”的意思是比喻“说得很漂亮，而实际上做不到或不准备去做”。英语可以译为 to mouth high-sounding words, to say fine-sounding things, to affect a high moral tone, to utter high-flown words。例如：

13. 这个官员爱唱高调，却很少办实事。
1) This official likes to mouth high-sounding words, but seldom does practical things.
2) This official often says fine-sounding things, but seldom does practical things.
3) This official likes to affect a high moral tone, but seldom does practical things.
4) This official often utters high-flown words, but seldom does practical things.

“高调”的第四个意思是比喻“引人注目的高姿态”。英语可以译为 high profile。例如：

14. 他在这件事情上一直保持高调。
He has kept a high profile on this matter.

“低调”的第一个意思是“唱歌或说话比一般频率低的音调”，即“低调门”。英语可以译为 low tune, low tone, low pitch, low-pitched。例如：

15. 她把调门儿起得太低了。
She has set the tune too low.
16. 这只猫叫起来声调很低。
The cat meows in a low tone.
17. 一些男人倾向于用低调门说话。
Some men tend to speak in a low-pitched voice.

“低调”的第二个意思是比喻“缓和而不张扬”。英语可以译为 low key。例如：

18. 你最好低调处理这件事。
It is advisable for you to handle the matter in a low key.
19. 大家都说他是个低调的人，因为他从来不在别人面前炫耀或吹嘘。
Everybody says he is a low-key person, because he never shows off or brags in front of others.
20. 总统发表了一个低调的讲话，希望使形势平静下来。
The president made a low-key speech, hoping to calm the situation.
21. 他们的婚礼办得很低调。
1) Their wedding was a very low-key affair.
2) The wedding was very low-keyed.

“低调”的第三个意思是形容“比较消沉和悲观的论调”。英语可以译为 depressing and pessimistic。例如：

22. 这位作家的作品的总倾向是低调的，强调死亡、流血和过分拥挤。
The general trend of the writer’s works is depressing and pessimistic, with the emphasis on death, blood and overcrowding.

“低调”的第四个意思是比喻“不引人注目的低姿态”。英语可以译为 low profile。例如：

23. 那个演员在私下保持低调。
The actor keeps a low profile in private.
24. 我建议他未来几天保持低调。
I advised him to keep a low profile for the next few days.
25. 这个学生保持低调，一直到考试结束。
The student kept a low profile until the exam was over.

42 零和游戏

汉语关键词：零、零和、零和游戏、零和博弈、零容忍

英语关键词：zero, zero-sum, zero-sum game, zero tolerance

句子：现在，“零和”观念正逐渐被“双赢”观念所取代。

误译：The zero-sum concept is now being gradually substituted for the win-win concept.

正译：The zero-sum concept is now being gradually substituted with/by the win-win concept.

解释：to substitute A for B的意思是“以A取代B”，其被动语态形式为 B is substituted with/by A。英语没有 B is substituted for A 的形式。

“零和”的意思是指“双方相同的获胜概率”。英语可以译为 zero-sum。例如：

1. 经济增长不是零和的。
   Economic growth is not zero-sum.
2. 我认为人们对世界常常采取零和观点，其实他们本不应该这样做。
   I think people often take a zero-sum view of the world when they shouldn't.
3. 我把“零和思维”定义为“对一切假使都质疑的思维”或“认为任何事情都有可能的思维”。
   I define zero-sum thinking as thinking that questions all assumptions or that considers anything as possible.
4. 零和经济是一种收益总和等于损失总和的体系。
   A zero-sum economy is a system in which the sum of the gains equals the sum of the losses.
5. 在一场严格的零和竞争中，一个演员获奖，而另一个演员输掉。
   In a strict zero-sum contest, one actor gains in prize while the other loses.
6. 许多人相信“哪里有赢家，那里必有输家”的零和观念。
   Many people believe in the zero-sum concept that wherever there are winners there must be losers.

“零和游戏”或“零和博弈”，英语可以译为 zero-sum game，其意思为 a situation in which what is gained by one person or group is lost by another person or group，即“一方获益而另一方受损的局面”。例如：

7. 零和游戏是一种一个玩家只能在另一个玩家输的情况下获胜的游戏。
   A zero-sum game is a type of game wherein one player can gain only at

the expense of another player.

8. 期货交易是一种零和游戏。
Futures trading is a zero-sum game.

9. 劳动力迁移不是零和游戏，由于创造了新的工作岗位，劳动力输出国和输入国是双赢的。
Labour mobility is not a zero-sum game: both senders and recipients win, as new jobs are created.

10. 在零和游戏中，人们总是试图隐藏自己的策略。
In zero-sum games, people always try to hide their strategies.

11. 各国之间对实力的追求不应再被视为一种零和博弈。
The pursuit of power among nations must no longer be seen as a zero-sum game.

12. 非零和游戏是双方皆赢或皆输的游戏。
A non-zero-sum game is one in which both sides can win or lose.

13. 在非零和游戏中，你们可能双赢，也可能共输。
In non-zero-sum games you can both do well, or both do poorly.

“零”作为修饰语，形容与数量增减相关的名词，英语可以译为zero，其意思为the lowest possible amount or level，即“最少量”、“最低点”或“最低程度”。例如：

14. 在英国，一些环境保护主义者呼吁建立零增长经济，作为通向真正可持续发展的唯一可能的途径。
In Britain, some environmentalists have called for the establishment of a zero-growth economy as the only possible route to real sustainable development.

14. 据说在美国，医院赚取零利润。
It is said that hospitals make zero profit in the United States.

15. 中国大陆从2009年7月1日起对原产自香港的部分产品实施零关税。
China's mainland implemented zero tariffs on part of the products originating from Hong Kong from July 1, 2009.

16. 在美国，许多经济学家宣称最佳货币政策应该力争零通货膨胀。
In the United States, many economists claim that optimal monetary policy should aim for zero inflation.

“零容忍”，英语可以译为 zero tolerance，其意思为the policy of applying laws very strictly so that people are punished even for offences that are not very serious，即“对轻微过失都不放过的严厉执法政策”。例如：

17. 只有全社会对腐败现象持“零容忍”态度，人们才能消除和减少腐败的发生。

Only when the whole society takes a zero tolerance attitude towards corruption, can people eliminate or reduce its occurrence.

18. 地方政府对青少年饮酒采取零容忍政策。

The local government adopts a zero tolerance policy on alcohol use by teenagers.

43 吹风会

汉语关键词： 吹风、吹冷风、吹风机、吹风会

英语关键词： get in a draught, dry one’s hair with a blower, blower, hair drier, hair dryer, discourage, make discouraging remarks on, brief, brief in advance, give a briefing, tip off, give a tip-off, briefing meeting, news briefing, press briefing, media briefing, advanced briefing, background briefing, briefing session, briefing

句子： 今天，外交部举行中外记者吹风会介绍温总理访问欧洲事宜。

误译： Today the Ministry of Foreign Affairs held a brief meeting for Chinese and international reporters about Premier Wen’s visit to Europe.

正译： Today the Ministry of Foreign Affairs held a briefing meeting for Chinese and international reporters about Premier Wen’s visit to Europe.

解释：

brief 的意思是 lasting only a short time，即“短暂的”。brief meeting 的意思是“短会”。“吹风会”的意思是“向记者发布新闻、解释一些关键问题的会议”。briefing 的意思是 a meeting in which people are given instructions or information，具有“吹风会”的含义。

“吹风”的第一个意思是“被风吹，受风寒”。英语可以译为 to get in a draught。例如：

1. 小心不要吹风着凉。

Be careful not to get in a draught and catch cold.

2. 你的病还没好，不要吹风。

Don’t get in a draught. You aren’t well yet.

“吹风”的第二个意思是“用吹风机吹干头发，使其定型”。英语可以译为 to dry one’s hair with a blower。例如：

3. 理发师正全神贯注地为顾客吹风。
With rapt attention, the hairdresser was drying the customer's hair with a blower.

“吹风机”，英语可以译为 blower, hair drier, hair dryer。例如：

4. 乒乓球悬浮在吹风机上方。
The ping-pong ball stays suspended above the hair dryer.

“吹冷风”的意思是“散布冷言冷语打击人的热情，或在别人头脑过热时劝其冷静”。英语可以译为 to discourage, to make discouraging remarks on。例如：

5. 他们把指标定得过高，要给他们吹吹冷风。
As they have set too high a target, you should discourage them.
6. 不要站在一边给我吹冷风。
Don't stand by and make discouraging remarks on me.
7. 他光吹冷风，不干实事。
He only makes discouraging remarks instead of doing solid work.

“吹风”的第三个意思是“有意透露意向或信息，使人知道”。英语可以译为 to brief, to brief in advance, to give a briefing, to tip off, to give a tip-off。例如：

8. 把这件事给他吹吹风。
1) Brief him on what this is all about.
2) Tip him off on what this is all about.
9. 开会之前，我想给你们吹吹风。
I would like to give you a briefing before the meeting.
10. 秘书长就会议情况给代表们吹了吹风。
The general secretary gave the representatives a briefing about the meeting.
11. 我先给你们吹吹风，大家好有个思想准备。
I'd like to give you a briefing, so that you can be mentally prepared.
12. 假如人们对决策众说纷纭，或者政府要出台新政策，最好先吹风，看一看公众反应和舆论。
If people hold widely different views on decision-making or the government is going to issue a new policy, it is advisable to brief it in advance so as to see the public reaction and public opinion.
13. 他吹风要咱们邀请他参加晚会。
He gave a tip-off that he wanted us to invite him to the party.

“吹风会”，英语可以译为 briefing meeting, news briefing, press briefing, media briefing, advanced briefing, background briefing, briefing session, briefing。例如：

14. 美国驻北京使馆就他们总统访华事宜举行了吹风会。
The U.S. Embassy to Beijing held a briefing meeting about their President's visit to China.
15. 这位官员在新闻吹风会上说，“这次核试验不针对任何一个国家，也不会对任何国家构成威胁。”
The official said on the news briefing, "This nuclear test was not directed at any country and nor does it constitute a threat to any country."
16. 白宫发言人主持了关于美国总统即将进行的亚洲之行的新闻吹风会。
The White House Spokesman hosted a press briefing on American President's upcoming trip to Asia.
17. 外交部就温总理访问埃及事宜举行媒体吹风会。
The Ministry of Foreign Affairs held a media briefing about Premier Wen's visit to Egypt.
18. 中午将在会议室举行关于这次会议的吹风会。
An advanced briefing on the conference will be held in the meeting room at noon.
19. 大会秘书处在会议之前为记者举行了背景吹风会。
The secretariat of the conference held a background briefing for reporters before the meeting.
20. 近80家公司参加了吹风会，热切地向发言者提问题。
Nearly 80 companies attended the briefing session and raised questions to the speakers eagerly.
21. 市政府给记者们举行了关于投资政策和投资环境的吹风会。
The city government held a briefing for reporters about its investment policy and investment environment.

44 流失文物

汉语关键词：流失、流失文物、水土流失、被掠夺、人才流失，退学、辍学、流失生

英语关键词：run off, soil erosion, lose, loss, looted, brain drain, outflow of talent，drop out of school, drop from school， school dropout, dropout student, dropout

句子： 我国驻联合国代表反对拍卖圆明园流失文物。

误译： China's Representative to U.N. is opposed to the auction of the lost relics originated from Yuanmingyuan.

正译： China's Representative to U.N. is opposed to the auction of the looted relics originated from Yuanmingyuan.

解释：

lost relics 的意思是"丢失的文物"。而"流失文物"指的是"历史上被掠夺而目前还未追讨回来的文物，英语应该译为 looted relics。

"流失"的第一个意思指"自然界的矿石、土壤自已散失或被水、风力带走，或河水等白白地流掉"。英语可以译为 to run off。例如：

1. 我们正在建造水库蓄积汛期的河水，以免流失。
   We are building up a reservoir to store the river water accumulated during the flood season, lest it might run off.
2. 工人们正设法堵住输油管道所有的漏洞，一点一滴的油也不让流失。
   The workers were trying to plug up all the leaks in the oil pipeline, not allowing a single drop of oil to run off.

"水土流失"，英语可以译为 soil erosion。例如：

3. 人们在荒丘上种植树木以防止和减少水土流失。
   People plant trees on the barren hillock to prevent and reduce soil erosion.

"流失"的第二个意思泛指"有用的或贵重的东西流散失去"。英语动词可以译为 to lose。名词可以译为 loss。例如：

4. 由于人们经常年复一年地在同一地域耕种农作物，土壤会流失自身所有的营养物质。
   As people often grow crops year after year in the same fields, the soil may lose all of its nutrients.
5. 当你把桔子切成小桔瓣时，会流失太多的汁。
   When you cut the orange into small segments, it will lose too much juice.
6. 市政府已采取有效措施制止国有资产流失。
   The municipal government has adopted effective measures to prevent the loss of state assets.
7. 钙补充剂有助于防止和减少钙质的流失，并强化骨骼。
   Calcium supplement helps to prevent and reduce calcium loss and also strengthen the bones.

"流失"的第三个意思是"被掠夺"的委婉语。英语可以译为 looted。例如：

8. 中国政府通过国际合作成功追回了这些流失文物。
   Through international cooperation, the Chinese Government succeeded in recovering these looted relics

"流失"的第四个意思是比喻"人员离开本地或本单位"，即"人才流失"。英语可以译为 brain drain, outflow of talent。例如：

9. 人才流失又称为人力资本逃逸。
   Brain drain is also known as human capital flight.
10. 人才流失可以简单地定义为大批技术人员从一个国家向另一个国家移民。
    Brain drain can be simply defined as the mass emigration of technically skilled people from one country to another country.
11. 移民常常会导致人才流失。
    Migration very often leads to brain drain.
12. 这个亚洲国家因为经济状况恶劣而遭受持续的人才流失。
    The Asian country suffered from a continual brain drain because of bad economy.
13. 阻止人才流失取决于创造一个良好的国内环境，而不是简单地为那些想出国的人设置障碍。
    Stopping the outflow of talent depends on creating a sound domestic environment rather than simply setting up barriers for those who wish to go abroad.

"流失"的第五个意思指"退学"或"辍学"。英语可以译为 to drop out of school, to drop from school。例如：

14. 现在，一些农村学生因贫穷而流失。
    Nowadays, some students in rural areas have dropped out of school because of poverty.
15. 由于他父亲供不起他的学费，这个男孩不得不退学，在工厂打工维持生计。
    As his father couldn't afford to pay for his tuition fee, the young boy had to drop from school and work in a factory to earn his own living.
16. 辍学会给一个学生造成恶劣影响。
    Dropping out of school can have dire impact on a student.
17. 我们必须采取积极行动防止农村学生流失。
    We must take active actions to prevent rural students dropping out of school.

"流失生"，英语可以译为 school dropout, dropout student, dropout。例如：

18. 这个流失生在街头到处游荡，不再上任何学校。
The school dropout wandered around in the streets and no longer attended any school.
19. 这些流失生需要经济帮助和心理咨询。
These dropout students need financial help and psychological consultation.
20. 当地教育部门正设法让流失生尽快复学。
The local educational department is trying to help the dropouts to go back to school.

45 话语权

汉语关键词： 话语、话语权
英语关键词： remark, words, what one says, discourse, say, have a say
句子： 发展中国家要求在气候变化问题上有更多的话语权。
误译： The developing countries want more rights of speech in the issues about climate change.
正译： The developing countries want more say in the issues about climate change.
解释：

right of speech 的意思是“发言权”，即“说话的权利”，其含义不如“话语权”强烈。“话语权”的“权”，不仅可以表示“权利”(right)，还可以表示“权力”(power)。英语的 say 作为名词，有 right or power to influence action or decision 的意思，即“影响行动或决定的权利或权力”，正好表达了“话语权”的内涵。

“话语”的第一个意思是“言语”或“说的话”。英语可以译为 remark, words, what one says。例如：

1. 我劝你不要相信他的似乎天真的话语。
I advise you not to believe his seemingly innocent remarks.
2. 她在旅途中话语不多，可是句句中听。
She had few words during the trip, but every sentence was pleasant to the ear.
3. 这位诗人的话语有力量，既有正面，又有负面的力量。
The poet’s words possess power—both positive and negative.
4. 他很少给我打电话，而且每次对我说的话语不多。
He seldom called me and every time said few words to me.

5. 她的话语感动得我们流下眼泪。
What she had said moved us to tears.

"话语"的第二个意思是指"由语句所构成的连贯的和完整的较大的语言交际单位，包括会话、段落、整篇文章等"，为语言学名词。英语可以译为 discourse。例如：

6. 这位语言学家正在研究话语分析的方法。
The linguist is studying the method of discourse analysis.
7. 话语分析的方法很复杂，如果不深入阅读是无法恰当理解的。
The method of discourse analysis is complex and cannot be properly understood without further reading.
8. 话语分析对在不同专业领域工作的学者来说，已逐渐具有不同的解释。
Discourse analysis has come to have different interpretations for scholars working in different disciplines.

"话语权"，英语可以译为 say。"拥有话语权"，英语可以译为 to have a say 例如：

9. 国力的提升，增强了中国的软实力，并为中国在国际社会赢得了更多的话语权。
The enhancement of national strength has improved China's soft power and won more say for China in the international community.
10. 人民群众在重要官员选拔中应该拥有话语权。
The masses of the people should have a say in the selection of important officials.
11. 过去，发展中国家在国际重大问题上没有话语权。
In the past, developing countries had no say in major international issues.
12. 我所要求的只是在这件事上有些话语权。
All I want is to have some say in this matter.

46 发言人

汉语关键词： 发言、发言权、发言者、发言人、发言稿、议长

英语关键词： right to speak, right of speech, voice, speak, make a speech, take the floor, speaker, Speaker, speech, spokesman, text of a speech

句子： 外交部发言人在新闻发布会上回答了外国记者提出的关于气候变化的问题。

误译： The Speaker of the Foreign Ministry answered the questions raised by international reporters about climate change at the press conference.

正译： The Spokesman of the Foreign Ministry answered the questions raised by international reporters about climate change at the press conference.

解释：

“发言人”的意思是“代表某一团体或组织发表意见的人”，译为 speaker 是不合适的。speaker 的第一个意思是 a person who gives a talk or makes a speech，即“讲演者”或“发言者”。speaker 的第二个意思是 the presiding officer in a legislative assembly or legislative body，即“立法机构的主持官员”，译为“议长”，要用大写。the Speaker of the British Upper House of Parliament 是“英国议会下院议长”；the Speaker of the American House of Representatives 是“美国国会众议院议长”。例如：

1. 据新闻记者报道，英国议会下院议长说，“企业的发展在反对贫困的斗争中是至关重要的。”
   According to the news reporters, the Speaker of the British Upper House of Parliament said, “The development of enterprises is crucial in the fight against poverty”.
2. 今天上午，美国国会众议院议长会见了正在访问美国的中国政府代表团。
   This morning, the Speaker of the American House of Representatives met China’s government delegation that was visiting America.

“发言人”应该译为 spokesman, spokeswoman, spokesperson，它的意思是 a person who speaks on behalf of a group or an organization。例如：

3. 这位发言人拒绝对这个问题进行评论。
   The spokesman declined to comment on this issue.
4. 一位政府女发言人否认了这些谣言。
   A spokeswoman for the government denied the rumours.
5. 这位女发言人阐明了政府在这一问题上的立场。
   The spokeswoman clarified the government’s position on this issue.
6. 这所大学的一位发言人说：“本大学欢迎残疾学生申请报考。”
   A spokesperson of the university said,“Our University welcomes the applications from the students with disabilities.”

“发言”的第一个意思是“发表意见”，用作动词。英语可以译为 to speak, to make a speech, to take the floor。例如：

7. 当他起立发言时，人们报以经久不息的掌声。
   When he rose to speak, he was accorded a prolonged ovation.

8. 我想就经济改革的必要性发言。
   I would like to speak about the need for economic reform.
9. 我在会上积极发言，表达了我的观点。
   I made an active speech at the meeting, expressing my views.
10. 她发言批评了这个新计划。
    She took the floor to criticize the new plan.
11. 现在我想请我们的贵宾首先发言。
    Now I'd like to invite our distinguished guest to take the floor first.

"发言者"，英语可以译为 speaker。例如：

12. 今晚我们的第一位发言者是来自哈佛大学的约翰逊教授。
    Our first speaker tonight is Professor Johnson from Harvard University.
13. 许多发言者在会议上强烈抨击了这个建议。
    Many speakers strongly attacked this proposal at the meeting.

"发言"的第二意思是"发表的意见"，用作名词。英语可以译为 speech。例如：

14. 我想将每位发言时间限制为10分钟。
    I would like to limit the time of each speech to ten minutes.
15. 他在大会上的发言正好切题。
    The speech he made at the meeting was just to the point.
16. 这位发言者很久、很久以前就死了，但是他的发言影响依然存在。
    The speaker died long, long ago but his speech still survived.
17. 他的书面发言具有深刻意义。
    His written speech is of profound significance.

"发言稿"，英语可以译为 text of a speech。例如：

18. 主席在会议上宣读了事先准备好的发言稿。
    The chairman read the prepared text of a speech at the meeting.

"发言权"的意思是"说话或发表意见的权利"。英语可以译为 right to speak, right of speech 或 voice。例如：

19. 没有调查，就没有发言权。
    1) He who makes no investigation has no right to speak.
    2) He has no right of speech without making any investigation.
20. 非洲国家在联合国安理会要求更多的发言权。
    African countries demand greater voice on UN Security Council.
21. 过去，妇女的发言权被剥夺，她们的希望被人不屑一顾。
    In the past, women's voices were silenced and their hopes were dismissed.

47

蜗居

汉语关键词： 蜗居、蜗居者、寄居、寄居者、旅居

英语关键词： humble abode, a nutshell of a house, live in a small room, confine oneself to a small room, one who lives in a nutshell of a house, live with a relative, stay with a relative, live away from home, sojourn, sojourner

句子： 现在国内正在热播电视连续剧《蜗居》。

误译： The TV series “Living in a Snail’s Shell” is hitting the small screen in China.

正译： The TV series “A Nutshell of a House” is hitting the small screen in China.

解释：

汉语可以用蜗牛壳比喻窄小的住处，有“蜗居”的说法。英语 snail 的意思是 a small soft creature with a hard round shell on its back, that moves very slowly，有“行动缓慢”的联想，但与“狭小”无关。这是它与汉语的文化差异。英语习语 slow as a snail 具有 very slow 的意思。at a snail’s pace 具有 very slowly 的意思。例如：

1. 我的互联网连接慢如蜗牛。
   My Internet connection is slow as a snail.
2. 我不愿意跟他徒步行走。他慢如蜗牛。
   I hate hiking with him. He’s slow as a snail.
3. 我骑的毛驴行走缓慢。
   The donkey on which I was riding moved at a snail’s pace.
4. 我感觉放假之前，时间过得很慢。
   I felt time moved at a snail’s pace before the holidays.
5. 这位老人慢慢地行走。
   The old man walked along at a snail’s pace.

“蜗居”的第一个意思是比喻“狭小的住所”，用作名词。英语可以译为 humble abode, a nutshell of a house。例如：

6. 有空请来蜗居小坐。
   Please drop in and visit with me in my humble abode when you have time.
7. 美国人很可能说“欢迎来到我们的蜗居”给请来的客人们打招呼。
   Americans are very likely to greet invited visitors with the phrase, “Welcome to our humble abode.”
8. 奢谈在像我们这样的蜗居里举行晚会是多么荒唐呀！
   How absurd it is to talk of giving a party in such a nutshell of a house as ours!

注意，narrow dwelling 表示的是“窄”，但是并不一定“小”，因而不一定是“蜗居”。例如：

9. 我的家是一所长条的窄房子，有许多房间，照明也好。
My home was a long narrow dwelling with many rooms, and good lighting.

10. 他站在他的窄房子的低矮屋顶下，伸手够天花板。
He stood under the low roof of his narrow dwelling and stretched out his hand to the ceiling.

“蜗居”的第二个意思是比喻“住在狭小的住所”，用作动词。英语可以译为 to live in a small room, to confine oneself to a small room。例如：

11. 他们一家五口人蜗居一间仅10平米的斗室。
In the past, the five people of his family lived in a small room which covered an area of only ten square metres.

12. 这三个打工族蜗居在北京郊区的一所寒冷的房间里。
The three odd-jobbers live in a small cold room in the suburbs of Beijing.

13. 这位孤独老人蜗居斗室。
This lonely old man confines himself to a small room.

“蜗居者”，英语可以译为 one who lives in a nutshell of a house。例如：

14. 这些蜗居者渴望早日搬进宽敞的房子。
Those living in a nutshell of a house are yearning to move into a spacious house.

“寄居”的第一个意思是“住在亲戚家中”。英语可以译为 to live with a relative, to stay with a relative。例如：

15. 她从小就一直寄居在姨妈家里。
Since she was a little girl, she has lived with her aunt.

16. 他从乡下到城里打工，寄居在表哥家里。
Coming from the countryside to do odd jobs in town, he stayed with his cousin.

“寄居”的第二个意思是“住在外地他乡”，或称“旅居”。英语可以译为 to live away from home, to sojourn。注意 sojourn 也可以用作名词。例如：

17. 这位老华侨多年寄居海外。
This old overseas Chinese has lived abroad for many years.

18. 这位来自海南岛的诗人长期寄居北方。
This poet coming from Hainan Island has long lived in North China.
19. 他在旅居非洲期间，学到了许多当地风俗。
When he sojourned in Africa, he learned a lot about native customs.
20. 尽管与世隔绝，而长期寄居在一个陌生的天地，他却保持没变。
Despite this isolation and this long sojourn in a strange world, he remained unchanged.

"寄居者"，英语可以译为 sojourner。例如：

21. 这些来自农村的打工族是处于城乡结合部的这个小村庄的寄居者。
Those odd jobbers coming from the rural areas are sojourners of the small village in the urban fringe area.

48 扫黄

汉语关键词：扫、清除、黄、黄色、黄段子、黄毒、扫黄、扫黄行动

英语关键词：sweep, sweep away, obscene, sexy, pornographic, salacious, blue joke, dirty joke, adult joke, indelicate joke, evil of pornography, wipe out pornography, sweep away pornography, crack down on pornography, crack down on pornographic products and publications, campaign against pornography, anti-pornography drive, anti-porno drive, anti-pornography campaign, anti-porno campaign

句子：我国各地正在开展手机网络扫黄行动。

误译：A campaign to sweep pornography in mobile phone network is being launched throughout our country.

正译：A campaign to sweep away pornography in mobile phone network is being launched throughout our country.

解释：

to sweep 的字面意思是 to clean a room or a surface, using a broom，即"用扫帚扫"，指具体动作。"扫黄"的"扫"具有"清除"的比喻意义，要译为 to sweep away，即 to get rid of sth completely。例如：

1. 教室已打扫干净。
The classroom has been swept clean.

2. 我妈妈演示给我看如何扫地。
   My mother showed me how to sweep the floor.
3. 从你的话语看，显然你是很少扫你住所前面的街道的。
   From your remark, it is obvious that you seldom sweep the street in front of your residence.
4. 当你扫楼梯时，你总是从顶上开始扫。
   When you sweep the stairs, you always start from the top.
5. 他的软弱破坏了他清除通向成功的障碍的决心。
   His weakness undermined his determination to sweep away the obstacles to his success.
6. 这场革命清除了旧的法律与秩序。
   The revolution swept away the old laws and orders.

“黄”或“黄色”，可以用来象征腐化堕落，特指色情。英语可以译为 obscene, sexy, pornographic, salacious。例如：

7. 这部小说的内容有点黄。
   The content of this novel is a bit obscene.
8. 互联网跟黄色电影和杂志在一起，成为受众最多的黄源。
   The Internet has become the most viewed source of pornography, along with sexy movies and magazines.
9. 手机上网成为黄色网站的“绿色通道”。
   The network access to mobile phones has become a “green channel” to pornographic websites.
10. 读黄色小说有害于年青人。
    Reading pornographic novels is harmful to young people.
11. 这位专家告诫青年学生不要读黄书。
    The expert warns the young students not to read pornographic books.
12. 以黄色书刊和影视片为其主要娱乐出口产品，美国已成为世界头号黄源。
    With pornographic publications, movies and videos as its major entertainment export, America has become the number-one supplier of pornography to the world.
13. 这位专家指出一些外国网络新闻网站专门报道丑闻和黄色新闻。
    The expert points out that some foreign news sites on the web exclusively report scandalous and salacious news.

“黄段子”，英语可以译为 blue joke, dirty joke, adult joke, indelicate joke。例如：

14. 他那样庸俗，总爱说黄段子，或者谈论别人的婚姻。
    He was so vulgar that he would often either crack a blue joke or talk

about other people's marriages.

"黄毒"，指"毒害人思想的淫秽书刊、音像制品等"。英语可以译为 evil of pornography。例如：

15. 黄毒已像瘟疫一样传播全世界。
The evil of pornography has spread like a plague throughout the world.
16. 扫除黄毒的途径是首先扫除黄源。
The way to get rid of the evil of pornography is first to get rid of the source of pornography.

"扫黄"的意思是"清理和消除黄色书刊及淫秽录像带"。英语可以译为 to wipe out pornography, to sweep away pornography, to crack down on pornography, to crack down on pornographic products and publications。例如：

17. 我们正在开展全国性手机网络扫黄行动。
We are launching a nationwide campaign to wipe out pornography on the networks for mobile phones.
18. 这位专家指出为了有效地扫黄，需要对互联网进行比较严格的限制。
The expert points out that tighter Internet restrictions are needed to crack down on pornography effectively.
19. 扫黄是一个长期而复杂的任务。
To crack down on pornographic products and publications is a long-term and complicated task.

"扫黄行动"，英语可以译为 campaign against pornography, anti-pornography drive, anti-porno drive, anti-pornography campaign, anti-porno campaign。例如：

20. 我们应该坚持不懈地开展"扫黄"、"打非"行动。
We should tirelessly carry on the campaign against pornography and illegal publications.
21. 网络扫黄行动是顺应民心之举。
The anti-pornography drive in the web is a deed that complies with the aspirations of the people.
22. 在中国，扫黄行动已扩展到手机游戏、在线小说、博客、视频、电台节目、手机网站、聊天室和即时通讯群组。
In China, the anti-porn drive has extended to mobile phone games, online novels, blogs, videos, radio programmes, mobile phone websites, chat rooms and instant messenger groups.

23. 地方政府在扫黄行动中端掉了十几个黄窝。
In the anti-pornography campaign, the local government destroyed a dozen of pornographic dens.

24. 在扫黄行动中，我市公安部门抓了几十个黄贩子。
In the anti-porno campaign, the public security department in our city arrested dozens of vendors of pornographic products and publications.

49 打黑

汉语关键词：打黑、打黑除恶、邪恶势力、黑人邪恶势力、邪恶魔力

英语关键词：evil force, black evil force, gang, crack down on gangs, crush gangs, attack against gangs, crack down on speculation and profiteering, since it got dark

句子：如果打黑不打它的保护伞，我们就会白打。

误译：If we attack against a black evil force without crushing its protective umbrella, we' ll fail to get rid of it completely.

正译：If we attack against a gang without crushing its protective umbrella, we' ll fail to get rid of it completely.

解释：

“打黑”的“黑”指的是“具有黑社会性质的犯罪团伙”。black evil force 或 black force of evil 有“邪恶势力”、“黑人邪恶势力”和“邪恶魔力”等歧义，不一定表示“犯罪团伙”。为避免歧义最好用 gang，它的意思是 an organized group of criminals，即“有组织的犯罪团伙”。例如：

1. Dick Cheney—The demonic black force of evil behind the current president, he is the corporate choice. Average people hate him, but CEOs don't ...and they write the checks.
迪克·切尼（美国布什政府时期的副总统）— 现任总统（指布什总统）背后的魔鬼般邪恶势力，他是公司企业的选择。普通人民痛恨他，而首席执行官们不恨他，……他们还给他开支票。

2. I remind them that there is a black force of evil in this world, which is not all fuzzy bunnies and warm sunny days.
我提醒他们说世界上有股邪恶势力，它决不是毛茸茸的兔子，也不是温暖的晴朗日子。

3. There was a White hero force fighting a black evil force, and they didn't have to throw in a bunch of minorities with the good guys to "even things up."
有一股白人英雄势力与一股黑人邪恶势力争斗，他们不需要有一批能“摆平事情”的好人组成的少数派掺合进来。
4. They find a tower with a spinning black evil force. They figure the spinning black evil force is Fate.
他们发现了一个带有旋转邪恶魔力的塔。他们判定这股旋转邪恶魔力就是命运之神。

“打黑”的第一个意思是“打击具有黑社会性质的犯罪团伙”，又称“打黑除恶”。英语可以译为 to crack down on gangs, to crush gangs, to attack against gangs。例如：

5. 当前，“打黑除恶”已成为反对刑事犯罪斗争的焦点。
At present, to crack down on gangs has become the focus point in the fight against crimes.
6. 重庆市自7月份开始打黑特别行动以来，警方已调查了数十名地方官员。
Since the beginning of the special operation to crush gangs in Chongqing in July, police have investigated dozens of local officials.
7. 在打黑行动中，为黑势力头目及成员提供保护伞的官员都将依法受到严惩。
In the fight to crack down on gangs, those officials who have provided protective umbrellas for gang bosses and gangsters will be severely punished in accordance with the laws.

“打黑”的第二个意思是“打击投机倒把和牟取暴利的活动”。英语可以译为to crack down on speculation and profiteering。例如：

8. 这位网民在博客中建议：我们应该在房地产市场掀起一场打黑行动。
In his blog, the netizen suggests that we should launch a campaign to crack down on speculation and profiteering in the real estate market.
9. 人们普遍关注最近足坛掀起的扫赌打黑行动。
People have generally paid attention to the campaign recently launched in football circles to sweep away gambling and to crack down on speculation and profiteering.

“打黑”的第三个意思是“从天黑起”。英语可以译为 since it got dark。例如：

10. 自打黑起，风中的寒意就真的降下来了。
The wind chill has really dropped since it got dark.
11. 妈妈打黑就没有闲着，为我张落着明天的行装。
Since it got dark, Mother has been busy preparing my package for tomorrow.

50 临时

汉语关键词： 临时

英语关键词： temporary, interim, provisional, makeshift, temporarily, for the time being, at the time when sth happens, on the spur of the moment, at the last moment, at the eleventh hour

句子： 临时借用一下自行车，好吗？很快就还你。

误译： May I borrow your bike temporarily? I' ll return it to you soon.

正译： May I borrow your bike? I' ll return it to you soon.

解释：

to borrow 的意思是 to take sth from sb to use temporarily,即“暂时使用别人的物品或金钱”。to borrow 已包含 temporarily(暂时)的意思。汉语用“临时”二字，是强调“暂时使用，不会长期使用”。许诺“用完后会立即归还”。因此，“临时”二字不必译出，可以省略 temporarily。

“临时”的第一个意思是“暂时”、“一时”、“短期”或“非正式的”，当形容词用。英语可以译为 temporary, interim, provisional, makeshift, temporarily, for the time being。temporary 的意思是 lasing or intended to last only for a short time, 与 permanent 的意思相对立，强调“不是永久的”。例如：

1. 你可以睡觉时好好想一想，再决定是否要接受这个临时工作。
   You can sleep on it before you decide whether you are going to take the temporary job.
2. 她不得不找一个临时工作来养活自己。
   She has to get a temporary work to keep herself alive.
3. 我们公司只有在休假替班、产假或工作量高峰期时，才会雇佣临时工。
   In our company, temporary workers are employed only for vacation relief, maternity leave or workload peaks.
4. 当他来到这个陌生小镇时，他不得不寻找临时住处。
   When he came to this small strange town, he had to seek for temporary accommodation.
5. 他们常常走到一起组建一个临时性或者有时是永久性的公司，用于解决一个特定的任务。
   They often come together to form a temporary or sometimes permanent company that serves to tackle a particular task.
6. 这位专家指出公众捐助只是解决穷人基本需求的一种临时措施。

The expert points out that public donation is only a temporary measure to address the basic needs of the poor.

7. 这个临时性文档包含了所有需要合并的记录。
   This temporary file contains all the records to be combined.
8. 至少我们已经找到了这一社会问题的临时解决办法。
   At least we've found a temporary solution to this social problem.
9. 这两国国家元首的会谈实际上是一次临时安排。
   The talk between the heads of state of the two countries was actually a temporary arrangement.
10. 持有自己国家颁发的驾驶执照的外国人可以在中国申请临时驾驶执照并驾车，而无须参加相关测试。
    Foreigners who have a driving license issued by their home countries can apply for a temporary driving licence and drive in China without having to take related tests.
11. 在那个亚洲国家，临时执照有效期最多为3个月。
    In that Asian country, the temporary licence can be valid for three months at most.
12. 由于我们打算买一所房子，我们怎样才能得到一笔大额临时贷款?
    How can we get a large temporary loan as we are trying to buy a house?
13. 一座塔吊突然倒塌，砸坏了一些临时性建筑物，但是幸好没有人受伤。
    A tower crane keeled over and crushed some temporary buildings, but fortunately nobody was hurt.
14. 我临时住在一个朋友家里。
    1) Temporarily, I stayed with a friend of mine.
    2) I stayed with one of my friends for the time being.

interim 的意思是 intended to last for only a short time until sb/sth more permanent is found，强调“过渡性的”。例如：

15. 这个拉美国家的临时政府是根据一部临时宪法执政的。
    The interim government of this Latin American country operated under an interim constitution.
16. 那个协议是旨在使该地区保持稳定的一项临时措施。
    The agreement is an interim measure aimed at stabilizing the region.
17. 给该委员会的委员们一个临时性报告是必要的。
    It is necessary to give the members of the committee an interim report.
18. 本周，中国驻这个非洲国家的临时代办将要上任。
    Chinese Charge d'Affaires ad interim to this African country will take up office this week.
19. 当大楼完工时，房产抵押按揭将用来偿还临时贷款。

When the building is finished, a mortgage on the property will be used to pay off the interim loan.

20. 市政府已对环境保护采取重大临时步骤。
The municipal government has taken a vital interim step towards environmental protection.
21. 这项临时协议将成为这两国之间后来的谈判与协议的基础和参照点。
This interim agreement will become the basis and reference point for subsequent negotiations and agreements between these two countries.
22. 约翰逊教授已被任命为该大学学术委员会临时主席。
Professor Johnson has been appointed Interim Chairman of the academic committee of the university.

provisional 的意思是 arranged for the present time only and likely to changed in the future，强调“是要变化的”。例如：

23. 我们需要为预备会议准备一份临时性报告。
We need to prepare a provisional report for the preparatory meeting.
24. 如果这个临时安排失败了，诉讼程序届时将会恢复。
If this provisional arrangement fails, proceedings would then resume.
25. 通过反复谈判，这两个国家最终就牛肉争议达成一项临时协议。
Through repeated negotiations, the two countries finally reached a provisional agreement in beef dispute.
26. 在我们达成一项合同之前，我们先同意达成一项临时合同。
Before we concluded a contract, we agreed on a provisional contract.
27. 随信附上一份临时议程以供参考。
A copy of the provisional agenda in enclosed for your information.
28. 完成学业时，将给所有学生颁发临时证书。
A provisional certificate will be issued to all students on completion of the programme.
29. 历史学家讨论认为俄国临时政府是一次失败。
The Russian Provisional Government is discussed by historians as a failure.
30. 临时法庭进社区，给居民提供了方便。
The provisional court in communities provides convenient access for residents.

makeshift 的意思是 used temporarily for a particular purpose because the real thing is not available，强调“替代的事物”。例如：

31. 这些业余演员在一个用木板搭的临时舞台上表演。
These amateur actors gave a performance on a makeshift stage of wood

planks.

32. 几个垫子充当临时的床。

A few cushions formed a makeshift bed.

33. 这个倒立的茶杯充做了临时烛台。

The upside down cup served as a makeshift candleholder.

"临时"的第二个意思是"临到事情发生的时候"，当副词用。英语可以译为 at the time when sth happens, on the spur of the moment, at the last moment, at the eleventh hour。例如：

34. 事先准备好，省得临时着急。

You should take precautions so that you may not be worried at the time when something happens.

35. 这是临时决定的。

This decision was made at the last moment.

36. 他平日不努力，考试前才临时抱佛脚。

1) As he doesn't work hard on usual days, he has to cram at the eleventh hour before the exam.

2) As he doesn't work hard on usual days, he has to make a frantic effort at the last moment before the exam.

37. 我临时找几个人帮我忙。

I tried to find some people to help me on the spur of the moment.

38. 我们不得不取消预订的房间，因为我们临时改变计划了。

We had to cancel our reservation, because we had changed our plan at the last moment.

51 围脖

汉语关键词： 围脖、围脖儿、围巾、微博、脖友、织围脖、微薄、微波、微波炉

英语关键词： scarf, muffler, neck warmer, microblogging, microblogging user, microblog, little, slender, slim, meagre, scanty, exiguous, small wave, ripple, microwave, microwave oven

句子： 这年头，没个"围脖"，还真不好意思跟人打招呼。

误译： In such years, if you don't have your own scarf, you may really feel ashamed of saying hollo to other people.

正译： In such years, if you haven't set up your own microblogging, you may really feel ashamed of saying hello to other people.

解释：

这个加引号的“围脖”，不是通常意义上的御寒用的围巾，而是“微博”的谐音。现在并没有不戴围巾就羞于跟人打招呼的习俗。这里的“打招呼”是指通过网络与人交流。“围脖”不能直译为 scarf，而要译为 microblogging（微博）。

“围脖”的第一个意思是“围在脖子上的围巾”，也称“围脖儿”。英语可以译为 scarf, muffler, neck warmer。例如：

1. 今天天气寒冷，出门要带帽子、围脖儿和手套。
   As it is cold today, you should put on your cap, scarf and gloves when you go out.
2. 冬天，他喜欢戴灰色方格围脖。
   In winter, he likes to wear a grey checked scarf.
3. 如果你在寒冷天气里跑步，你应该戴个围脖儿。
   If you are running in cold weather, you should have a scarf around your neck.
4. 她解开了她戴着的红色围脖。
   She loosened the red muffler that she had worn.
5. 套头围脖能够拉上去盖着鼻子，而且因为它自身安全而对小孩子们是理想的。此外，它织起来也快。
   A neck warmer can be pulled up to cover the nose and is ideal for small children because it's inherently safe. And it's quick to knit.

“围脖”的第二个意思是“微博”的谐音，即“微型博客”。英语可以译为 microblogging。“脖友”是“微型博客用户”，可以译为 microblogging user。“织围脖”是指写微博和发微博的过程，可以译为 to microblog。例如：

6. “围脖”是一种网络服务，为“脖友”们提供了新的相互交流的平台。
   Microblogging is a kind of network service, which provides a new platform for the microblogging users to communicate with each other.
7. 现在人们在通过电脑、或者手机来“织围脖”。
   Now people are microblogging through computers or mobile phones.
8. 去年下半年，微博在中国的年轻网民群体中迅速流行起来。
   In the second half of last year, microblogging quickly became popular among the younger groups of netizens in China.
9. 通过微博，你可以把所见、所闻和所思，用一句话写下来，篇幅不超过140个汉字。
   Through microblogging, you can write down what you have seen, heard

and thought about in one sentence within a space of fewer than 140 characters.

10. 微博无疑是分享与发现眼下正在发生的事情的最好方式。
Microblogging is without a doubt the best way to share and discover what is happening right now.
11. 如果你想使用正确的工具来做这个工作，你很可能需要一个专门的微博平台。
If you want to use the right tool for the job, you're probably going to need a specialized microblogging platform.
12. 这种多媒体微博将会简化你的在线生活。
This sort of multimedia microblogging will simplify your online life.
13. Twitter是世界上最知名的微博网站，目前有3,200万个独立访问用户。
Twitter is the best-known microblogging website of the world, which has 32 million independent visiting users now.

“微薄”的意思是“微小单薄”或“数量少”。英语可以译为 little, slender, slim, meagre, scanty, exiguous。例如：

14. 他竭尽自己微薄的力量来帮助这些残疾人。
1) He exerted what little strength he had to help these handicapped people.
2) He did what little he could to help these handicapped people.
15. 他靠写作的微薄收入生活。
1) He lives on his slender earning from his writing.
2) He lives on his slim income from his writing.
16. 我父亲靠微薄的收入养活全家。
1) My father supported the whole family with his meagre income.
2) My father kept the whole family alive with his meagre earnings.
17. 这个寡妇靠她微薄收入与女儿住在一起。
The widow lived with her daughter on her scanty income.
18. 这个青年人在一个建筑工地打工，收入相当微薄。
The young man works as an odd-jobber at a construction site, earning an exiguous income.

“微波”的第一个意思是“细小的水波”。英语可以译为 small wave, ripple。例如：

19. 虽然在微波荡漾水中的倒影有些模糊不清，却显得更加美丽。
Although the reflection is blurry on the water with small waves moving, it looks more beautiful.
20. 初升的太阳在平静海面的荡漾微波上闪烁着金光。

The rising sun sparkled gold across the ripples of a gentle sea.

"微波"的第二个意思是"波长为 1 米至 1 毫米的无线电波"。英语可以译为 microwave。例如：

21. 微波通信已经用于电信业中，而没有给野生动物造成任何危害。
Microwave communications links have already been used in the telecommunications industry without doing any harm to wildlife.
22. 对微波传输的通常反应是忧虑，因为微波被公众普遍视为危险的辐射形式。
The common reaction to microwave transmission is one of concern, as microwaves are generally perceived by the public as dangerous forms of radiation.

"微波炉"，英语可以译为 microwave oven。例如：

23. 我妈妈正用微波炉加热食物。
My mother is heating up the food in a microwave oven.
24. 这种爆米花在微波炉里加热很快就会爆开花。
This popcorn pops quickly in the microwave oven.
25. 金属盘子不能放在微波炉里加热。
You can't put metal dishes in a microwave oven.

52 蚁族

汉语关键词： 蚁族、蚁群、蚁穴、蚁巢、蚂蚁洞

英语关键词： ant clan, ant tribe, ant community, ant colony, ant nest, ant hole

句子： "蚁族"是对高校毕业生低收入聚居群体的形象比喻。

误译： Ant family is a vivid metaphor of the groups of low-income college graduates who settle in a compact community.

正译： Ant tribe is a vivid metaphor of the groups of low-income college graduates who settle in a compact community.

解释：

笔者观察到"蚁族"有 ant family, ant clan, ant tribe 和 ant community 等译法。family 的第一个意思是 a group consisting of one or two parents and their children，即 nuclear family（核心家庭）；第

二个意思是 a group consisting of one or two parents, their children and close relations，即 extended family(外延家庭)；第三个意思是 all the people who are related to each other, including those who are now dead，即"家族"；第四个意思是 a group of related animals and plants,动物分类译为"科"。例如:Tigers belong to the cat family.(虎属于猫科。)这里的"蚁族"不是有血缘关系的同一家庭或家族，也不是一种昆虫分类的名称，译为 ant family 是不合适的。

clan 有 a group of people who are connected because of a particular thing 的意思。将"蚁族"译为 ant clan 是可以接受的。例如：

1. "蚁族"指白天从事不稳定工作，晚上聚居于城乡结合部的收入微薄的大学毕业生群体。
   Ant clan refers to the group of college graduates with meagre income, who do insecure jobs in the daytime, and settle in the urban fringe areas at night.
2. 这些低收入高校毕业生与蚂蚁有相同特点，例如弱小、群居和勤奋，因此被称为"蚁族"。
   As these low-income university graduates have the same characteristics as ants, for example, they are weak, gregarious and hard-working, they are called "ant clan".

tribe 有 a group of people, especially of one profession 的意思。将"蚁族"译为 ant tribe 也是可以接受的。例如：

3. "蚁族"是继农民、农民工和下岗职工之后我国的第四个弱势群体。
   Next to farmers, rural migrant workers and laid-off workers, ant tribe is the fourth disadvantaged group in our country.
4. "蚁族"这个概念在中国大学毕业生中已被广为认可
   The concept of "ant tribe" has been widely acknowledged by collage graduates in China.
5. 日益显现的"蚁族"现象已在我国引起极大关注和重视。
   The ever-emerging phenomenon of ant tribes has aroused great concern and attention in our country.

community 有 a group of people who share the same religion, race, job, etc. 的意思。将"蚁族"译为 ant community 也是可以接受的。例如:

6. 对北京、上海、广州、武汉和西安等大城市的调查显示：每个城市都有惊人数量的蚁族。
   The survey made in such big cities as Beijing, Shanghai, Guangzhou, Wuhan and Xi'an shows that there is an amazing number of ant communities in each city.

7. 在某种程度上，“蚁族”是一个被人漠视和鲜为人知的群体，也是一个少有人关注和同情的群体。
   To a certain degree, ant community is a group of people who are neglected and rarely known, and also a group of people who are scarcely shown concern and sympathy for.

“蚁群”，英语可以译为 ant colony。例如：

8. 蚁群由一只蚁后和无数勤劳而无生育能力的工蚁组成。
   An ant colony is formed by a queen ant and numerous industrious and sterile worker ants.
9. 蚁后是蚁群中的一只成年的、有生育能力的雌蚂蚁，它通常会成为该蚁群中所有其他蚂蚁的母亲。
   A queen ant is an adult, reproducing female ant in an ant colony, which generally will be the mother of all the other ants in that colony.
10. 工蚁喂养和照料蚁群的幼虫。
    A worker ant feeds and cares for the colony’s young.
11. 如果一只工蚁发现了一个好的食物源，它会一路留下气味，使蚁群其他的蚂蚁能够找到食物。
    If a worker ant has found a good source for food, it leaves a trail of scent so that the other ants in the colony can find the food.
12. 单个一只蚂蚁并不聪明，但是一群蚂蚁就变聪明了。
    A single ant isn’t smart, but a colony of ants are.

“蚁穴”的第一个意思是“蚁巢”，英语可以译为 ant nest。例如：

13. 蚂蚁在土壤里或在一棵朽树里筑巢。
    Ants make a nest in the soil or inside a decayed tree.

“蚁穴”的第二个意思是“蚂蚁洞”，英语可以译为 ant hole。例如：

14. 她在靠近蚂蚁洞之处放了一些食糖，以阻止蚂蚁走向更远的地方。
    She put some sugar close to the ant hole to dissuade the ants from travelling further afield.
15. 千里之堤，溃于蚁穴。
    1) One ant-hole may cause the collapse of a thousand-li dyke. (直译)
    2) A long solid dyke may collapse because of an ant hole in it. (直译)
    3) Slight negligence may lead to great disaster. (意译: 小失误能酿大祸。)
    4) A little neglect may breed great mischief. (意译:小疏忽能成大害。)
    5) A small leak may sink a great ship. (英语对应谚语：小漏能沉大船。)
    6) A tall building will be burned down by a spark from a chimney’s chink. (英语对应谚语：烟囱裂缝冒出的一个火星能使一座高楼夷为平地。)

53 假球、赌球、黑哨

汉语关键词：假球、赌球、黑哨

英语关键词：match-fixing, match rigging, rigged match, rigged ballgame, football fraud, soccer fraud, ballgame betting, betting, gambling, referee cheating, referee trick, match-fixing referee, unfair referee

句子：这位足坛老将关于打击假球的呼吁得到了球迷们的支持。

误译：The appeal made by the veteran footballer for attacking the false ball won support from his fans.

正译：The appeal made by the veteran footballer for attacking match-fixing won support from his fans.

解释：

“假球”的意思是球赛造假，用违法手段预定比赛结果。“假球”指的是“不真实的比赛”，是一种违法行为，而不是“假的球”，不能字对字译为false ball。“假球”，英语可以译为match-fixing, match rigging, rigged match, rigged ballgame, football fraud, soccer fraud。例如：

1. 2009年11月，公安部发动了全国性足球打假扫赌行动。
   The Ministry of Public Security launched a nationwide crackdown on football match-fixing and gambling in November, 2009.
2. 中国最近发动了足球反假球、反腐败行动，逮捕了20多名体育官员。
   China has recently launched a crackdown on match-fixing and corruption in football with the arrests of more than 20 sports officials.
3. 中国警方在全国范围足球反腐风暴中已拘留一些涉嫌假球和赌球的人。
   Chinese police have detained a few people on suspicion of match- fixing and gambling in a nationwide crackdown on soccer corruption.
4. 在过去几个月里，一些官员、足球球员和俱乐部经理因涉嫌假球或赌球而被拘留或逮捕。
   A number of officials, football players and club managers have been arrested or detained in the past few months on suspicion of football match-rigging or gambling.
5. 随着足球领导班子高层官员在全国性打假球、反赌球行动中接受调查，中国足球又发生震荡。
   Chinese soccer has been rocked again with top officials of the sport's leading body under investigation amid the nationwide clampdown on match-rigging and gambling.

6. 在有组织的体育赛事中，当完全或部分按照预定结果进行而违犯游戏规则、甚至法律时，就出现了假球现象。
In organized sports, a rigged match occurs when it is played to a completely or partially pre-determined result, violating the rules of the game and even the law.
7. 这些足球球员被爆料曾受贿而踢了一场假球。
These footballers were exposed to have been bribed into playing a rigged ballgame.
8. 数月前，我国开始了一场根除足球假球贻害的行动。
A few months ago, a drive began in our country to eradicate the blight of football fraud.
9. 反假球行动给了我们重振中国足球发展的信心和希望。
The crackdown on soccer fraud has given us confidence and hope to revitalize the development of Chinese soccer.

"赌球"的意思是以足球、篮球等比赛结果、球员以及相关事实进行赌博的行为。英语可以译为 ballgame betting, betting, gambling。例如：

10. 像在赌场里见到的赌博、以及赌球等等，对我们大多数人来说，真的是一件机遇和命运之事。
Gambling, as seen in casinos, ballgame betting, etc., is really a matter of chance and fate for most of us.
11. 警方与体育官员取缔了一个涉嫌在欧洲职业足球比赛中操纵球赛和赌球的犯罪团伙。
Police and sport officials have dismantled a criminal ring suspected of match-fixing and betting in European professional football.
12. 湖南省警方最近追查到3个通过互联网组织足球赌球的犯罪团伙。
Police in Hunan Province have recently tracked down three criminal groups that organized betting on soccer via the Internet.
13. 地方政府已采取行动关闭组织网络足球赌球的非法赌博运营商。
The local government has taken action to close illegal gambling operators who organized the online betting in football.
14. 这个人因经营网络足球赌球而被地方法院判处3年徒刑。
The man was sentenced to three years in prison by a local court for running online gambling in soccer.

"黑哨"的第一个意思是裁判员收受贿赂或受人指使违反公平性原则的行为。英语可以译为 referee cheating, referee trick。例如：

15. 我们必须划清黑哨与球员欺诈行为之间的界限。
We must draw a distinction between the referee cheating and a player's devious act.

16. 据报导那个国家的足球联赛充满了假球、黑哨、服用兴奋剂和假摔。
It is reported that the soccer league in that country is full of match fixing, referee tricks, doping and penalty diving.

“黑哨”的第二个意思是违反公平性原则的裁判员。英语可以译为 match-fixing referee, unfair referee。例如：

17. 这名黑哨以受贿罪被监禁两年。
The match-fixing referee was imprisoned for two years on a charge of taking bribes.
18. 我们队的队长和总教练决定撤出比赛，作为对这位黑哨的抗议。
The captain and the head coach of our team decided to withdraw from the match as a protest against the unfair referee.

54 保障性住房

汉语关键词： 保障、住房、保障性住房、外壳

英语关键词： housing, indemnificatory housing, ensure, protect, guarantee, assurance, safeguard

句子： 我们必须加快保障性住房建设，以解决低收入家庭的住房困难。

误译： We must speed up the construction of protective housing so as to tackle the difficulty in housing for low-income families.

正译： We must speed up the construction of indemnificatory housing so as to tackle the difficulty in housing for low-income families.

解释：

housing 的第一个意思是 houses, flats, etc. for people to live in, 即“人的住房”。housing 的第二个意思是 a hard cover that protects part of a machine, 即“机器部件的外壳”。虽然 to protect 有“保障”的意思，但是 protective housing 的意思不是“保障性住房”，而是“防护箱”。比如，protective housing for a battery in a car 的意思是“汽车蓄电池保护器”。保障性住房指“政府为中低收入住房困难家庭所提供的限定标准、限定价格或租金的住房”。英语可以译为 indemnificatory housing。indemnificatory 的意思是 protective against damage or loss, especially in the form of a promise to pay for any that happens, 即“补偿性的”。例如：

1. 保障性住房包括廉租住房、经济适用住房和政策性租赁住房。
Indemnificatory housing consists of low-rent housing, affordable housing and policy-regulated rental housing.
2. 建设保障性住房，与低收入家庭的切身利益密切相关，是各级政府的重要任务。
The construction of indemnificatory housing, which is closely related to the immediate benefit of low-income families, is an important task for the government at various levels.

“保障”的第一个意思是“保护生命、财产和权利等，使不受侵犯和破坏”，作动词用。英语可以译为 to ensure, to protect。例如：

3. 地方政府已采取保护性措施安置地震灾民，并保障他们的人身安全。
The local government has adopted protective measures to resettle the quake-afflicted people and ensure their personal safety.
4. 儿童必须学会如何保障他们的自身安全。
Children must learn how to protect their own personal safety.
5. 我们必须依法保障农民工的人身自由。
We must ensure the rural migrant workers' personal freedom according to the law.
6. 宪法最基本的价值是限制政府权力和保障公民权利。
The basic value of the constitution is to restrict the power of the government and to protect the rights of the citizens.
7. 这项法律旨在保障全体公民的合法权益。
This law is designed to protect the legitimate rights of all citizens.
8. 保障民生是各级政府的重要责任。
To ensure people's well-being is the important responsibility for the government at all levels.

“保障”的第二个意思是“确保，使充分实现”，作动词用。英语可以译为 to guarantee。例如：

9. 请放心，还款是有保障的。
Please rest assured that repayment is guaranteed.
10. 自从他找到新工作，他的生活就有了保障。
Since he got a new job, his life has become guaranteed.
11. 我们要尽一切努力保障农产品供给，以稳定其价格。
We must make every effort to guarantee the supply of agricultural products, so as to steady their prices.

“保障”的第三个意思是“起保障作用的事物”，作名词用。英语可以译为 guarantee, assurance, safeguard。例如：

12. 加强安全管理和采取有效措施是实现安全生产的保障。
To enforce safety management and adopt effective measures are the guarantee to realize the safety in production.
13. 许多雇员收入低微，缺少必要的保障。
Many employees are lowly paid and lack necessary assurance.
14. 大多数侵权产品通常质量低劣，或者缺少必要的保障。
Most infringing products usually have inferior qualities or lack necessary guarantees.
15. 为改善民生，我们需要机构性保障。
To improve people's well-being, we need institutional guarantee.
16. 我们需要更强有力的法律保障来保护消费者。
We need stronger legal safeguards to protect the consumers.
17. 保障制度的设计应有助于缩小城乡差距。
The designing of the safeguard system should be helpful to narrowing the gap between urban and rural areas.

55 丢面子

汉语关键词： 面子、丢面子、丢脸 、保全面子
英语关键词： outside, outer part, image, respect, pride, face, lose face, save face, feelings, powder
句子： 他这件事做错了，觉得很丢面子。
误译： He felt he had lost his face because of the mistakes he made in this matter.
正译： He felt he had lost face because of the mistakes he made in this matter.
解释：

"丢面子"或"丢脸"有"丧失体面"的意思。这个汉语比喻，被英语接受，译为 to lose face，意思是 to be less respected or look stupid because of sth you have done。注意 to lose face 已成为固定词组，中间不可以加人称代词所有格。

"面子"的第一个意思是"物体的表层"。英语可以译为 outside, outer part。例如：

1. 这条被子的里子和面子都是新的。
Both the inside and the outside of the quilt are new.

2. 这件大衣的衬里是布的，面子是毛皮的。
   This overcoat has cloth on the inside and fur on the outside.
3. 这件袍子的面子很好看。
   The outside of the robe looks very nice.
4. 这双布鞋的面子穿破了。
   The outer part of the cloth shoes is worn-out.

“面子”的第二个意思是“形象”，为贬义。英语可以译为 image。例如：

5. 有些官员好大喜功，爱搞面子工程。
   Some officials like to do image projects because they crave for grandeur and success.
6. 纳税人的钱不能用来搞面子工程。
   The money collected from taxpayers can't be used for image projects.
7. 一切伤害人民感情的面子工程必须坚决制止。
   All the image projects that hurt people's feelings must be stopped resolutely.

“面子”的第三个意思是“尊重”或“自尊”，为褒义。英语可以译为 respect, pride。例如：

8. 这位影星在演艺圈里很有面子。
   This film star enjoys due respect in the entertainment circles.
9. 李教授是个要面子的人。
   Professor Li is a person with a strong sense of pride.
10. 我觉得你嘲笑他说英语的方式而伤了他的面子。
    I think you've hurt his pride by laughing at the way he speaks English.
11. 凡是有人的地方，就会有面子问题。
    Wherever there are people, there is the issue of pride.
12. 他由于死要面子而拒绝接受帮助。
    He refused to accept help out of a false sense of pride.

“面子”的第四个意思是“表面的虚荣”，为贬义，英语可以译为 face。“保全面子”，可以译为 to save face，意思是 to avoid or help avoid embarrassment。例如：

13. 使他人丢面子常常可能是不可避免的。
    Causing other people to lose face may be unavoidable at times.
14. 他们可以不失面子地接受这个建议。
    They can accept the advice without losing face.
15. 她被解雇了，但是她为保全面子，逢人便讲她辞职了。
    She was fired, but she saved face by telling everyone she'd resigned.

16. 他不惜一切代价试图挽回面子。
 He tried to save face at all costs.
17. 帮助人们挽回面子，涉及到给他们尊严无损地摆脱困境的方法。
 Helping someone save face involves giving them a way to exit the situation with their dignity intact.
18. 帮助她挽回面子并保持作为一个人的尊严非常重要。
 Helping her save face and retain her dignity as a human being was important.
19. 他这个人很爱面子。
 He is very much concerned about face-saving.
20. 在我们的交际中恰当选择礼貌策略对保持面子是非常重要的。
 The proper choice of politeness strategy in our communication is of vital significance for keeping face.

"面子"的第五个意思是"私人间的情面"。英语可以译为 feelings。例如：

21. 看在老朋友的面子上，你高抬贵手吧。
 Will you please show mercy to me, considering the feelings of an old friend of yours?
22. 我不便驳他面子，只好同意了。
 As I couldn't refuse to consider his feelings, I had to agree.
23. 他太固执，一点也不顾我们的面子。
 He was too stubborn to show any consideration for our feelings.
24. 他是个对朋友重面子的人。
 He is a person who shows great considerations for his friends' feelings.
25. 他是个不讲面子的人。
 He is a person who shows no consideration for other people's feelings.
26. 你总得给我们大家留点面子吧。
 You should have to take our feelings into consideration.
27. 最后他对我撕破面子。
 Finally he cast aside all considerations of my feelings.
28. 碍于面子，我最后只好答应她了。
 Being affected by her feelings, I could not but make a promise to her at last.

"面子"的第六个意思是"粉末"。英语可以译为 powder。例如：

29. 这个纸口袋里装的全是药面子。
 The paper bag is filled with powdered medicine.

56 孩奴

汉语关键词： 孩奴、儿童奴隶、童奴、黑奴家长

英语关键词： outside, outer part, image, respect, pride, face, lose face, save face, feelings, powder

句子： “孩奴”指那些不得不在子女身上花费很大部分收入的年轻家长。

误译： “Child slaves” refer to the young parents who have to spend a large part of their income on their children.

正译： “Child-enslaved parents” refer to the young parents who have to spend a large part of their income on their children.

解释：

child slave 的意思是child who serves as a slave，即“儿童奴隶”或“童奴”。例如：

1. 由于地震带来的严重后果，海地儿童奴隶的数量将会大大增长。
   As a bad consequence of the earthquake, there will be an increasing number of child slaves in Haiti.
2. 报纸报道说一个巴基斯坦男孩在4岁时以相当于12美元的价钱被卖给一家地毯厂当儿童奴隶。
   The newspaper reported that a Pakistani boy was sold to a carpet industry as a child slave at the age of 4 for the equivalent of 12 USD.
3. 据报道警方从一个非法工厂救出了十几个童奴劳工。
   Police was reported to have rescued a dozen of child slave workers from an illegal factory.
4. 这位新闻记者描述了西非贩卖儿童奴隶的情况。
   The news reporter depicted child slave trade in West Africa.
5. 这篇文章揭露了一个东南亚国家的农场的童奴劳工状况。
   The article exposed the child slave labour on a farm in an Asian country.

“孩奴”是我国近来出现的新词，指的是家长，不是孩子，在英语中没有现成的对应词，国内有人译为children’s slaves或slaves to their children。但是这些译法没有说出家长“被孩奴”的特点。不妨译为child-enslaved parent。例如：

6. 这篇文章的标题是《如何不当孩奴？》
   The article is entitled How Not To Be Your Children’s Slave?
7. 这位作家谈论了家长如何培养有责任心的孩子，和避免当“孩奴”

的感觉。

The writer talked about how a parent can bring up responsible children and avoid feeling like a slave to them.

8. “孩奴”是一生都在为子女打拼，为子女忙碌，失去了体现自我生存价值的父母。

The child-enslaved parents are those who struggle and keep themselves busy for their children all their lives, thus being deprived of the embodiment of their own value of existence.

9. 生儿育女费用高，望子成龙压力大，“孩奴”现象困扰着世界许多国家。

As people have too high costs of children-rearing and too heavy pressures caused by their high expectations for their children, the phenomenon that parents are being enslaved to their children is perplexing many countries in the world.

10. 类似“房奴”和“孩奴”之类的现象，主要来自社会压力，很大程度上消解了人们的幸福感和自我实现的满足感。

Such phenomena as being mortgage slaves and child-enslaved parents are mainly originated from social pressures, which have, to a great extent, dissolved people's sense of happiness and their sense of satisfaction with self-realization.

11. “房奴”加上“孩奴”，意味着“终身为奴”。

Being a mortgage slave and a parent enslaved to your child implies that you will get enslaved all your life.

12. 除了生育抚养，“孩奴”们把大部分钱花费在为孩子的教育上。

Besides raising children, the child-enslaved parents have most of their money spent on education for their children.

13. 一些80后新生代年轻人恐惧未来，拼命挣钱准备当“孩奴”。

As some young people of the post-80's generation fear the future, they are working hard to make money, thus getting prepared to become child-enslaved parents.

14. “孩奴”的说法是城镇一些年轻夫妇的一种夸张的自嘲。

Such a saying as “a child-enslaved parent” is an exaggerated self ridicule by some young couples in the cities or towns.

从国外的博客上看到有人用 enslaved parent 表示“孩奴”。这需要有清楚的上下文。enslaved parent 原指美国“黑奴家长”，与 free parent（自由民家长）相对应。使用 enslaved parent 时要谨慎。例如：

15. 你们从来都不用打扫卫生，因为你们有女佣人或孩奴。

You never have to clean because you have a maid or an enslaved parent.

16. 假如我是一个黑奴家长，我会尽我所能，避免生养孩子。
If I were an enslaved parent, I would do everything in my power to avoid having children.

57 植入广告

汉语关键词： 插播广告、植入广告、植入式营销

英语关键词： commercial inserts, insert commercials, spot announcement, product placement, product placement marketing, embedded marketing, embed a product

句子： 春晚植入广告过多引发质疑。

误译： Too many commercial inserts at the CCTV New Year's Gala have been called in question.

正译： Too much product placement at the CCTV New Year's Gala has been called in question.

解释：

commercial inserts 的意思是"插播广告"，指打断正常电视节目的播放而插入强迫观众看的广告，与"植入广告"是两码事。作为名词，"插播广告"也可以译为 spot announcement。例如：

1. 电视台利用插播广告打断节目。
Television stations interrupt programmes with commercial inserts.
2. 这个电视频道最近播放了一些不平常的插播广告。
This television channel has recently broadcast several unusual commercial inserts.
3. 插播广告是在主要广播节目或电视节目之间呈现的。
A commercial spot announcement is presented between major radio or television programmes.
4. 任何作为一种营销手段的插播广告的成功与否，是通过听众对该广告所宣传产品的反应情况来衡量的。
The success of any spot announcement as a selling device is measured by the listener's response to the product advertised.

作为动词，"插播广告"可以译为 to insert commercials。例如：

5. 根据规定，电视台不得任意插播广告。

According to the regulations, TV stations cannot insert commercials freely.

6. 有些观众投诉说电视台在娱乐节目播放过程中不顾时间规定常常插播广告。

Some viewers complained that the TV station often inserted commercials during the entertainment programming regardless of the timing.

“植入广告”指把产品及其服务具有代表性的视听品牌符号融入影视或舞台产品中，以求给观众留下印象，是一种营销手段。英语可以译为product placement。例如：

7. 植入广告是一种将产品融入电视节目、电影等传媒产品之中以进行宣传的广告形式。

Product placement is a form of advertisement which incorporates a product into such a media product as a television programme or a film so as to publicize it.

8. 植入广告在电视、电影、视频游戏和书籍中让人不易察觉地宣传产品。

Product placement subtly advertises products in television, movies, video games and books.

9. 植入广告在故事片、电视节目或其他不易明显觉察是广告形式的传媒中展示品牌产品。

Product placement shows a brand name product in a feature film, television programme, or other medium not typically perceived to be an advertising.

10. 植入广告是一种广告形式，即在通常没有广告的语境，像电影、电视节目的台词或新闻节目中，植入品牌产品或服务。

Product placement is a form of advertisement, where branded goods or services are placed in a context usually devoid of ads, such as movies, the story line of television shows, or news programmes.

“植入广告”又称“植入式营销”，英语可以译为product placement marketing或embedded marketing。例如：

11. 近年来，植入式营销在新闻媒体上一直非常流行。

Product placement marketing has been very popular among the news media in recent years.

12. 许多公司没有适当规划就匆忙投入植入式营销运动，而这正是为什么大多数努力得不偿失的原因。

Many companies have rushed into product placement marketing campaigns without proper planning, and that's why most efforts have failed to pay for themselves.

13. 如果你把你的品牌和网站植入我们的世界范围的视频产品，你就会看到植入式营销的效果。
If you embed your brand and website into our worldwide video products, you will see the impact of embedded marketing.
14. 这位专家认为在新闻频道和儿童及青少年频道应该禁止植入式营销。
The expert holds that embedded marketing should be prohibited in news channels and channels for children and young adults.

作为动词，“植入广告”可以译为 to embed a product。例如：

15. 制造商成功地在一个电视节目的情节中植入广告，使其容易被人记住。
The manufacturer succeeded in embedding the product in the plot of a TV show, making it memorable.

58 假唱

汉语关键词： 假唱、胡唱、乱唱、对口型、假唱歌手、真唱、唱歌音准
英语关键词： false singing, lip-synch, lip-sync, lip synchronization, lip-synch singer, lip-sync singer, true singing, sing live, live singing
句子： 这个歌星被指责在歌舞晚会上假唱。
误译： The star singer was accused of false singing at the song-and-dance show.
正译： The star singer was accused of lip-synching at the song-and-dance show.
解释：

false singing 的意思是 bad singing，即“胡唱”、“乱唱”、“唱歌音不准”、“唱得很糟糕”与 true singing（唱歌音准）是相对的。“假唱”不能字对字地译为 false singing。例如：

1. 说到“胡唱”，我在猜你的意思是“唱得很糟糕”。
By false singing, I'm guessing you mean BAD singing.
2. 这个考生分辨不出说到的音哪个唱得准，哪个唱得不准。
The examinee was unable to discriminate between true and false singing of the notes in question.
3. 因为这个人胡唱，我的耳朵疼死了。
My ears are hurting because of this false singing man.

4. 他观察到歌手们已很长时间沉溺于雕虫小技和胡唱乱唱的方法来赢得掌声。
He observes that singers have long indulged in trinkets and a false singing method to win applause.

"假唱"的意思是"歌唱或戏曲演员以放录音充当现场演唱"。英语动词可以译为 to lip-synch, to lip-sync，其意思是 to move your mouth, without speaking or singing, so that its movement match the sound on a recorded speech or song，或 to move the lips in synchronization with a recorded speech or song，即"对口型"。例如：

5. 这位业余歌手不愿意以虚情假意去假唱糊弄听众。
The amateur singer is reluctant to cheat the audience by lip-synching with a false display of affectation.
6. 这个职业歌手在由地方电视台播放的音乐会上被抓住假唱。
The professional singer was caught lip-syncing during a concert broadcast by the local TV station.
7. 这个歌星在舞台上假唱欺骗了她的歌迷。
The star singer cheated her fans by lip-synching on stage.
8. 这名歌手因在演出中假唱而向公众示道歉。
The singer apologized to the public for having lip-synced prerecorded songs in the show.

lip synchronization, lip synch 或 lip sync 的意思是 combination of audio and video recording in such a way that the sound is perfectly synchronized with the action that produced it，即"对口型"，是一种后期配音的技术手段。例如：

9. 对口型是使插入声音力求与原演员口型相配的过程。
Lip synchronization is a process where the insertion of audio attempts to match the lip movements of the original actors.

"假唱歌手"，英语可以译为 lip-synch singer 或 lip-sync singer。例如：

10. 假唱歌手最怕被要求做即兴表演。
A lip-synch singer is mostly afraid of being asked to make an improvised performance.
11. 这个我所遇到过的最烂的假唱歌手依然在表演。
The worst lip-synch singer that I have ever met is still performing!
12. 我们在严肃音乐节目里找不到任何假唱歌手。好像他们认为作为歌手，真唱是必须的。
We can't find any lip-sync singer in serious music programmes. It seems

that they think playing live music is certain as a singer.

同样地,"真唱"不能字对字地译为 true singing,因为它的意思是"唱歌音准"。"真唱"是在现场用自己的声音演唱,动词可以译为 to sing live,名词可以译为 live singing。例如:

13. 如果你儿子具有唱歌音准的天赋,你就应该鼓励他通过上声乐课提高他的演唱能力。
    If your son had a true singing talent, you should encourage him to enhance his singing abilities through voice lessons.
14. 这个男孩要在舞台上真唱。
    The boy wanted to sing live on stage.
15. 那些能很好地真唱的歌手应受到我们的尊敬。
    Those singers who can sing live well deserve our respect.
16. 观众们愿意听真唱,胜过听放录音的假唱。
    The audience prefers live singing to recorded singing.
17. 我认为这是我见到的最好的真唱表演。
    I think this is the best live singing performance that I have ever seen.
18. 全家人举行了真唱表演来庆祝老爷爷的80大寿。
    The whole family celebrated the 80th anniversary of the old grandfather's birthday by conducting a live singing performance.

59 召回

汉语关键词: 召回、召集、召开、召见、召唤

英语关键词: recall, call back, call in, call together, assemble, hold, convene, convoke, call in one' s subordinates officially, summon sb to the interview, summon an envoy of a foreign country, call

句子: 最近丰田召回了800多万辆问题汽车。

误译: Toyota has recently returned more than 8 million problematic cars.

正译: Toyota has recently recalled more than 8 million problematic cars.

解释:

to return 的意思是 to give back,在这里指制造商将汽车归还消费者,是错误翻译。to recall 的意思是 to take back,指制造商从消费者那里收回汽车,这才是正确翻译。

“召回”的第一个意思是“上级调回或叫回派出的人员”。英语可以译为 to recall，即 to order sb to return。例如：

1. 这名年轻官员被上级召回北京。
   The young official was recalled to Beijing by his superior.
2. 这个亚洲国家出于安全考虑召回了它的外交代表。
   The Asian country recalled its diplomatic envoy due to security concerns.
3. 两国分别召回各自的大使。
   The two countries respectively recalled their ambassadors home.
4. 2009年，伊朗宣布临时召回驻英国大使。
   In 2009, Iran declared that it would temporarily recall its ambassador to Britain.
5. 这些青年人被召回服现役。
   These young people were recalled to active duties.
6. 这些休假的军官被召回执行军事任务。
   These officers on leave were recalled to military duty.

“召回”的第二个意思是“生产商收回有问题的产品加以改正”。英语可以译为 to recall, to call back, to call in，即 to ask sth to be returned, often because there is sth wrong with it。例如：

7. 该汽车制造商将召回有缺陷的产品，加以修理、替换或退款。
   The auto manufacturer will recall defective products for repairs, replacement or refund.
8. 该公司已召回所有出故障的吹风机。
   The company has called back all the faulty hairdryers.
9. 该玩具公司已决定在全世界范围内召回那些有缺陷的产品。
   The toy company has decided to call in the defective products all over the world.
10. 有严重故障的汽车已被制造商召回。
    Cars with serious faults have been called in by the manufacturers.

“召集”的意思是“通知人们聚集起来”。英语可以译为 to call together, to assemble。例如：

11. 队长召集全体队员开会。
    The leader called all the team members together for a meeting.
12. 班校长召集全体教师开会。
    The headmaster assembled all the teachers for a meeting.

“召开”是的意思是“召集人们开会”。英语可以译为 to call, to hold, to convene, to convoke。例如：

13. 秘书长应理事国请求召开安理会会议。
The General Secretary called a meeting of the Security Council at the request of its members.
14. 下周我们将召开研讨会讨论技术在教育中提供的机会。
We shall hold a symposium next week to discuss the opportunities technology presents in education.
15. 首相计划在星期一召开内阁紧急会议解决国家巨额预算赤字问题。
The Prime Minister planned to convene an emergency meeting of his cabinet on Monday to address the state's huge budget deficit.
16. 大学校长决定召开会议讨论关于科学教育的问题。
The president of the university decided to convoke a meeting to discuss the issues related to science education.

"召见"的第一个意思是"上级叫下级来见面"。英语可以译为 to call in one's subordinates officially, to summon sb to the interview。例如：

17. 部长有事将召见下属。
The Minister will officially call in his subordinates on business.
18. 当他值班时，他受到导师的召见。
He was summoned to the interview by his supervisor while he was on duty.

"召见"的第二个意思是"外交部通知外国驻本国使节前来商谈有关事宜"。英语可以译为 to summon an envoy of a foreign country。例如：

19. 我外交部召见美国大使。
The U.S. Ambassador was summoned to China's Foreign Ministry.

"召唤"的意思是"呼唤"。英语动词可以译为 to call；名词可以译为 call。例如：

20. 新的生活在召唤着我们。
We are called to new life.
21. 这是时代的召唤。
This is the call of the times.

60 尊严

汉语关键词：尊严

英语关键词：dignity, dignified

句子：我们的目标是让人民生活得更加幸福，更有尊严。

误译：We are aimed at letting people to live more happily and with more dignity.

正译：We are aimed at letting people live more happily and with more dignity.

解释：

英语表示“让某人做某事”，要用 to let sb do sth 结构。to let 后跟“名词/代词 + 不定式”组成的复合宾语，其中不定式 do sth 前面要省去 to。其实这样的错误很容易避免。连初学者都知道应该说 Let's go，而不会说 Let's to go。

“尊严”的第一个意思是“可尊敬的或不容侵犯的身份、地位或人格”。英语可以译为 dignity。例如：

1. 中国积贫积弱，受尽屈辱，没有外交尊严的时代一去不复返了。
   The days are gone forever when China was poor, weak, humiliated and with no diplomatic dignity.
2. 对人来说，最重要的东西是尊严。
   To man, the most important thing is dignity.
3. 世界上每个人都想享有尊严，而且每个人都值得享有尊严。
   Everybody in the world wants dignity, and they deserve it.
4. 这位社会学家认为像克隆一类的生殖技术容易触犯人的尊严。
   The sociologist holds that reproductive technologies such as cloning are prone to violate human dignity.
5. 许多人批评这个电视商业广告，因为它触犯了人的尊严。
   Many people criticized this TV commercial advertisement for its violation of human dignity.
6. 任何酷刑或其他残酷的、非人道的或侮辱人格的处理或惩罚都是对人的尊严的一种冒犯。
   Any act of torture or other cruel inhuman or degrading treatment or punishment is an offence to human dignity.
7. 沉默现在是我唯一能保持我的尊严完整无损的方法。
   Silence is now the only way for me to keep my dignity intact.
8. 他意识到他作为一名高官的责任，总是保持人格的尊严。
   He is aware of his duties as a high official and always maintaining the

dignity of his personality.

9. 作为人，我们有权维护我们的尊严。
   As human beings, we are entitled to preserve our dignity.
10. 应该允许垂危病人死得有尊严。
    The terminally ill should be allowed to die with dignity.
11. 当你无家无业时，很难保持自己的尊严。
    It is difficult to preserve your dignity when you have no job and no home.
12. 拥有知识的人拥有尊严与荣耀。
    He who has knowledge has dignity and glory.
13. 他的演说充满了骄傲和尊严。
    His speech is full of pride and dignity.
14. 我们必须坚决捍卫国家独立、主权和尊严。
    We must resolutely safeguard our national independence, sovereignty and dignity.
15. 像人一样，动物也有感情、思想和尊严。
    Animals have feelings, thoughts and dignity like men.

“尊严”的第二个意思是“庄重肃穆，尊贵威严”，为形容词。英语可以译为 dignified。例如：

16. 这本书记录了一位简朴而尊严的老学者的生平和工作。
    The book records the life and work of a simple yet dignified old scholar.
17. 她觉得父亲很高大，样子很尊严。
    She feels that her father is very tall and dignified in his appearance.
18. 这位妇女样子很尊严，而且总是仰着头。
    The woman was very dignified in appearance and she always kept her head up.
19. 在这位作家的著作中，社会中最卑贱的人成为尊严的人。
    The most lowly people of society became dignified beings in the writer's works.
20. 这座佛像十分尊严。
    The statue of Buddha looks very dignified.
21. 他登上尊严的讲台，开始讲演。
    He rose to the dignified platform and began to make a speech.
22. 我感到非常荣幸给我提供这样一个尊严的讲台与你们分享我的经历。
    I feel privileged to be offered such a dignified platform to share my experiences with you.
23. 他在整个审讯过程中，保持着尊严的沉默。
    Throughout his trial, he maintained a dignified silence.
24. 他尊严地做出回应，同意她对他说的话。
    He reacted in a dignified manner, accepting what she told him.

61

拆弹部队

汉语关键词： 拆弹、拆除炸弹、拆除炸弹引信、引爆炸弹、拆弹专家、拆弹官员、拆弹部队、拆弹小组

英语关键词： hurt locker, disassemble a bomb, disarm a bomb, disable a bomb, dismantle a bomb, dispose a bomb, defuse a bomb, diffuse a bomb, detonate a bomb, bomb-disposal expert, bomb technician, bomb-disposal officer, defusing officer, bomb-disposal force, bomb disposal-team, bomb-disposal squad, bomb squad

句子： 这部获奥斯卡奖影片讲述了一个美国拆弹小组在伊拉克的故事。

误译： The Oscar-winning film tells about an American hurt locker in Iraq.

正译： The Oscar-winning film tells about an American bomb-disposal squad in Iraq.

解释：

获奥斯卡奖电影 The Hurt Locker 讲述了一个美国拆弹小组在伊拉克的故事，中文片名干脆将它叫做《拆弹部队》。但是，hurt locker 自身的意思与拆弹部队毫无关系。hurt locker 是个俚语，有 mental or physical pain 的意思，是一种精神或身体痛苦的状态。有人将它解释为 a period of immense, inescapable physical or emotional pain，是身心极其痛苦的一段时间。还有人将它解释为 the place of ultimate pain，是身心极其痛苦的境地。美国大兵俚语（G.I. slang）的意思是 being injured in an explosion，即"被炸伤"，更有遭受痛苦境遇的内涵。

"拆除炸弹"或"拆弹"，英语可以译为 to disassemble a bomb, to disarm a bomb, to disable a bomb, to dismantle a bomb, to dispose a bomb。例如：

1. 一个能拆除炸弹的机器人可以使人不必进入危险地带。
   A robot that can disassemble a bomb prevents a human from getting into harm's way.
2. 作为一名拆弹专家，你必须在三分钟以内拆除炸弹阻止爆炸，以拯救无辜的平民。
   As a bomb-disposal expert, you must disarm the bomb within three minutes to stop the explosion so as to save innocent civilians.
3. 这些拆弹专家靠技术和运气来拆除炸弹。
   These bomb-disposal experts rely on both skill and luck to disarm a bomb.
4. 我应该剪断哪种颜色的电线才能拆除炸弹呢？
   What colour wire should I cut to disable a bomb?

5. 这种机器基于军方已用来拆弹的机器人。
The machine is based on a robot already used by the military to disable bombs.
6. 昨天在市中心一条繁忙道路发现两件可疑物品，随后被拆弹专家拆除。
Two suspicious objects were found on a busy road downtown yesterday and were later dismantled by bomb-disposal experts.
7. 这位拆弹专家在试图拆除信件炸弹时视死如归。
The bomb-disposal expert faces death trying to dismantle a letter bomb.
8. 当安全小组正在赶往现场拆除炸弹时，发生了爆炸。
The explosion occurred when the security team was on its way to the scene to dispose a bomb.

to defuse a bomb 的意思是 to remove the fuse from a bomb so that it cannot explode，即“拆除炸弹引信”。例如：

9. 这个警察成功地拆除了恐怖分子在一个繁忙街道的角落里安置的炸弹的引信。
The policeman succeeded in defusing a bomb planted by the terrorists in the corner of a busy street.

现在有人用与 to defuse 发音相近的 to diffuse 取而代之，将“拆除炸弹引信”说成是 to diffuse a bomb。本来 to diffuse 的意思是 to spread sth widely in all directions，即“传播”或“散布”，与“拆除”毫无关系。但是互联网上屡见 to diffuse a bomb 的说法，看来这个说法也被接受。例如：

10. 这个拆弹小组派出他们最称职的组员去儿童医院拆除炸弹。
The bomb squad sent their best-qualified man to diffuse a bomb in the Children's Hospital.

“引爆炸弹”，英语可以译为 to detonate a bomb。例如：

11. 警方说今天他们在一个公共汽车站附近发现了一枚汽车炸弹，将其引爆。
The police said that they had discovered and detonated a car bomb near a bus station today.

“拆弹专家”和“拆弹官员”，英语可以译为 bomb-disposal expert, bomb technician, bomb-disposal officer, defusing officer。例如：

12. 几位拆弹专家被派去拆除没有爆炸的装置的引信。
A few bomb-disposal experts were sent to defuse the device which had

failed to explode.

13. 这家银行发生爆炸，造成一名拆弹专家身亡。
A bomb explosion in the bank killed a bomb technician.
14. 一名英国拆弹专家在阿富汗南部试图拆除一枚定时炸弹时被炸死。
A British bomb-disposal expert was killed while trying to defuse a time bomb in southern Afghanistan.
15. 一名专业拆弹官员将可疑物品放置在火车站的防爆罐内。
A professional defusing officer placed the suspected objects in the bomb bin in the railway station.

“拆弹部队”和“拆弹小组”，英语可以译为 bomb-disposal force, bomb disposal-team, bomb-disposal squad, bomb squad。例如：

16. 市政府已成立了一支拆弹部队来应对炸弹威胁。
The municipal government has established a bomb-disposal force to deal with bomb threat.
17. 一个拆弹小组奉召到机场清除机上可疑物品。
A bomb-disposal team was called to the airport to remove the suspicious objects from the plane.
18. 这个拆弹小组的两名成员试图拆除在一座大型购物中心发现的未爆的炸弹。
Two members of the bomb-disposal squad tried to defuse an undetonated bomb found in a shopping mall.
19. 这个拆弹小组调查了可疑物品，但结果却是虚惊一场。
A bomb squad investigated the suspicious objects, but it turned out to be a false alarm.

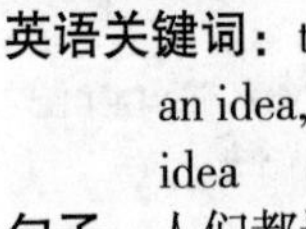

62 出点子

汉语关键词： 想点子、出点子、想主意、出主意、出谋划策、献计献策、支招儿

英语关键词： think over an idea, think of an idea, find an idea, produce an idea, create an idea, generate an idea, give an idea, give out an idea, offer an idea, provide an idea

句子： 人们都说他会出点子。

误译： Everybody says he is good at thinking over ideas.

正译：Everybody says he is good at generating ideas.

解释：

to think over an idea 的意思是 to consider an idea carefully, especially before reaching a decision，即“在做出决定之前仔细考虑一个已提出的点子”，与“出点子”无关。例如：

1. 他仔细考虑了这个点子，看它是否行得通。
   He thought over the idea to see whether it would work.
2. 我们仔细考虑了一个外国人向我们提出的点子。
   We thought over the idea proposed to us by a foreigner.

“出点子”有“想出或生成主意”和“给出或提供主意”等两层意思。前者英语可以译为 to think of an idea, to find an idea, to produce an idea, to create an idea, to generate an idea。后者英语可以译为 to give an idea, to give out an idea, to offer an idea, to provide an idea。“出点子”有许多意思相近的说法，像“出主意”、“想点子”、“想主意”、“出谋划策”、“献计献策”和“支招儿”等。例如：

3. 我要我的朋友们帮助我为新年晚会出点子。
   I asked my friends to help me to think of ideas for the New Year’s party.
4. 我想出一个点子来改进我们的产品。
   I thought of an idea to improve our product.
5. 他绞尽脑汁想出一个跟我想出的主意类似的点子。
   He racked his brains to find an idea similar to the one I was thinking of.
6. 我最终想出一个从没在我脑海里闪过的点子，而它是行得通的。
   I finally found an idea that hadn’t crossed my mind, and it worked.
7. 当我们不得不凭空出点子的时候，不幸的是我们并不总是那样成功。
   Unfortunately we are not always so successful when we have to produce an idea out of nothing.
8. 令人高兴的是，这个小组想出了全体成员都同意的主意。
   Happily, the group produced an idea that all its members agreed on.
9. 他想出了一个与我的建议不同的点子。
   He created an idea that was different from my suggestion.
10. 我想出了一个他们都强烈支持的点子。
    I created an idea that they all strongly supported.
11. 我为解决这个问题出了一个点子。
    I generated an idea for the solution of the problem.
12. 他为小公司出点子将挑战变为机遇。
    He generated ideas for small companies to turn challenges into opportunities.
13. 企业成长取决于你出新点子的能力。

Business growth depends on your ability to generate new ideas.

14. 他就如何经营企业给我出谋划策。
    He gave me an idea about how to run a business.
15. 这位健康专家就如何保持健康给观众出点子。
    The health expert gave ideas to the audience about how to keep fit.
16. 他正设法出点子使人们更容易了解形势。
    He was trying to give out an idea to make it easier for people to understand the situation.
17. 这位工程师出了将对整个系统有价值的点子。
    The engineer gave out ideas that would be valuable to the entire system.
18. 我献计献策供公众考虑。
    I'd like to offer an idea for public consideration.
19. 居民们就如何使他们的小区保持清洁和安全献计献策。
    The inhabitants offered ideas on how to keep their residential area clean and safe.
20. 这位老人就如何经营饭馆给他的儿子支招儿。
    The old man provided an idea for his son on how to run a restaurant.
21. 这位股评家定期给希望在股票市场的人们支招儿。
    The stock analyst regularly provides ideas for the people who wish to make investment in the stock market.

63 馊点子

汉语关键词： 点子、馊点子、馊、主意、踩点子、鼓点子、点子公司

英语关键词： go sour, spoil, idea, lousy idea, rotten idea, drop, speck, beat, drumbeat, keep time in dancing, a little, a bit, a small amount of, point, right spot, heart of the matter, idea-generation company, consulting company, consultancy company

句子： 你的馊点子太过分了。

误译： Your sour idea has gone too far.

正译： 1) Your lousy idea has gone too far.
2) Your rotten idea has gone too far.

解释：

"馊"的原义指"饭菜等变质而发出酸臭味"。英语可以译为 to go sour, to spoil。例如：

1. 这牛奶在保质期内就馊了。
   The milk has gone sour within the guarantee period.
2. 我忘记把剩饭放到冰箱里；现在都馊了。
   I forgot to put the left-over food in the refrigerator; now it's all spoiled.

“馊点子”，就是“不高明的主意”。lousy 和 rotten 都有 very bad 的意思。“馊点子”，英语可以译为 lousy idea, rotten idea。但是，sour 有 disagreeable, unpleasant, unfriendly 等含义。sour idea 的意思是“人们不同意、不喜欢或不欢迎的想法”，不是“馊点子”。例如：

3. 他认为立即提高税收将是个馊点子。
   He thought that tax rises right away would be a lousy idea.
4. 我个人认为那是个馊点子。
   I personally think it's a rotten idea.
5. 我决不会考虑你的不受欢迎的想法。
   I won't take your sour idea into consideration.

“点子”的第一个意思是“液体的小滴”。英语可以译为 drop。例如：

6. 雨点子越来越大，落得越来越快。
   Raindrops got bigger and bigger and fell faster and faster.
7. 雨点子不停地打在湖面上。
   Raindrops kept hitting the surface of the lake.
8. 雨点子不断地落在我头上。
   Raindrops kept falling on my head.
9. 雨点子打在树叶上，发出沙沙的声音。
   Raindrops hit the leaves with rustling sounds.
10. 雨点子在窗上留下了斑点。
    The raindrops left spots on the windows.
11. 我能听到雨点打在屋顶上，咚咚作响。
    I can hear the raindrops drumming on the roof.

“点子”的第二个意思是“点状的痕迹”。英语可以译为 speck。例如：

12. 他的衣服上有几个油点子。
    There are some specks of grease on his clothes.
13. 飞奔的汽车溅了我一身泥点子。
    The running car splashed specks of mud over me.
14. 她发现她的新鞋上有个泥点子。
    She found there was a speck of mud on her new shoe.
15. 他的衬衣上有几个泥点子。
    He got a few specks of dirt on his shirt.

16. 如果你的搅拌盆里哪怕有一个油点子或水点子，蛋清就会瘪了。
The egg whites will deflate if there is even a speck of grease or moisture in your mixing bowl.

“点子”的第三个意思是“打击乐的节拍”。英语可以译为 beat of a percussion instrument。“鼓点子”，英语可以译为 drumbeat。例如：

17. 村民们随着鼓点子翩翩起舞，来表达他们的感情。
The villagers danced to the drumbeat to express their feelings.
18. 每当我听到这个特别的曲调，我就禁不住随着鼓点子跳起舞来。
Each time I hear this particular tune, I can't help but dance to the drumbeat.

“踩点子”，英语可以译为 to keep time in dancing 。例如：

19. 他对我们讲了跳街舞踩点子的要领。
He told us the basic requirements for keeping time in dancing hip-hop.

“点子”的第四个意思是“少量”。英语可以译为 a little, a bit, a tiny amount of。例如：

20. 他在中药店抓了点子药吃，病就好了。
He got well after he took a little medicine he had got from a traditional Chinese drug store.

“点子”的第五个意思是“关键”、“要害”或“要点”。英语可以译为 point, right spot, heart of the matter。例如：

21. 他一下子就说到了点子上。
1) He said to the point at once.
2) He spoke to the point at once.
22. 他抓工作抓到点子上了。
In his work, he put his finger on the right spot.
23. 他的话说到点子上了。
His remark went to the heart of the matter.

“点子”的第六个意思是“主意”或“办法”。英语可以译为 idea。例如：

24. 他的点子真多。
He is full of ideas.
25. 他净是鬼点子。
He is full of tricky ideas.
26. 你听说过她的新点子吗?
Did you hear about her new idea?

27. 这是他的第一个馊点子。
    That is his first rotten idea.
28. 通过电子邮件传送大量文件可真是个坏点子。
    It is really a bad idea to send huge files through Email.
29. 忧虑不会带来什么好点子。
    Worry never comes up with good ideas.
30. 我想同我的朋友们制作一部视频，但是我出不了什么点子。
    I want to make a video with my friends, but I can't come up with any ideas.
31. 他用不同想法思考，想出新的点子。
    He thought different thoughts and came up with new ideas.
32. 当我们努力想点子的时候，讨论可能很有帮助。
    Discussion can be quite helpful when we try to come up with an idea.

“点子公司”是出谋划策或从事管理咨询的公司。英语可以译为 idea-generation company, consulting company, consultancy company。例如：

33. 这家点子公司为各种生活和商务领域提供创造性解决方案。
    This idea-generation company delivers creative solutions for every area of life and business.
34. 国内外的点子公司正在争夺中国市场份额。
    Both domestic and foreign consulting companies are battling for market shares in China.
35. 这家点子公司成立于2006年，它是由一队来自酒店业和其他商业部门的高层管理人员组建。
    This consultancy company was established in 2006 and it is formed by a team of executives coming from hospitality industry and other commercial sectors.

64 做文章

汉语关键词： 文章、做文章、写文章

英语关键词： article, essay, writings, hidden meaning, implied meaning, insinuation, idea, write an article, write an essay, make a fuss over, make an issue of, do something great

句子： 为什么有人总拿中国做文章？

误译： Why are some people always writing articles about China?
正译： Why are some people always making a fuss over China?
解释：

在这句话里，"做文章"不是指"写文章"的具体动作，而是比喻抓住一件事借题发挥，以达到某种目的。

"做文章"的第一个意思是"写文章"。英语可以译为 to write an article, to write an essay。例如：

1. 你可以在你的自由时间呆在家里做文章。
You can stay at home and write articles in you own free time.
2. 如果你遵循做文章的格式，你在写作中肯定会有改进。
If you follow the format of writing an essay, you will make a definite improvement in your writing.
3. 你应当做的事是找到做文章的要求和格式。
What you should do is to find out the requirements and the format of writing an essay.

"做文章"的第二个意思是比喻"抓住一件事发议论或在上面打主意"。英语可以译为 to make a fuss over, to make an issue of。例如：

4. 她总是就一点儿小事大做文章。
She was always making a fuss about a trifling matter.
5. 在这样一件区区小事上做文章，毫无道理。
There is no sense making such a fuss about such an unimportant matter.
6. 他想抓住这件事做文章。
He tried to seize upon the matter and make an issue of it.
7. 在这样鸡毛蒜皮的事情上做文章似乎太愚蠢了。
It seemed silly to make an issue of such a trifle.
8. 当然我会帮助你，没有必要就这件事做文章。
Of course I'll help you, and there's no need to make an issue of it.
9. 我被他的话语弄得烦恼，但是没有就这件事做文章。
I was upset by his remarks, but didn't make an issue of it.
10. 既然那只是一个小小的分歧，咱们就别在这件事上做文章了。
Since it's only a small disagreement, let's not make an issue of it.
11. 我死也不明白他们怎么竟然厚脸皮想在这件事上做文章。
I can't for the life of me understand how they have the gall to try to make an issue of it!

"做文章"的第三个意思是比喻抓住某个机会、利用某个条件有所作为。英语可以译为 to do something great。例如：

12. 县政府正充分利用本地资源做文章。
The county government is making full use of the local resources to do something great.

“文章”的第一个意思是“篇幅不很长的单篇作品”。英语可以译为 article, essay。例如：

13. 他访问了北京以后，写了一篇对这座城市印象的文章。
After he visited Beijing, he wrote an article about his impression of the city.
14. 他从文章中删去打印错误的字母。
He erased the misprinted letter from his article.
15. 这个大学生做了一篇命题文章。
The student wrote an article on the given topic.
16. 这个集子共有12篇文章。
There are 12 essays in this collection.

“文章”的第二意思是泛指著作。英语可以译为 writings。例如：

17. 这个学物理的学生对黑格尔的文章感兴趣。
The student of physics is interested in the writings of Hegel.
18. 她的文章充满了激情、灵感和喜悦。
Her writings are filled with passion, inspiration, and joy.

“文章”的第三意思是“曲折隐晦的含义或情节”。英语可以译为 hidden meaning, implied meaning, insinuation。例如：

19. 他发现她的话里面有文章。
He found there was some hidden meaning in her remarks.
20. 他的建议中大有文章，可是我弄不明白。
There is some implied meaning in his suggestion, but I can’t figure it out.
21. 我知道这里有文章。
I know there is an insinuation here.

“文章”的第四意思是“主意或点子”。英语可以译为 idea。例如：

22. 他肚子里文章多。
He has a lot of ideas in his mind.

65

网络红人

汉语关键词： 红人、网络红人、网络明星、网络名人、走红、红得发紫、红极一时

英语关键词： favourite, highly favoured person, blue-eyed boy, fair-haired boy, white-haired boy, Internet star, online star, star on line, Internet celebrity, web celebrity, blue-eyed boy on the Internet, have good luck, be in luck, become popular, achieve popularity, be much in favour, be much in demand, be extremely popular, enjoy great popularity for a time, be all the rage for a time

句子： 犀利哥从来没有想过当“时尚偶像”或网络红人。

误译： Brother Sharp never wanted to be a “fashion icon” or a blue-eyed person on the Internet.

正译： Brother Sharp never wanted to be a “fashion icon” or a blue-eyed boy on the Internet.

解释： blue-eyed person 是“蓝眼睛的人”。blue-eyed boy 的意思是favourite, 或 person who is liked better by sb and receives better treatment than others，即“受宠爱的人”或“红人”。

“网络红人”，又称“网络明星”或“网络名人”，是“走红于网络的平民”。英语可以译为 Internet star, online star, star on line, Internet celebrity, web celebrity, blue-eyed boy on the Internet。例如：

1. 这篇文章讲述了一个网络红人的兴起。
   The article talked about the rise of an Internet star.
2. 随着网络的迅速广泛传播，在公众中出现了越来越多的网络红人。
   With the rapid and wide spread of the network, there have appeared more and more online stars in public.
3. 这个乞丐无缘无故很快变成了网络红人。
   The beggar soon became a star on line for no reason at all.
4. 自身作为一个网络红人，这位女演员警告说网络是个危险的地方。
   Being an Internet celebrity herself, the actress warns that the Web is a dangerous place.
5. 互联网几乎天天都在制造网络红人。
   Almost every day, the Internet is creating web celebrities.
6. 网络红人是走红于网络的平民。
   A blue-eyed boy on the Internet is an ordinary person who is popular on the Web.

“红人”的第一个意思是“受上级赏识宠信的人”或“受重用的人”。英语可以译为 favourite (with sb in power), highly favoured person, blue-eyed boy(英), fair-haired boy(美)。例如：

7. 这位秘书被她的同事们认为是她老板的红人。
   The secretary was considered by her colleagues as the favourite with her boss.
8. 这个年青人在公司里被当作红人对待。
   The young man was treated as a highly favoured person in his company.
9. 由于迈克成为老板的红人，就没有人喜欢他了。
   Nobody likes Mike since he's become the boss's blue-eyed boy.
10. 迈克是总经理的红人，他被选定以便快速提升。
    Mike is the general manager's fair-haired boy, and he's been marked out for quick promotion.

“红人”的第二个意思是“走红的人”。英语可以译为 blue-eyed boy, fair-haired boy, white-haired boy。例如：

11. 这名政客以压倒多数票当选，成为党内的红人。
    The politician won the election by an overwhelming majority, and became his party's blue-eyed boy.
12. 马克因能言善辩而成为新闻界的红人。
    Mark has become the fair-haired boy of press circles because of his eloquence.
13. 这个年轻人被当作成一个红人，他受到特殊待遇，好像他比其他所有的人略胜一筹。
    Thc young man is regarded as a white-haired boy who gets special treatment as if he were above everybody else.

“走红”的第一个意思是“遇到好运气”，或称“走红运”。英语可以译为 to have good luck, to be in luck。例如：

14. 没有人总是走红。
    Nobody can always have good luck.
15. 他由于一路走红，而步步高升。
    As he is in luck all the way, he has been promoted quickly.

“走红”的第二个意思是“受欢迎”或“吃得开”。英语可以译为 to become popular, to achieve popularity, to be much in favour, to be much in demand。例如：

16. 这个女演员在娱乐圈很快就走红了。
    The actress soon became popular in the circles of entertainment.

17. 这个小演员唱京剧唱红了。
The young actor became popular for singing Beijing opera.
18. 这个歌手靠这首歌一夜走红。
The singer achieved popularity overnight for this song.
19. 这个年轻作家因其网络小说在大学生中间非常走红。
The young writer achieved immense popularity among college students for his online fiction.
20. 最近，这种网络游戏十分走红。
Recently this kind of online game has been much in favour.
21. 这种节能冰箱在市场上十分走红。
This type of energy-saving refrigerator has been much in demand in the market.

"红得发紫"，英语可以译为 to be extremely popular。例如：

22. 虽然这个演员长得很丑，他在娱乐圈却红得发紫。
Though the actor is ugly-looking, he is extremely popular in the circle of entertainment.

"红极一时"，英语可以译为 to enjoy great popularity for a time, to be all the rage for a time。例如：

23. 这个电影演员曾吸引了许多注意力，红极一时。
The film star attracted considerable attention and enjoyed great popularity for a time.
24. 这个理论曾红极一时，但是后来结果是错误的。
The theory was all the rage for a time, but turned out to be wrong.

66 清明扫墓

汉语关键词： 清明、清明节、扫墓

英语关键词： visit a grave, visit a tomb, pay tribute to sb at sb's grave/tomb, pay homage to sb at sb's grave/tomb, pay respect to sb at sb's grave/tomb, good government and prevalence of justice, sober and calm, clear and bright, Tomb-Sweeping Day, Mourning Day

句子： 人们清明扫墓缅怀死者。

误译：On Tomb-Sweeping Day, people go to sweep the graves in memory of the dead.
正译：On Tomb-Sweeping Day, people pay tribute to the dead at their tombs.
解释：

“扫墓”原指在亲人的墓地打扫，培土和祭奠，现在也指在烈士墓或纪念碑前举行纪念活动。to sweep a grave 和 to sweep a tomb 是字对字直译，过于强调打扫坟墓的动作，而不能概括祭奠先人的意思。“扫墓”，英语可以译为 to visit a grave, to visit a tomb, to pay tribute to sb at sb’s grave/tomb, to pay homage to sb at sb’s grave/tomb, to pay respect to sb at sb’s grave/tomb。例如：

1. 昨天，我陪一个朋友的妻子去扫墓，这个朋友死于一场车祸。
Yesterday, I visited a grave with the wife of a friend who died in an auto accident.
2. 人们在清明节去给故去的亲人扫墓，或去革命烈陵园扫墓。
On Tomb-Sweeping Day, people visit family tombs or go to mausoleums of revolutionary martyrs.
3. 这位老妇人在清明节去给故去的丈夫扫墓。
On Tomb-Sweeping Day, the old lady paid tribute to her late husband at his grave.
4. 上星期日，我们给一位在解放战争的一次战役中阵亡的无名战士扫墓。
Last Sunday, we paid homage to an unknown soldier at his tomb, who died in a battle during the Liberation War.
5. 清明节，村民们给他们的先人扫墓。
On Tomb-Sweeping Day, the villagers paid respect to their ancestors at their graves.

“清明”的第一个意思是“法度严明，秩序井然”。英语可以译为 clean/good government and prevalence of justice。例如：

6. 人民反对贪腐，期盼清明之治。
The people are opposed to corruption and expect a good government and prevalence of justice.
7. 先烈们为中国解放，为政治清明而奋斗牺牲。
The revolutionary martyrs struggled and died for the liberation of China and for a good government and prevalence of justice.

“清明”的第二个意思是“头脑明白清楚”。英语可以译为 sober and calm。例如：

8. 在混乱中，他保持神志清明。
In confusion, he kept sober and calm in mind.

9. 由于我的神志是清明的，我决不会跟着这个狂人一道发狂。
As my mind is sober and calm, I won't go mad with the mad man.
10. 欲望愈少，心灵愈清明。
Less desire makes you more sober and calmer in mind.

"清明"的第三个意思是"清澈明亮"。英语可以译为clear and bright。例如：

11. 今天天气清明。
It is clear and bright today.
12. 今夜月色清明。
Tonight, the moon is clear and bright.
13. 在布满星辰的天空，新月清明。
The new moon is clear and bright in the star-filled sky.

"清明"的第四个意思是"二十四节气中的一个节气"，即"清明节"。英语可以译为 Tomb-Sweeping Day, Mourning Day。有人译为 Pure Brightness Day 或 Qingming Day，不懂中国文化的西方人不会了解其中的含义，两种译法都需要解释。还是用 Tomb-Sweeping Day，容易被西方人理解。例如：

14. 清明节在公历每年4月4日、5日或6日。
Tomb-Sweeping Day falls on April 4, 5 or 6 every year according to Gregorian calendar.
15. 民众在清明节这一天有扫墓的习俗。
The folks have the custom of paying tribute to the deceased on Mourning Day.
16. 清明节是传统节日，而现在已成为法定节假日。
Tomb-Sweeping Day was a traditional festival, but now it has become an official public holiday.
17. 清明时节雨纷纷，路上行人欲断魂。
1) A drizzling rain keeps falling on Mourning Day; The traveler has his heart broken on the way.
2) It drizzles endless on Tomb-Sweeping Day; The traveler on the way feels himself lost in dismay.
18. 农谚说：清明前后，种瓜点豆。
As an agricultural proverb goes, before and after Mourning Day, it is the time for planting melons and dibbling beans.
19. 清明节正在临近，到了悼念死者的时候了。
Tomb-Sweeping Day is approaching and it is time to mourn those who have passed away.

67 胶囊公寓

汉语关键词： 胶囊、公寓、胶囊公寓、胶囊旅馆、公寓楼

英语关键词： capsule, flat, apartment, capsule hotel, capsule apartment, apartment building, apartment house, lodging house

句子： 北京最近出现一种不到两平方米的“胶囊公寓”。

误译： Beijing has recently appeared a kind of “capsule apartment” which covers an area of fewer than two square metres.

正译： In Beijing there has appeared a kind of “capsule apartment” which covers an area of fewer than two square metres.

解释：

这种字对字的译法容易出现语法错误。to appear 是不及物动词，后面不能跟宾语，即不能出现在“主 + 谓 + 宾”结构中。但是，to appear 可以出现在“主 + 谓 + 地点状语”结构中。这句话的主语太长，要用“there + appear”结构。

“胶囊旅馆”源自日本，英语可以译为 capsule hotel。例如：

1. 胶囊旅馆是日本的一种旅馆，提供大量极小的房间。
   A capsule hotel is a type of hotel in Japan with a large number of extremely small rooms.
2. 在东京的胶囊旅馆里，每位客人住在大约3×4×6 英尺的狭小的供睡觉用的空间里。
   In capsule hotels in Tokyo, each guest stays in a small sleeping space, which is about 3 feet by 4 feet by 6 feet.

“胶囊公寓”，英语可以译为 capsule apartment。例如：

3. 这个“胶囊公寓”包括一间2.5平方米的私人房间和公共区域。
   This capsule apartment comprises a 2.5-square-metre private room and common area.
4. 这个“胶囊公寓”占地不到两平方米，备有电视、上网条件和一张小书桌。
   The capsule apartment covers an area of less than 2 square metres, featuring TV, Internet connection and a small desk.
5. 一位退休老工程师最近建造了他的第一批“胶囊公寓”，是专为“蚁族”设计的。

An old retired engineer has recently built up his first group of capsule apartments designed exclusively for “ant tribe” members.

6. 最近，一位78岁老人在北京建造了8间“胶囊公寓”，每间面积不到两平方米。

   In Beijing, a 78-year-old man has recently had eight units of “capsule apartment” built, each of which covers an area of less than two square metres.

7. 这个“胶囊公寓”虽然很小，但是你在里面可躺，可坐，可看电视和上网。

   Though the capsule apartment is very small, you can lie, sit, watch television and get on line inside it.

“公寓”的第一个意思是“分户居住的多层或高层建筑，有若干成套的单户独用的房间，设备较好”。英语可以译为flat(英)，apartment(美)。例如：

8. 他想买一所两居室的公寓做投资用。

   He wants to buy a flat with two bedrooms for investment.

9. 他租了一套旧公寓，它需要重新装修了。

   He rented an old flat, which needed redecorating.

10. 这对年轻白领夫妇盼望尽快搬进自己的公寓。

    This young white-collar couple expects that they can sooner move into their own apartment.

11. 这个年轻人正在寻找一所靠近他工作地点的新装修的公寓。

    The young man is looking for a newly-furnished apartment near his workplace.

“公寓楼”，英语可以译为apartment building, apartment house。例如：

12. 在城市郊区，我拥有一座供出租用的公寓楼。

    In the suburbs of the city, I own an apartment building which I rent out.

13. 我把公寓楼卖给了一个正在购买商业物业的投资者。

    I sold an apartment house to an investor who was buying up commercial properties.

“公寓”的第二个意思是“旧时租期较长、房租按月计算的旅馆，居住人多为求学或谋事者”。英语可以译为lodging house。例如：

14. 他离开父母，搬进公寓，开始自己谋生。

    He left his parents and moved into a lodging house, starting to make his own living.

15. 她住在为附近学院学生开办的一家公寓里。

She lived in a lodging house for students from nearby colleges.

16. 这个学生在附近从一位女房东那里租了一个公寓。
The student rented a lodging house from a landlady in the neighbourhood.

"胶囊"，英语可以译为 capsule。例如：

17. 我着凉了，就吃了两粒感冒胶囊。
As I had a cold, I took two cold capsules orally.
18. 这个病人不喝水就吞下了胶囊。
The patient swallowed the capsule without drinking water.

68 拆迁

汉语关键词： 拆、拆开、拆散、拆卸、拆除、拆掉、拆毁、拆迁、拆迁户、拆迁居民、拆迁工程、拆台、拆墙角、挖墙脚、拆东墙补西墙、拆字、测字

英语关键词： open, take apart, unravel, dismantle, disassemble, pull down, knock down, tear down, demolish, pull down the old houses and resettle the inhabitants, get resettled, household to be resettled, inhabitant to be resettled, resettlement project, cut the ground from under sb' s feet, undermine, pull the rug out from under sb, rob Peter to pay Paul, divine by means of taking apart a Chinese character, decipher a character by means of taking it apart for divination, analyze the component parts of a Chinese character for divination, glyphomancy

句子： 为了拓宽道路，这一带的居民将要拆迁。

误译： In order to widen the road, the residents in this area will pull down their old houses and resettle themselves.

正译： In order to widen the road, the residents in this area will get resettled.

解释：

"拆迁"的"拆"，指拆除土地上原有的建筑物；"迁"，指迁移和安置原土地使用者。如果主语是有关部门或开发商，他们要负责拆除和安置两件事，英语可以直译为 to pull down the old houses and resettle the inhabitants。如果主语是被拆迁的居民，他们不管拆除，而只要被安置，英语则只需译为 to get resettled。例如：

1. 这家开发商已承包这个地区的拆迁。
The developer has contracted to pull down the old houses and resettle the inhabitants in this area.
2. 我们已在这所房子住了30年，但是很快就要拆迁了。
We have lived in this house for 30 years, but soon we'll get resettled.

"拆迁户"，英语可以译为 household to be resettled。"拆迁居民"，英语可以译为 inhabitant to be resettled。例如：

3. 按照协议，这些拆迁户可以回迁原地。
According to the agreement, these households to be resettled can move back to their original places.
4. 我们必须维护拆迁居民的根本利益。
We must protect the fundamental interest of the inhabitants who are to be resettled.

"拆迁工程"，英语可以译为 resettlement project。例如：

5. 在这个棚户区启动的拆迁工程旨在造福穷苦百姓。
The resettlement project launched in this shantytown is intended to benefit the impoverished people.

"拆"的第一个意思是"把合在一起的东西打开"，即"拆开"、"拆散"或"拆卸"。英语可以译为 to open, to take apart, to unravel, to dismantle, to disassemble。例如：

6. 他慢慢拆开信封，从里面取出信来。
He slowly opened the envelope and took out the letter from it.
7. 这个学生拆散发动机，仔细研究它的组成和结构。
The student took apart the engine and carefully studied its composition and structure.
8. 我妈妈正在拆一件旧毛衣，它窟窿太多而不能穿了。
My mother was unraveling an old sweater that had too many holes to be wearable.
9. 他拆卸自行车，一直拆到基本零件。
He dismantled the bicycle down to nuts and bolts.
10. 这位车工彻底拆卸了这个车床，然后清洗、调整和给所有零件上润滑剂。
The turner completely disassembled the lathe, and then cleaned, adjusted, and lubricated everything.

"拆"的第二个意思是"毁坏除掉"，即"拆除"、"拆掉"或"拆毁"。英语可以译为 to pull down, to knock down, to tear down, to demolish。例如：

11. 工人们正在拆除那些危房。
The workers were pulling down those crumbling houses.
12. 他们为了建造新房子，而拆掉了这些旧房子。
They knocked down these old houses to build up new ones.
13. 这座摇晃的大楼已被拆除。
The rickety building has been torn down.
14. 他们决定拆除这座桥，而不是寻求修缮它。
They decided to demolish the bridge instead of seeking to repair it.

"拆台"，英语可以译为 to cut the ground from under sb's feet。例如：

15. 由于他的竞争对手们债台高筑，他就趁机拆他们的台。
As his competitors were heavily in debt, he seized the opportunity to cut the ground from under their feet.
16. 当我们推出这个新产品时，我们拆了竞争对手的台。
When we launched the new product, we cut the ground from under our competitors' feet.

"拆墙角"或"挖墙脚"，英语可以译为 to undermine, to pull the rug out from under sb。例如：

17. 你应该明白在每个组织里你都会找到企图拆墙角的人。
You should understand in every organization you will find people who try to undermine the company.
18. 这个被开除的雇员想挖公司的墙角。
The employee who had been dismissed intended to pull the rug out from under the company.

"拆东墙补西墙"，英语可以译为 to rob Peter to pay Paul。例如：

19. 如果你通过向我借钱去还银行贷款，那就像是拆东墙补西墙。
If you pay the bank loan through borrowing money from me, it is just like robbing Peter to pay Paul.
20. 他用交房租的钱付煤气费账单，那就像是拆东墙补西墙。
He paid the gas bill with the rent money, which was just robbing Peter to pay Paul.

"拆字"或"测字"，英语动词可以译为 to divine by means of taking apart a Chinese character, to decipher a character by means of taking it apart for divination, to analyze the component parts of a Chinese character for divination，名词可以译为 glyphomancy。例如：

21. 测字先生通过拆字来占卜。
    A glyphomancer makes divinations by means of taking apart a Chinese character.
22. 算命先生通过拆字来占卜。
    The fortune-teller deciphered the Chinese character by means of taking it apart for divination.
23. 他拆字占卜。
    He analyzed the component parts of a Chinese character for divination.
24. 相信测字可以预知未来是迷信。
    The belief in divining the future through glyphomancy is nothing but a superstition.

69

撞车

汉语关键词： 撞、撞车

英语关键词： collide, collision, happen to be at the same time, overlap, knock down, bump into, crash, meet by chance, come across, run across, run into, try, have a try, dash, barge

句子： 由于两家电影厂争拍同一题材影片，这两部电影的情节撞车了。

误译： As the two studios scrambled to produce a film on the same subject, the plots of the two films collided with each other.

正译： As the two studios scrambled to produce a film on the same subject, the plots of the two films overlapped with each other.

解释：

这里“撞车”是“碰巧一样”的意思。to collide 的意思是 to strongly disagree in opinion，即“意见冲突”，不表示“情节或内容雷同”。to overlap 的意思是 to cover part of the same area of sth，即“部分范围重叠”，有“撞车”的比喻意义。例如：

1. 他们经常在政策决策上相互冲突。
   They regularly collide with each other over policy decisions.
2. 观众发现这两部电视连续剧内容撞车。
   The viewers found the contents of the two TV series overlapped with each other.

“撞车”的第一个意思是“车辆相撞”。英语动词可以译为 to collide，名词可以译为 collision。例如：

3. 昨天，两辆卡车在这里撞车了。
   Yesterday, two trucks collided with each other here.
4. 这辆汽车与货车在浓雾中迎面撞车了。
   1) The car and the van collided head-on in thick fog.
   2) The car collided head-on with the van in thick fog.
5. 由于今天早晨有浓雾，公路上发生了撞车事故。
   As there was heavy fog this morning, there occurred accidents of collision on the highway.

“撞车”的第二个意思是比喻“时间冲突或内容重复”。英语可以译为 to happen to be at the same time, to overlap。例如：

6. 由于安排不周，这两个约会撞车了。
   Due to an improper arrangement, the two appointments happened to be made at the same time.
7. 这两个会议撞车了，我只能参加一个。
   As the two meetings happen to be held at the same time, I can attend only one of them.
8. 员工轮休应该统一安排，以免撞车。
   The staff's off-work rotation should be arranged in a unified way so as to avoid overlapping.
9. 咱们申报的项目选题跟别的单位撞车了。
   The subject of the project we have applied for overlaps with that of another unit.

“撞”的第一个意思是“运动着的物体跟别的物体猛然相碰”。英语可以译为 to knock down, to bump into, to crash, to collide。例如：

10. 小心，别让汽车撞上。
    Take care not to be knocked down by a car.
11. 这辆汽车撞倒了一个正在过人行横道线的老人。
    The car knocked down an old man who was walking on the zebra crossing.
12. 我在走进会议室时跟他撞了个满怀。
    When I entered the meeting room, I bumped into him.
13. 她跑得那样快，结果撞到一棵大树上，她的眼镜掉了。
    She ran so quickly that she bumped into a tree and her glasses came off.
14. 这架巨型客机撞到靠近村庄的高山上。
    The giant passenger plane crashed against the mountain near the village.

15. 这个男孩跌倒时，他的头部撞到桌子上。
As the boy fell, his head collided with the table.

“撞”的第二个意思是“遇见”或“碰见”。英语可以译为 to meet by chance, to come across, to run across, to run into。例如：

16. 没想到他在国外撞见了一位老乡。
Unexpectedly, he met a townsman by chance in a foreign country.
17. 我在上班的路上撞见了一件有趣的事。
On my way to office, I came across something interesting.
18. 我不想见他，可是偏在大街撞上他。
I didn't want to see him, but I ran across him in the street.
19. 我在回家的路上撞见一个多年失去联系的中学同学。
On my way home, I ran into a classmate from high school, with whom I had been out of touch for years.

“撞”的第三个意思是“试探”。英语可以译为 to try, to have a try。例如：

20. 让我来撞一撞运气。
Let's me try my luck.
21. 去撞一撞看，说不定能成。
You may go and have a try, and you might succeed as well.

“撞”的第四个意思是“莽撞地行动”或“猛闯”。英语可以译为 to dash, to barge。例如：

22. 他在大街上横冲直撞。
He dashed around madly in the street.
23. 只见山后撞出一彪人马。
A detachment of troops were seen dashing from behind the hill.
24. 他横冲直撞穿过人群。
He barged his way through the crowds.

70 体面

汉语关键词：体面、体面劳动

英语关键词：face, dignity, labour with honour, respectable, honourable, with honour, decent, glorifying, glorious, have good looks, look smart

句子： 我们要不断提高劳动者的报酬，让他们体面地劳动。

误译： We must constantly increase the pay of the labourers, so as to let them work with decency.

正译： We must constantly increase the pay of the labourers, so as to let them labour with honour.

解释：

decency 的意思是 honest, polite behaviour that follows accepted moral standards and shows respect for others，即“正派”或“彬彬有礼”。to work with decency 具有“对别人尊重”的内涵。而“体面地劳动”包含“别人对劳动者尊重”的内涵，应译为 to labour with honour。

“体面”的第一个意思是“面子”、“名誉”、“体统”或“身份”。英语可以译为 face, dignity。例如：

1. 对那些强烈主张那个错误想法的人们来说有失体面。
   It is a loss of face for those who strongly stood for that wrong idea.
2. 他认为这个工作不够体面。
   He considered the job beneath his dignity.
3. 双方认为那个和平建议是他们能够体面地接受的一个建议。
   Both sides thought that the peace proposal was one they could accept with dignity.
4. 等他们年老时，他们想能够体面而受到尊重地退休。
   When they got old, they wanted to be able to retire with dignity and respect.

“体面”的第二个意思是“有尊严的”。英语可以译为 respectable, honourable, with honour。例如：

5. 他曾经有高薪的工作和体面的家庭，却因沉溺赌博，而犯了挪用公款罪。
   He used to have a high-paid job and a respectable family, but committed a crime of embezzling public funds as a result of being addicted to gambling.
6. 世上最体面的人是劳动者。
   The most respectable people of the world are labourers.
7. 他急切想与债权人达成体面的妥协。
   He was anxious to make an honourable compromise with the creditors.
8. 体面劳动使劳动者感到光荣。
   Honourable labour makes labourers feel glorified.
9. 在整个谈判的年代里，他们一直坚持体面的和平。
   Throughout the years of negotiations, they have insisted on peace with honour.

10. 为了达成协议，我们决定做出体面的让步。
To reach agreement, we decided to make a concession with honour.
11. 这个公司的总经理打算体面地退休。
The general manager of the company intended to retire with honour.

“体面”的第三个意思是“像样的”、“过得去的”。英语 decent 的意思是 of a good enough standard or quality，即“像样的”、“过得去的”。例如：

12. 他得到了一份当项目经理的体面职业。
He has got a decent job as a project manager.
13. 当时没受过大学教育就能找到一份体面工作是可能的。
At that time, it was possible to secure a decent job without a college education.
14. 由于他搬进自己的公寓，他的家庭最终得到了一个体面的住处。
As he moved into his own apartment, his family finally got a decent place to live in.
15. 我衷心希望我的每位朋友都能过上体面而幸福的生活
I sincerely wish every friend of mine could live a decent and happy life.
16. 这两位学者对体面的生活究竟是什么有着不同的定义。
The two scholars differ in their definitions of what exactly constitutes a decent living.
17. 世界文明的命运取决于为全人类提供体面的生活水准。
The destiny of world civilization depends upon providing a decent standard of living for all mankind.
18. 人们穿着体面的衣服，涌向广场参加庆祝会。
People dressed themselves decently and flocked to the square for the celebration.

“体面”的第四个意思是“光荣”、或“光彩”。英语可以译为 glorifying, glorious。例如：

19. 勤劳致富是件体面事。
To achieve prosperity through industrious work is a glorifying matter.
20. 好吃懒做可不是件体面事。
To be gluttonous and lazy is by no means a glorious matter.

“体面”的第五个意思是“好看”或“漂亮”。英语可以译为 to have good looks, to look smart。例如：

21. 这姑娘长得很体面，很大方。
The girl has good looks and ease of manner.
22. 他身穿新西服，样子很体面。
He looks smart in his new suit.

71 安全

汉语关键词：安全

英语关键词：safety, security, safe, secure

句子：我们必须加强学校及其周遍的安全工作。

误译：We must strengthen safety work in and around school.

正译：We must strengthen security work in and around school.

解释：

safety 的意思是 the state of being protected from danger and harm，强调的是"安全状态"。security 的意思是 the activities involved in protecting a country, building or person against attack, danger, etc，强调的是"保卫安全的活动或措施"。上 Google 搜索，发现 strengthen security work 有 4,420 条结果，其中近 3,600 条来自国外网页，而 strengthen safety work 仅有 4 条结果，其中 2 条来自国外网页。这句话的"安全工作"有采取安全措施的含义，译成 strengthen security work 较合适。

"安全"的第一个意思是"没有危险"或"不受威胁"。英语名词可以译为 safety, security；形容词可以译为 safe, secure。例如：

1. 保护你自己人身安全的最好方式，就是采取明智的预防措施。
   The best way to protect your personal safety is to take wise precautions.
2. 警方关注这个12岁女孩的安全，她已失踪一个星期了。
   The police are concerned for the safety of the 12-year-old girl who has been missing for one week.
3. 这位政客被拘押，是为了他自己的安全。
   The politician was kept custody for his own safety.
4. 所有学校领导不论何时都应把学生的安全放在首位。
   All school authorities should always put the safety of their students in the first place.
5. 消费者在购买、使用商品和接受服务时享有人身、财产安全不受损害的权利。
   In buying or using commodities or in receiving services, consumers are entitled to their personal safety and the safety with regard to their property.
6. 最终这名水手成功地游到了安全地带。
   Finally the sailor succeeded in swimming to safety.

7. 这是一个儿童们可以安全地玩耍的地方。
This is a place where children can play in safety.
8. 这位作者在文章中指出网络暴力威胁校园安全。
In his article, the author points out that network violence threatens campus safety.
9. 政府已采取有效措施维护校园安全。
The government has adopted effective measures to maintain school safety.
10. 这位学者认为军事因素在国家安全中占有重要地位。
The scholar holds that military factors occupy an important position in national security.
11. 据报导，该国政府已在全城部署了安全部队。
It is reported that the government of that country has deployed security forces throughout the city.
12. 联合国安全理事会负有维持国际和平与安全的责任。
The United Nations Security Council is charged with the maintenance of international peace and security.
13. 粮食安全就是所有人在任何时候都能在物质上和经济上获得足够、安全和富有营养的食物以满足其健康而积极生活的膳食需要。
Food security exists when all people, at all times, have physical and economic access to sufficient, safe and nutritious food for a healthy and active life.
14. 这位专家说这些塑料玩具对幼小儿童是不安全的。
The expert says these plastic toys are not safe for small children.
15. 我们的职责是为学生、教员、职员和校园来访者提供一个安全环境。
Our mission is to provide a safe and secure environment for students, faculty, staff and campus visitors.

security 还有the state of feeling safe from danger的意思。例如：

16. 有了社会安定，百姓才有安全感。
Only with social stability, will ordinary people have a sense of security.
17. 当事实上她已在危险之时却感到安全。她已使自己身陷一种虚假的安全感。
She had a feeling that she was safe when in fact she was in danger. She'd allowed herself to be lulled into a false sense of security.

“安全”的第二个意思是“没有事故”或“不出事故”。英语名词可以译为 safety；形容词可以译为 safe。例如：

18. 安全操作机器对其操作者的安全是至关重要的。
Safe operation of a machine is essential to the safety of its operators.

19. 这家航空公司有极佳的安全记录。
The airline has an excellent safety record.
20. 这些小学生安全地穿过了马路。
These primary school children crossed the road in safety.
21. 那些执意不遵循安全标准的人将受到纪律处分。
Those who choose not to follow the safety standards will be subject to disciplinary action.
22. 他们在生产中采取了严格的安全措施。
They have adopted strict safety measures in production.
23. 这名工人因未能遵守安全预防措施而受到惩处。
The worker was punished for having failed to observe the safety precautions.
24. 许多人都担心这种治疗方法的安全性。
Many people are worried about the safety of the treatment.
25. 这些专家正在就如何改善该城市的道路安全状况进行热烈讨论。
These experts are having a heated discussion about how to improve road safety in this city.
26. 这架飞机虽遭一群飞鸟撞击而轻微受损，但安全返航。
The plane made a return flight in safety, though it had been slightly damaged from a collision with a flock of flying birds.
27. 这架直升机在大雾中安全着陆。
The helicopter made a safe landing in heavy fog.
28. 员工和环境是影响安全施工的两个因素。
The staff and the environment are two factors that affect safe construction.

72 释放

汉语关键词： 释放

英语关键词： release, free, set free, discharge, emit, liberate

句子： 这个含冤入狱的农民被无罪释放。

误译： The farmer who was wrongfully put into prison on a false charge has been released without crime.

正译： The farmer who had been wrongfully put into prison on a false charge has been released without charge.

解释：

without crime 的意思是"没有犯罪"。在这里,"无罪"的意思是"没有罪名",应该译为 without charge。又,"含冤入狱"发生在"无罪释放"之前，应该用过去完成时表达。

"释放"的第一个意思是"放出被拘押者或服刑者，使其恢复人身自由"。英语动词可以译为 to release, to free, to set free, to discharge；名词可以译为 release。例如：

1. 这个被误判犯谋杀罪的人已被释放出狱。
   The man who had been wrongfully convicted of murder has been released from prison.
2. 他刑满释放后，立刻回家去了。
   After he was released upon completion of sentence, he went back home directly.
3. 由于这名犯人生了重病，他已取保释放。
   As the prisoner is seriously ill, he has been released on bail.
4. 最后，双方同意释放战俘。
   Finally, both parties agreed to release the prisoners of war.
5. 这位被抓并当作人质的老人，在患重病后被释放。
   The old man who had been captured and held hostage, was released after becoming seriously ill.
6. 这些恐怖分子说他们只有在某些条件下才会释放人质。
   The terrorists say that they will release their hostage only on certain conditions.
7. 法庭做出最终判决，拒绝释放这名犯人。
   The court rendered a final judgment, refusing to discharge the prisoner.
8. 他已入狱三年了，即将从狱中释放。
   He's been behind bars for three years and he is about to be freed from prison.
9. 他们决定释放这些战俘以换取赎金。
   They decided to set free the prisoners of war in return for some ransom.
10. 这个人在承认盗窃行为以后被有条件地释放了。
    The man was conditionally discharged after admitting the theft.
11. 政府一直努力争取使被索马里海盗劫持的人质获得释放。
    The government has been working to secure the release of the hostages held by the Somali pirates.
12. 这个犯人有望早点获得释放。
    The prisoner can expect an early release from prison.

“释放”的第二个意思是“把内含的能量或物质放出来”。英语动词可以译为 to release, to emit, to liberate；名词可以译为release。例如：

13. 20世纪30年代，人们发现原子可以分裂而释放出大量的能量。
In the 1930’s, it was found that the atom could be split, releasing huge quantities of energy.
14. 原子反应堆能够有效地释放原子能。
The atomic reactor can efficiently release atomic energy.
15. 反应过程中能释放出剧热。
Intense heat is released in the reaction.
16. 牛在消化食物时，会释放出甲烷。
Cattle release methane when they digest their food.
17. 精神压力会导致人体释放增加胰岛素阻抗性的激素。
Stress causes the body to release hormones that increase insulin resistance.
18. 这条蛇咬了我，把致命的毒液释放进我的血管里。
The snake bit me, releasing its deadly venom into my bloodstream.
19. 如果能量足够大，这个电子就会释放出来。
If the energy is sufficient, this electron will be emitted.
20. 一大块木头燃烧时释放出大量的热。
A chunk of wood liberates considerable heat during combustion.
21. 这种肥料的养分释放缓慢。
The nutrients of this kind of fertilizer make a slow release.

“释放”的第三个意思是“把内在的情感发泄出来”。英语可以译为 to release。例如：

22. 对任何年纪的任何人来说，大哭一场以释放情感是完全可以的。
It’s totally alright for anyone at any age to cry to release their sentiment.
23. 她放声大哭，把所有积郁的情感都释放出来。
She burst into tears, releasing all her pent-up emotions.
24. 音乐是人们释放感情的一个渠道。
Music is a channel for people to release their feelings.
25. 人们需要负责任地释放自己的愤怒感情。
People need to release their feelings of anger in a responsible way.

73 绑架

汉语关键词： 绑架、绑架者、绑匪、绑票、人质、赎人、赎金、撕票、劫持、劫汽车、劫火车、劫机、劫持者、劫机者、劫机犯

英语关键词： kidnap, kidnapper, kidnapping, abduct, abductor, abduction, manipulate, hijack, hijacking, hostage, ransom, kidnap sb for ransom, hold sb for ransom, kill the hostage, hijack a car, car-hijacking, hijack a train, train-hijacking, hijack an airplane, hijacking of aircraft, aircraft hijacking, skyjacking, aircraft piracy, aerial piracy, hijacker, skyjacker

句子： 有些人试图借助网络绑架民意。

误译： Some people tried to kidnap public opinion by means of the network.

正译： Some people tried to manipulate public opinion by means of the network.

解释：

to kidnap 的意思是 to take sb away illegally and keep them as a prisoner, especially in order to get money for returning them，即“为取得钱财而劫持人”，绑架的对象是人。而“绑架民意”的意思是“强行控制民意”，绑架的对象不是人，而是“人民的意见和愿望”。应译为 to manipulate public opinion。

“绑架”的第一个意思是“用强力劫持人”。英语动词可以译为 to kidnap, to abduct，名词可以译为 kidnapping, kidnap, abduction。例如：

1. 前几天，两名中国石油工人在也门被绑架。
   A few days ago, two Chinese oil workers were kidnapped in Yemen.
2. 这些恐怖分子秘密绑架了一名西方国家的外交官。
   The terrorists secretly kidnapped a diplomat of a Western country.
3. 这些匪徒威胁要绑架这个有钱人家的孩子。
   The bandits threatened to kidnap the child from a rich family.
4. 根据一位警官所说，一名15岁男孩被绑架勒索。
   According to a police official, a 15-year-old boy was kidnapped for ransom.
5. 这名罪犯因绑架罪被判处死刑。
   The culprit was sentenced to death for kidnapping.
6. 这名罪犯对绑架的指控供认不讳。
   The criminal admitted the charge of kidnap.
7. 据报道，一名4岁孩子在幼儿园大门口遭到绑架。
   It was reported that a 4-year-old kid was abducted at the gate of the kindergarten.

8. 这名女学生被报道说在从学校回家的路上遭到绑架。
   The school-girl was reported to have been abducted on her way home from school.
9. 绑架儿童是一种严重而令人痛苦的犯罪行为。
   Child abduction is a serious and traumatic crime.

“绑架”的第二个意思是“用不正当手段操纵、控制或左右”。英语可以译为 to manipulate, to hijack 等。to hijack 的意思 to use or take control of sth, especially a meeting, in order to advertise one's own aims and interests，即“操纵、控制会议等”。例如：

10. 这些暴力和专制政治集团企图利用选举绑架民意。
    These violent and dictatorial political groups tried to use elections to manipulate the will of the people.
11. 这位经济学家认为我国的房地产业现在不仅绑架了老百姓和政府官员，而且绑架了金融机构，甚至绑架了中国经济和整个社会。
    The economist holds that the real estate industry of our country has now manipulated not only ordinary masses of people and government officials, but also financial institutions, and even China's economy and the whole society.
12. 主席必须保证人们不会为了他们自己的议事日程而绑架会议。
    The chairman must make sure that people do not hijack the meeting for their own agenda.
13. 一个超级大国为了自身的目的和利益而绑架了这个国际会议。
    A superpower hijacked this international meeting for its own aims and interests.

“绑架者”或“绑匪”，英语可以译为 kidnapper, abductor。例如：

14. 绑架者向银行家的家人索要100万美元的赎金
    The kidnappers demand a ransom of one million dollars from the banker's family.
15. 绑匪被捕，失踪的孩子被平安地送回家中。
    The abductor was arrested and the missing child was returned safely to his family.

“人质”，英语可以译为 hostage。例如：

16. 一名妇女和两名儿童在银行抢劫案中被扣押为人质。
    A woman and two children were taken hostage during the bank robbery.
17. 这名在伊拉克被扣押当人质两年半的外国记者最近第一次讲述了他的磨难。

The foreign journalist who had been kept as a hostage in Iraq for two and half years has recently spoken for the first time of his ordeal.

18. 这名被恐怖分子扣押当人质将近一年的新闻记者已经获得释放。
The news reporter who had been held hostage by the terrorists for almost a year has been released.
19. 这名生重病的人质最近被释放了。
The hostage who had been seriously ill has recently been freed.
20. 政府正在谈判人质释放的事宜。
The government is negotiating the release of the hostages.

"赎人"的意思是"用钱财赎回人质"，英语可以译为 to ransom。例如：

21. 这名被绑架的儿童被赎回，没受伤害而返回家中。
The kidnapped child was ransomed and returned home unharmed.

"赎金"的意思是"赎回人质所用的钱财"，英语可以译为ransom。例如：

22. 这名人质拒绝为了他的释放而支付赎金。
The hostage refused to pay ransom for his release.

"绑票"的意思是"匪徒把人劫走，强迫被绑架者的家属出钱赎人"。英语可以译为 to kidnap sb for ransom, to hold sb for ransom。例如：

23. 我邻居家的小男孩被绑票了。
My neighbour's little boy was kidnapped for ransom.
24. 这个有钱人被绑票，受到威胁，并受到匪帮成员的严刑拷打。
The wealthy man was held for ransom, threatened and tortured by members of the gang.

"撕票"的意思是"绑匪杀死人质"，英语可以译为 to kill the hostage。例如：

25. 当这些绑匪未能得到他们索要的赎金时就撕票了。
The kidnappers killed the hostage when they failed to get the ransom they had demanded.

"劫持"的意思是"挟持"、"要挟"，英语可以译为 to hijack；名词可以译为 hijacking, hijack。例如：

26. 昨天，一群海盗在公海上劫持了一艘日本船。
Yesterday, a group of pirates hijacked a Japanese ship on the high seas.
27. 船只正在被劫持，人质正在被扣押，索马里海岸线已变成一个战争区域。
Ships are being hijacked, hostages are being taken, and the Somalia coastline has become a war zone.

28. 这个地区最近发生了一系列劫持事件。
There have been a series of hijackings recently in this area.
29. 大约30名可疑海盗在执行一项未遂的劫持任务以后，正被扣押在一艘俄罗斯战舰上。
About 30 suspected pirates are being held on board a Russian warship after carrying out an unsuccessful hijack.

“劫汽车”，英语动词可以译为 to hijack a car；名词可以译为 car hijacking。例如：

30. 几名匪徒在一个偏远地区的公路上劫持了一辆汽车。
A few gangsters hijacked a car on the highway in a remote area.
31. 这名罪犯用武力从司机那里劫持了这辆汽车。
The criminal hijacked the motor vehicle from its driver by force.
32. 有两个人被指控与去年年底在城市郊区劫持汽车有关联。
Two men were charged in connection with a car-hijacking in the suburbs of the city at the end of last year.

“劫火车”，英语动词可以译为 to hijack a train；名词可以译为 train- hijacking。例如：

33. 据报载，一组恐怖分子企图劫持一列装载核装置的火车。
According to the newspaper, a group of terrorists attempted to hijack a train carrying a nuclear device.
34. 昨天，在我出生的村庄附近发生了一起劫火车的事件。
Yesterday, a train-hijacking took place close to the village where I was born.

“劫机”，英语动词可以译为 to hijack an airplane；名词可以译为 hijacking of aircraft, aircraft hijacking, hijacking, skyjacking, aircraft piracy, aerial piracy。例如：

35. 两名武装人员在这次班机由伦敦飞往开罗时劫持了飞机。
Two armed men hijacked the airplane on a flight from London to Cairo.
36. 频繁发生劫机事件，是相对近来的现象。
The frequent hijacking of aircraft is a relatively recent phenomenon.
37. “劫机”指的是一个武装人员或集团控制了一架飞机。
Aircraft hijacking refers to the take-over of an aircraft by an armed person or group.
38. 对机场劫机的怀疑已证明是错误的。
The suspicion of a hijacking at the airport has proven to be false.
39. 这次劫机是一个胆大妄为的人的胆大妄为的行为。
The skyjacking was a desperate act by a desperate man.

40. 当这些机组人员面临劫机威胁时，他们保持沉着冷静。
When the aircrews were faced with an aircraft piracy threat, they remained calm and sober.
41. 劫机在一定程度上与国际恐怖主义紧密相关。
Aerial piracy is to some extent closely related to international terrorism.

"劫持者"，英语可以译为 hijacker。例如：

42. 这些劫持者用手榴弹武装着。
The hijackers were armed with hand grenades.
43. 他与劫持者保持着直接联系。
He's in direct contact with the hijackers.

"劫机者"或"劫机犯"，英语可以译为 hijacker, skyjacker。例如：

44. 万幸的是，这名劫机者还没来得及进入驾驶舱就被制止住了。
Thankfully, the hijacker was stopped before he was able to enter the cockpit.
45. 警方相信这名劫机犯肯定有犯罪记录，受过军事训练，而且熟悉这家航空公司。
The police believed that the skyjacker must certainly have had a criminal record, military training, and familiarity with the airline company.

74 践踏

汉语关键词： 践踏

英语关键词： tread on, trample on, step on, ride roughshod over, tread underfoot, violate

句子： 一个国家不能践踏另一个国家的核心利益。

误译： A country cannot tread another country's core interests.

正译： A country cannot tread on another country's core interests.

解释：

to tread 作为及物动词，意思是 to crush or press sth with your foot，即"踩压或踩坏东西"。英语没有 to tread one's interest 的搭配。to tread 作为不及物动词，意思是 to put your foot down while you are stepping or walking，强调"踩向某个东西"的具体动作。英语有 to tread on one's interest 的搭配，相当于 to violate one's interest，比喻"践踏利益"的意思。

“践踏”是个贬义词，它的第一个意思是“用脚踩人或植物，使之受伤害或毁坏”。英语可以译为 to tread on, to trample on, to step on。例如：

1. 我们要防止牲畜践踏庄稼。
   We must prevent domestic animals from treading on the crops.
2. 请不要践踏幼苗。
   Please don't trample on the seedlings.
3. 路边的草坪不能任人践踏。
   The lawns by the roadside can't be trampled on by anybody at their will.
4. 路是从没路的地方践踏出来的。
   The road was formed as a result of being trampled on in a place where there had been no road at all.
5. 溃败的军士仓皇逃窜，自相践踏。
   The defeated soldiers fled in panic, trampling on each other.
6. 请勿践踏青草。
   Please don't step on the grass.

“践踏”的第二个意思是比喻“摧残蹂躏百姓”。英语可以译为 to ride roughshod over。例如：

7. 这个恶棍仰仗权势践踏乡亲。
   Depending on the power relations, the bully rode roughshod over his fellow townsmen.
8. 这批恶势力随心所欲地践踏百姓。
   The evil forces ride roughshod over the ordinary people at whim.

“践踏”的第三个意思是“违反或侵犯权利、法律、真理、准则、民意等”。英语可以译为 to trample on, to tread underfoot, to violate。例如：

9. 这个南美洲国家的政府践踏了民意。
   The government of the South American country trampled on the views of ordinary people.
10. 这些示威者相信他们的政府已经反复践踏了他们的宪法权利。
    The demonstrators believed that their government had repeatedly trampled on their constitutional rights.
11. 我们决不允许侵略者肆意践踏我国的独立和主权。
    We will not allow the aggressors to wantonly trample on the independence and sovereignty of our country.
12. 这名官员已变得如此无耻而践踏真理和法律，且不顾人民的意愿。
    The official has become so shameless as to trample on truth and law, regardless of the people's will.

13. 互联网言论自由并不赋予你践踏别人权利的权利。
Free speech on the Internet doesn't give you the right to trample on the rights of other people.
14. 他们真正想做的是践踏中华民族的尊严和分裂中国。
What they really mean to do is to trample on the dignity of the Chinese nation and to split China.
15. 过去，西藏的农奴主在神权农奴制下践踏了西藏人民的尊严和人权。
In the past, the serf owners in Tibet trampled on the dignity and human rights of the Tibetan people under the theocratic feudal serfdom.
16. 一位瑞士专家指出植物应受到尊重，岂能被践踏。
A Swiss expert points out that plants deserve respect, which can by no means be trampled on.
17. 这家报纸指出：实际上，美国是践踏人权最严重的国家。
The newspaper points out that the United States is the worst country where human rights are trod underfoot.
18. 你在行使自己权利的时候，不可践踏别人的基本权利。
While you are exercising your own rights, you cannot tread others' basic rights underfoot.
19. 公民言论自由的宪法权利不容践踏。
The citizens' constitutional right to freedom of speech cannot be violated.
20. 这位专家认为国际关系准则已被践踏。
The expert holds that the principles guiding international relations have been violated.
21. 公民的隐私权应得到保护，而不可践踏。
A citizen's right of privacy should be protected and cannot be violated.
22. 这位女顾客在超市被搜身，她作为公民的基本权利遭到践踏。
As the female customer was given a frisk at the supermarket, her fundamental right as a citizen was violated.

75 留守

汉语关键词： 留守、留守儿童

英语关键词： leave sb behind to safeguard the capital city, leave sb behind to safeguard the second capital city, stay behind for garrison duty, stay behind for defence, stay behind for liaison duty, stay behind to take care of sth, be left behind in a place, child left behind, left-behind child

句子：父母都到城里打工去了，而留守儿童与爷爷、奶奶呆在村子里。

误译：Their parents have gone to the city to do odd jobs, while the left-over children stay with their grandparents in their village.

正译：Their parents have gone to the city to do odd jobs, while the left-behind children stay with their grandparents in their village.

解释：

left-over 的意思是 not used up，即“没有用完的”或“剩下的”，用来修饰物品，如 left-over food(剩饭)；而不能用来修饰人。在这里，“留守的”的意思是“遗留在原地没有动的”，应译为 left-behind。例如：

1. He had a little left-over money at the end of the month, so he went to see a film.
   他在月底还有一点剩余的钱，于是就去看了一场电影。
2. We know about how the dinosaurs lived from their left-behind eggs and footprints.
   我们通过恐龙遗留的蛋和脚印来了解它们是怎么生活的。

“留守”的第一个意思是“古代皇帝离开京城时命大臣驻守”、或“皇帝平时派官员在陪都或行都督守”。英语可以译为 to leave sb behind to safeguard the capital city, to leave sb behind to safeguard the second capital city。例如：

3. 皇帝御驾亲征，派一位元帅留守京城。
   The emperor led his army to go out for a battle, leaving a marshal behind to safeguard the capital city.
4. 皇帝返回京城时，命一位亲王留守陪都。
   When the emperor returned to the capital city, he ordered a prince to stay behind to safeguard the second capital city.
5. 这员将军受命留守行都，以备紧要时政府进驻。
   This general was ordered to stay behind to safeguard the temporary capital city, where the government would be stationed in case of emergency.

“留守”的第二个意思是“军队进发时，留驻部分人员以为守备”。英语可以译为 to stay behind for garrison duty, to stay behind for defence。例如：

6. 总司令命令说第一师将派往前线，而第二师将留守。
   The General-in-Chief ordered that the First Division would be sent to the front while the Second Division would stay behind for garrison duty.

7. 奇怪的是，这支打了胜仗的队伍并没有继续前进，而是就地留守。
Strangely enough, this victorious army did not continue to move forward, but stayed on the spot for defence.
8. 当一支进犯的敌军逼近时，我军需要留守。
When an aggressive enemy army is close, our army needs to stay behind for defense.

"留守"的第三个意思是"机关、团体等离开原驻地时留下少数人在原驻地负责联系工作"。英语可以译为 to stay behind for liaison duty。例如：

9. 这个小组奉命留守。
This group of people stayed behind for liaison duty as ordered.

"留守"的第四个意思是"居留下来看管"。英语可以译为 to stay behind to take care of sth。例如：

10. 全家人都搬到新房子去了，让这个老仆人留守老宅子。
The whole family had moved to the new house, letting the old servant stay behind to take care of the old house.

"留守"的第五个意思是"被留下来守在一个地方"。英语可以译为 to be left behind in a place。例如：

11. 孩子们都长大出国了，只剩下父母留守空巢。
The children have all grown up and gone abroad, only having their parents left behind at the empty nest.
12. 当他们的父母到城里寻找更好的社会和经济机遇时，生活在农村的孩子常常留守在原来的村子里。
The children living in rural areas are often left behind in their original villages when their parents travel to urban areas for better social and economic opportunities.

"留守儿童"，英语可以译为 child left behind, left-behind child。例如：

13. 据统计，目前我国农村留守儿童人数将近2,000万人。
According to statistics, there are nearly 20 million children left behind in the rural areas of our country.
14. 农村留守儿童的心理问题正逐渐成为严重的社会问题。
The psychological issue of these left-behind children in rural areas is gradually becoming a serious social problem.

76

吃醋

汉语关键词： 醋、醋意、醋劲儿、醋坛子、醋罐子、打翻醋坛子、吃醋、食醋、吃干醋、争风吃醋

英语关键词： vinegar，jealous，jealousy，person eaten up with jealousy，jealous man, jealous woman，eat vinegar，be jealous，be jealous for no reason at all，uncalled-for jealousy, vicarious jealousy，be bitterly and openly jealous of each other

句子： 他爱吃醋，不让妻子跟陌生男人说话。

误译： He loves to eat vinegar, not allowing his wife to talk with an unfamiliar man.

正译： He is so jealous that he doesn't allow his wife to talk with an unfamiliar man.

解释：

汉语的“吃醋”有“感到嫉妒”的比喻意义。在这里，“爱吃醋”表示的是嫉妒的心态，而不是吃酸味的醋。

“醋”的第一个意思是调味用的酸味液体。英语可以译为 vinegar。例如：

1. 醋是一种常用的调味品，可刺激食欲。
   Vinegar is a common condiment, which can stimulate appetite.
2. 我发现醋的气味刺鼻，我忍受不了醋的味道。
   I find the smell of vinegar unpleasant and I cannot stand the taste of vinegar.
3. 厨房里传来一股熬醋的气味，使他很难受。
   From the kitchen there came a smell of boiling vinegar, which made him very sick.

“醋”的第二个意思是比喻“嫉妒”，英语可以译为 jealous。“醋意”或“醋劲儿”，比喻“嫉妒心”，英语可以译为 jealousy。例如：

4. 她听到丈夫夸奖别的女人，顿生醋意。
   When she heard her husband praising other women, she suddenly burned with jealousy.
5. 为什么一个婚姻幸福的男人竟然这样没有理性地变得醋意大发？
   Why should a happily married man suddenly become eaten up with jealousy in such an unreasonable manner?
6. 当你醋劲儿十足的时候，很容易让人相信你的生活正失去控制。
   When you are consumed with jealousy, it's easy to believe that your life is spinning out of control.

7. 你的醋劲儿又上来了。
   You are being jealous again.
8. 似乎没有花多大功夫就醋海生波，使她头脑模糊。
   It doesn't seem to take much for a storm of jealousy to cloud her mind.

"醋坛子"或"醋罐子"，比喻"在男女关系上嫉妒心很强的人"。英语可以译为 person eaten up with jealousy, jealous man, jealous woman。例如：

9. 什么东西在主导这个"醋坛子"的思维过程?
   What is dominating the thought process of the person eaten up with jealousy?
10. 她的男朋友是个大醋罐子。
    Her boyfriend is an insanely jealous man.
11. 她心胸太狭窄,是个十足的醋坛子。
    Being narrow-minded, she is a very jealous woman.

"打翻醋坛子",英语可以译为 to be overwhelmed by jealousy。例如：

12. 当她的男朋友被她的一个同屋抢走时，她打翻了醋坛子。
    She was overwhelmed by jealousy when her boyfriend was stolen from her by one of her roommates.

"吃醋"的第一个意思是字面意思，即"食醋"。英语可以译为 to eat vinegar。例如：

13. 胃溃疡患者不宜食醋。
    Gastric ulcer patients should not eat vinegar.
14. 糖尿病患者应少吃醋。
    Diabetic patients should eat less vinegar.
15. 他吃面条的时候，总是吃点醋。
    When he has noodles, he always eats a little vinegar.

"吃醋"的第二个意思是"产生嫉妒情绪，多指在男女关系上"。英语可以译为 to be jealous。例如：

16. 当他发现他的女朋友爱别人的时候，他吃醋了。
    He was jealous when he discovered that his girlfriend loved someone else.

"吃干醋"的意思是"为与自己无关的事情而嫉妒"。英语动词可以译为 to be jealous for no reason at all；名词可以译为 uncalled-for jealousy, vicarious jealousy。例如：

17. 他这个人爱吃干醋，别理他。
    Just forget him, for he often becomes jealous for no reason at all.
18. 这不关你的事，你不要吃干醋。
    Don’t be jealous for no reason at all, for it’s none of your business.
19. 爱吃干醋是一种病。
    Extreme uncalled-for jealousy is a sickness!
20. 出于一种吃干醋的感觉，我摇了摇头。
    I shook my head out of a sense of vicarious jealousy.

“争风吃醋”的意思是“因追求同一异性而互相嫉妒争斗”，英语可以译为 to be bitterly and openly jealous of each other。例如：

21. 看到一对父子因一个女人争风吃醋而反目成仇，真是太可笑了。
    It is ridiculous to see a father and a son turn to foe, being bitterly and openly jealous of each other because of a woman.
22. 这些女子因一个男子而互不信任，争风吃醋。
    These women distrusted each other and were bitterly and openly jealous of each other because of a man.

77 跨界

汉语关键词： 跨界、跨界音乐

英语关键词： transboundary, across the borders, cross-border, crossover music, crossover

句子： 跨界的时尚价值在于让毫不相干和甚至矛盾、对立的元素产生灵感火花和奇妙创意。

误译： The fashionable value of crossing the border lies in letting the irrelevant, and even contradictory and controversial elements produce sparks of inspiration and wonderful creativity.

正译： The fashionable value of crossover lies in letting the irrelevant, and even contradictory and controversial elements produce sparks of inspiration and wonderful creativity.

解释： to cross the border 的意思是“穿越边界”的动作。而这句话的“跨界”代表一种新锐的生活态度与审美方式的融合。“跨界”这个词译自英语 crossover。

"跨界"的第一个意思是"跨越边界"。英语可以译为 transboundary, across the borders, cross-border。例如：

1. 跨界污染对周边国家和地区，甚至对全球环境可能造成严重危害，而相应地会产生国际法律责任。
Transboundary pollution may do serious harm to surrounding nations and regions, and even to the environment of the world, which will correspondingly give rise to international legal duty.
2. 作为一个跨界而居的民族,布里亚特蒙古族深受俄罗斯民族的影响,其服饰也已欧化。
As a people living across the borders, the Buriat-Mongolians have been deeply influenced by the Russians and their costumes have been Europeanized.
3. 本公司提供跨界巴士服务。
Our company provides cross-border bus and coach service.

"跨界"的第二个意思是"两个领域或两种不同类型事物的交叉、融合或混合"。英语可以译为 crossover。例如：

4. 一些流行产品背后都隐藏着跨界的概念。
The crossover concept is hidden behind some popular products.
5. 恐怖分子与犯罪组织的跨界已引起严重的社会问题。
The crossover between terrorists and criminal organizations has caused serious social problems.
6. 这名歌手进行了传统民间音乐与西方流行音乐的跨界表演。
The singer gave a crossover performance of traditional folk music and Western pop.
7. 去年，她的一个专辑获得第49届格莱美音乐奖最佳古典跨界专辑奖提名。
Last year, one of her albums was nominated for the Best Classical Crossover Album of the 49th Grammy Awards.
8. 虽然他坚定地说他将坚持古典传统而不会做跨界音乐，但是他也渴望尝试非常规的实验。
While saying firmly that he will stay in the classical tradition rather than do crossover, he is keen to try the odd experiment.
9. 在这个领域，公司间的跨界合作受到鼓励，共同信息库得到共享。
In this field, crossover cooperation among companies is encouraged and common information bases are shared.
10. 人们在争论跨界设计是设计师创新的土壤，还是商业炒作的手段。
People are arguing whether crossover design is the soil for designers to make creations or a means for people to make commercial speculations.

11. 专家们称之为跨界营销的东西正变得越来越流行。
What the experts call crossover marketing is becoming increasingly popular.

“跨界音乐”，英语可以译为 crossover music, crossover。例如：

12. 跨界音乐是当下音乐领域的时髦，它兼容不同音乐门类，以古典与流行的跨界为主要标志。
Crossover music is currently a fashion in music circles, which incorporates different music genres and is mainly marked with classical-popular crossover.
13. 这只单曲曾是风靡欧洲和全世界的真正的跨界音乐名曲。
This single has been a real crossover hit around Europe and the world.

“跨界”的第三个意思是“跳出原有格局和旧有经验或做法，重新思考与行动”。英语可以译为 crossover。例如：

14. 在现代商业社会中，跨界不仅是一种合作方式，也是一种思维方式和营销方式。
In modern commercial society, crossover is not only a means of cooperation, but also a way of thinking and a way of marketing.
15. 所谓“跨界”，时尚界称之为混搭；科学界称之为边缘学科；创意界称之为旧元素新组合，或者换种说法就是：把不搭界的东西相加在一起而产生的一种新价值。
The so-called “crossover” is named as “mix and match” in fashion circles, as “interdisciplinary subject” in scientific circles, and as a new combination of old elements in innovation circles, or in other words, it is a new value created by putting unrelated things together.
16. 显然，跨界不是简单的商战技巧，而是一种企业或品牌的创新战略。
Obviously, crossover is not a simple tactics used in commercial wars, but a new strategy of innovation for an enterprise or a brand.

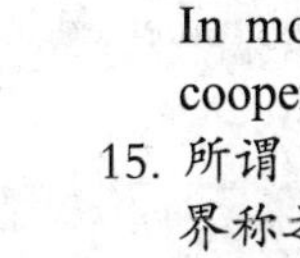

78 泡汤

汉语关键词： 泡汤

英语关键词： be immersed in soup, be immersed in water, be drowned, bathe in a hot spring, dawdle, loiter, come to nothing, dash to pieces， fall through, waste, bust, cancel

句子： 倾盆大雨淹没街道，许多汽车泡汤了。
误译： The torrents of rain flooded the street, and many cars drowned.
正译： The torrents of rain flooded the street, and many cars were drowned.
解释：

在这里，“泡汤”有“被水淹没”的意思。to drown 的意思是 to complete cover sth in water，即“淹没”，为及物动词。“汽车泡汤”，就是“汽车被淹没”，应该用被动语态。

“泡汤”的第一个意思是“浸泡在汤里”。英语可以译为 to be immersed in soup。例如：

1. 他喜欢米饭泡汤吃。
He likes to eat the rice immersed in soup.
2. 我认为吃米饭泡汤对胃不好。
I don't think that eating the rice immersed in soup does any good to the stomach.
3. 许多旅游者大老远来品尝这种用鱼头煮的美味的泡汤面条。
Many tourists come from afar to taste this delicious noodles immersed in soup cooked with fish head.

“泡汤”的第二个意思是“被水淹没”。英语可以译为 to be drowned, to be immersed in water。例如：

4. 连下了几天暴雨，停放在低洼处的汽车都泡汤了。
It rained hard for a few days in succession. As a result, the cars which were parked in the low-lying areas were all drowned.
5. 一场大雨使盐池里晒的盐全泡汤了。
A heavy rainfall drowned the brine in the solar salt field, which had been evaporated in the sun.
6. 这场倾盆大雨过后，至少有20辆汽车在被水淹的地下车库泡汤了。
After the heavy rainfall, at least 20 cars were immersed in water in the flooded underground car park.

“泡汤”的第三个意思是“在温泉里沐浴或洗浴”。英语可以译为 to bathe in a hot spring。例如：

7. 冬天，他喜欢到温泉泡汤。
In winter, he enjoys bathing in a hot spring.
8. 冬天在温泉泡汤后，要注意保暖和休息。
In winter, make sure that you should keep warm and take a good rest after taking a bath in hot spring.
9. 他经常在混合有各种药草和芳香油的矿泉里泡汤。

He often takes a bath in a spa where the water is mixed with herbs and aromatic oils.

“泡汤”的第四个意思是“怠工”或“磨洋工”。英语可以译为 to dawdle, to loiter。例如：

10. 现在干活泡汤的吃不开了。
    Those who dawdle over their work have now become unpopular.
11. 现在很少有人工作泡汤了。
    Nowadays few people can afford to loiter on the job.

“泡汤”的第五个意思是“落空”。英语可以译为 to come to nothing, to dash to pieces, to fall through, to waste, to bust, to cancel。例如：

12. 这笔生意泡汤了，但是双方都没有怨气。
    The deal came to nothing, but there were no hard feelings on either side.
13. 由于管理不善，他的投资全部泡汤了。
    As a result of bad management, his investment came to nothing at all.
14. 这个斥资过亿元打造的景观工程最后泡汤了。
    The scenic project on which more than a hundred million yuan had been spent finally came to nothing.
15. 不幸的是，我们这么多天的努力就白白泡汤了。
    Unfortunately, so many days' efforts of ours came to nothing at all.
16. 由于干旱歉收，村民丰收的希望泡汤了。
    Due to the crop failure caused by drought, the villages' hope for good harvest dashed to pieces.
17. 由于父母供不起，她去美国留学的计划泡汤了。
    As her parents couldn't afford to support her, her plan to go to study in the United States fell through.
18. 他认为花在这个计划上的钱至少一半已经泡汤了。
    He thinks that at least half of the money spent in the plan has been wasted.
19. 由于金融危机，对许多人来说，美国之梦泡汤了。
    As a result of the financial crisis, the American Dream busted for a lot of people.
20. 听说工会组织的春游要泡汤。
    I hear that the spring outing organized by the trade union will be cancelled.

79 缩水

汉语关键词： 缩水、缩水率、抽水

英语关键词： soak sth in water to make it shrink, shrink in the wash, shrinkage, shrinkage rate, shrink, lose in value, decline in value

句子： 近来全球股市暴跌使市值大幅缩水。

误译： The recent global stock market crash has made the market value to shrink by a big margin.

正译： 1) The recent global stock market crash has made the market value shrink by a big margin.

2) The recent global stock market crash has caused the market value to shrink by a big margin.

解释：

to make sb do sth 具有“使某人做某事”的意思。其中的 sb do sth 是动词 to make 的复合宾语。不定式 do sth 前面要省略 to。如果用 to cause sb to do sth 表示“使某人做某事”的意思，不定式 do sth 前面则不可省略 to。

“缩水”的第一个意思是“将纺织品等放进水中浸泡使其收缩”，这是一个动作。英语可以译为 to soak sth in water to make it shrink。例如：

1. 这块布料缩过水了吗？
   Did you soak the cloth in water to make it shrink?
2. 我妈妈在裁剪裙子之前，先将这块布料缩水。
   Before my mother cut out a skirt, she soaked the cloth in water to make it shrink.

“缩水”的第二个意思是“某些纺织品浸水后因纤维吸水膨胀而收缩”，也称“抽水”，这是一种现象。英语可以译为 to shrink in the wash。例如：

3. 羊毛织物在热水里会缩水。
   Woolen fabrics will shrink in hot water.
4. 这件毛衣因洗涤不当而缩水了。
   The sweater shrank because it was washed badly.
5. 在热水中洗毛线会使毛线收缩。
   Washing wool in hot water will make it shrink.
6. 这块布料在水洗后缩水了。
   This cloth shrank after being washed in water.
7. 这件T恤衫会缩水吗？

Will this T-shirt shrink in the wash?

8. 牛仔裤会缩水。

The jeans will shrink in the wash.

9. 这种布料不缩水。

1) This cloth doesn't shrink in the wash.

2) This cloth won't shrink when it's washed.

10. 热水容易使一些衣服缩水、起褶和褪色。

Hot water tends to make some clothing shrink, wrinkle, and fade.

11. 我们测试了一件百分之百纯棉衬衣在洗涤、晾干和熨烫后缩水多少。

We tested how much a 100% cotton shirt shrinks after going through the wash, being dried, and being ironed.

“缩水率”的意思是“纺织品或其他物品缩水量占缩水前原量的百分比”。英语可以译为 shrinkage 或 shrinkage rate。例如：

12. 买棉布衣服时，你应该考虑到它们的缩水率。

When buying cotton clothes, you should take their shrinkage into account.

13. 这台烘干设备用于棉纺、印染和服装等行业的缩水率试验。

The stoving equipment is used for shrinkage test in cotton textile, dyeing and clothes trade.

14. 这种材料的缩水率为10%左右。

This material has a shrinkage of around 10 per cent.

15. 这个坯体的缩水率为6%。

This clay body has a shrinkage rate of 6%.

“缩水”的第三个意思是比喻“内容、数量或价值在原有基础上缩小和减少”。英语可以译为 to shrink, to lose in value, to decline in value。例如：

16. 这所学校的学生人数已经缩水。

The number of students in this school has shrunk.

17. 人手不足已使我们工厂的年产量缩水。

Shortage of hands has shrunk our plant's yearly output.

18. 最近，该公司股值缩水一半多。

The equity of the company has recently shrunk by over 50%.

19. 与去年2,200亿相比，奢侈品市场今年预计将缩水至1,980亿。

The luxury market is expected to shrink to $198 billion this year, compared with $220 billion last year.

20. 据报道，从7月到9月，美国经济缩水0.33个百分点。

It is reported that the United States economy shrank by three-tenths of one percent from July through September.

21. 由于这家影视公司股值下跌，这个影星的身价缩水一千万美元。
    As the equity of this film and television company dropped, the film star lost ten million dollars in value.
22. 全球经济衰退导致一些亿万富翁的身价大大缩水。
    The global economic recession caused some billionaires to decline greatly in value.

80 包装

汉语关键词： 包装、包装纸、包装袋、包装盒、包装箱

英语关键词： pack, packing, package, packaging, packing paper, wrapping paper, packing bag, packing box, packing case

句子： 这个唱片公司最近包装并推出了一名青年歌星。

误译： The record company has recently packed and promoted a young pop star.

正译： The record company has recently packaged and promoted a young pop star.

解释：

to pack 和 to package 作为及物动词，都有 to put sth into a container so that it can be stored, transported or sold 的意思，包装的对象物是商品。但是，to package 还有 to present sb/sth in a particular way 的意思，即“经形象设计使美化”。但是 to pack 没有这种用法。例如：

1. 这个女演员已被包装，推出并进入市场。
   The actress has been packaged, promoted and put onto the market.
2. 这家报社对把新闻包装成娱乐形式进行了尝试。
   The newspaper company made an attempt to package news as entertainment.

“包装”的第一个意思是“把商品包裹起来或装进盒子、瓶子等容器，以起到保护和装饰作用”。动词可以译为 to pack, to package。名词可以译为 packing。例如：

3. 售货员用纸盒把礼品包装起来。
   The shop assistant packed the gift into a paper box.
4. 这件产品是用塑料袋包装的。
   This product is packed in a plastic bag.

5. 这件礼物包装得真漂亮。
   This gift was really beautifully packaged.
6. 他们的产品总是包装得非常吸引人。
   Their products are always attractively packaged.
7. 食品用礼品盒包装。
   The food is packaged in a gift box.
8. 快餐机器人将很可能会包装食品。
   Fast-food robots will probably package food.
9. 音乐是上乘的，专辑是用塑料盒包装的。
   The music is good and the album is packaged in a plastic casing.
10. 书商精心包装待寄的书籍，这样在运输过程中损坏的可能性就变得最小化了。
    The book-seller carefully packages its books for mailing so that the possibility for damage in transit is minimized.
11. 合法公司发现他们的声誉受到危及，而且他们的利润受到假冒产品的威胁，这些假冒产品包装得跟真品一模一样。
    Legitimate companies have found their reputations jeopardized and their profits threatened by fake products that are packaged to look exactly like the real thing.
12. 损失归咎于包装不当。
    The loss is attributed to inadequate packing.
13. 对仪器包装，请务必小心。
    Please be careful as regards the packing of the instruments.

“包装”的第二个意思是指“包装用的材料、容器等”或指“商品包装的形式”，为名词。英语可以译为 packing, packaging。例如：

14. 这些货物的包装完整无损。
    The packing of the goods is in good order.
15. 这件礼品的包装很美观、雅致。
    The packing of the gift is beautiful and elegant.
16. 这件礼物的包装很别致。
    The packing of the present is quite unique.
17. 这个工人在专利产品的包装上标明专利号。
    The worker indicated the number of the patent on the packing of a patented product.
18. 在消费品产业中，对消费者做出购买决定，包装的质量如同产品自身一样起决定作用。
    In the consumer goods industry, the quality of the packaging is as decisive as the product itself for the consumer’s buying decision.

"包装纸"，英语可以译为 packing paper，wrapping paper。例如：

19. 他们用一卷高质量的包装纸保护运输中的易碎物品。
They protected fragile items in transit with a high-quality roll of packing paper.
20. 包装纸可以用来包食物，以达到卫生和美观的目的。
Wrapping paper can be used for food for sanitary and aesthetic purposes.

"包装袋"，英语可以译为 packing bag。例如：

21. 一个小包装袋可以在一个挂篮或支架上节省大得令人惊奇的空间。
A small packing bag can save a surprising amount of space in a pannier or on a rack.

"包装盒"，英语可以译为 packing box。例如：

22. 我父亲送我一个照相机当作生日礼物，照相机装在一个包装盒里。
My father gave me a camera as a birthday gift, which came with a packing box.

"包装箱"，英语可以译为 packing case。例如：

23. 盖完日期戳以后，成品盒奶运送出流水线，自动地或用手放入包装箱，以便运输。
After the date is stamped, the finished milk carton moves off the conveyor, and is packed either automatically or by hand into a packing case, for shipment.

"包装"的第三个意思是"比喻对人或事物进行形象设计，使美化和有特色，而更具有吸引力或商业价值。"英语可以译为 to package。例如：

24. 这家电影公司精心包装了它的演员、导演、制片人和作者。
The film company carefully packaged its actors, directors, producers and writers.
25. 这个电影公司用明星制包装它的女演员。
The film studio used the star system to package its actresses.
26. 经过包装，这个影星的面貌焕然一新。
Having been packaged, the film star took on an entirely new look.

81

封闭

汉语关键词：封闭、封闭疗法、打封闭

英语关键词：close, closed, close down, block, seal, seal off, seal up, cap, shut down, block therapy, with block therapy

句子：我听说这所学校实行封闭式管理。

误译：I hear that this school is managed in a close way.

正译：I hear that this school is managed in a closed way.

解释：

作为形容词，close 的意思是 near，即“近的”，与 far（远的）相对立。in a close way 的意思是 closely，即“近距离地”或“亲近地”。例如：

1. 近距离用奶瓶喂奶可以刺激眼神交流。
   Bottle feeding in a close way may encourage eye contact.
2. 我喜欢与人们亲近地工作。
   I enjoy working with people in a close way.

作为形容词，closed 的意思是“封闭的”，与 open（开放的）相对立。例如：

3. 他们生活在一个封闭社会里，与世隔绝。
   They live in a closed society, isolating themselves with outside world.
4. 我们决不能封闭起来搞建设。
   Wc can by no means construct our country in a closed way.
5. 这些航天员正在封闭环境中进行训练。
   These astronauts are being trained in a closed environment.
6. 这些运动员正在进行封闭式训练。
   These athletes are having a closed-door training.
7. 这个水处理系统是一个不允许空气进入的封闭系统。
   The system for water handling is a closed system that does not permit air to enter.
8. 像开放式基金一样，封闭式基金从大投资者，也从小投资者那里融资。
   Like open-end funds, closed-end funds gather money from large and small investors alike.

“封闭”的第一个意思是“严密盖住，或彻底封口，使处于隔绝状态”。英语可以译为 to close down, to seal, to seal off, to cap。例如：

9. 我们不能封闭信息，而应该很好地认识外面世界。
We mustn't close down information, and we should have a good knowledge of the outside world.
10. 地方当局试图封闭他们不喜欢的信息。
The local authorities tried to close down the information they disliked.
11. 这个工人用火漆封闭了瓶口。
The worker sealed the bottle with wax.
12. 英国石油公司的工程人员正在试图封闭一个向墨西哥湾泄漏原油的油井。
BP engineers were trying to seal off an oil well which was leaking crude oil into the Gulf of Mexico.
13. 这些石油工人成功地封闭了正在喷油的油井。
The oil workers succeeded in capping the oil well which was spewing oil.

“封闭”的第二个意思是“严密关闭，使不能通行”。英语可以译为 to block, to seal up, to seal off。例如：

14. 警察封闭了通往事故现场的道路。
Police has blocked the road leading to the scene of the accident.
15. 大雪封闭了城里所有的道路。
Heavy snow blocked all the roads in the city.
16. 这些叛乱者推开家具来封闭这所房子底层的门窗。
These rebels pushed the furniture around to block the doors and windows on the bottom floor of the house.
17. 这些罢工者封闭了大楼的门窗。
These strikers sealed up the doors and windows of the building.
18. 在意大利，警察未能封闭被一大群示威者占领了四天的飞机场。
In Italy, police failed to seal off the airport which had been occupied by a large group of demonstrators for four days.

“封闭疗法”，英语可以译为 block therapy。“打封闭”，英语可以译为 with block therapy。例如：

19. 你可以打封闭治疗这种病症。
You may treat the disease with block therapy.

“封闭”的第三个意思是“中断或停止服务”。英语可以译为 to close, to close down。例如：

20. 这个欧洲国家由于来自冰岛火山的火山灰而被迫封闭了7个飞机场和几十次航班。
The European country was forced to close seven airports and dozens of flights due to volcanic ash from the volcano in Iceland.

21. 由于大雪，机场被封闭了。
Due to heavy snow, the airport was closed down.
22. 这个火车站已经封闭，准备重建。
This railway station has been closed down, getting ready for reconstruction.

“封闭”的第四个意思是“查封”。英语可以译为 to close down, to shut down。例如：

23. 警方封闭了这个赌场。
Police closed down the gambling house.
24. 住在附近的居民一直请求警察封闭这个妓院。
The residents who live nearby have been calling for the police to close down the brothel.
25. 警察封闭了这个制假窝点。
Police shut down the illegal workshop where counterfeit products were made.

82 三俗

汉语关键词： 三俗、庸俗、低俗、媚俗、媚世、庸俗化、抵制

英语关键词： boycott, resist, vulgar, vulgarity, vulgar taste, distasteful, coarse, distastefulness, low taste, cater to one's vulgar taste, pander to one's vulgar taste, pander to one's base interest, fish for cheap popularity

句子： 艺人在演出中应自觉地抵制三俗。

误译： Entertainers should consciously boycott vulgarity and distastefulness or fishing for cheap popularity in their performance.

正译： Entertainers should consciously resist being vulgar and distasteful or fishing for cheap popularity in their performance.

解释：

“三俗”指的是“庸俗、低俗、媚俗”。“抵制”的意思是“阻止某种事物，使其不能侵入或发生作用”。“抵制三俗”就是“阻止庸俗、低俗和媚俗”。to boycott 的意思是 to refuse to buy, use or take part in sth as a way of protesting，即“拒绝购买、使用或参加”，将“抵制”视为一种抗议的方式，用在这里不合适。to resist 的意思是 to refuse to accept sth and try to stop it from happening，即“拒绝接受某种事物，而且努力阻止其发生”，用在这里合适。例如：

1. 这些环保主义者组织了一场示威活动呼吁人们抵制象牙产品。
These environmentalists organized a demonstration to call for people to boycott ivory products.
2. 董事长抵制了一切要他辞职的企图。
The chairman of the board resisted all attempts to make him resign.

"庸俗"的意思是"粗俗"、"平庸鄙陋"、"不高尚"、"不高雅"。英语形容词可以译为 vulgar；名词可以译为 vulgarity, vulgar taste。例如：

3. 在这个演员的庸俗表演中，我发现没有什么令人愉悦或有艺术性的东西。
I found nothing entertaining or artistic in this actor's vulgar performance.
4. 同事们相互吹捧是庸俗的。
That colleagues flatter each other is vulgar.
5. 从这位公众人物当众的行为，我们可以看出他是多么庸俗，多么丑陋。
From the public figure's acts in public, we can see how vulgar and ugly he is.
6. 他哼着一个庸俗的小调。
He hummed a vulgar tune.
7. 有一些流行音乐被认为是庸俗的和宣扬暴力的。
Some of the popular music is considered vulgar and violent.
8. 许多人认为这本书有庸俗的味道。
Many people think that this book has vulgar tastes.
9. 庸俗的出版物是中国走向市场经济行动的一个负面结果。
Vulgar publications are a negative result of China's move to a market economy.
10. 我们为他的笑话之庸俗感到气愤。
We were offended by the vulgarity of his jokes.

"庸俗化"，可以译为 to vulgarize。例如：

11. 曾一度经历庸俗化的哲学，需要在分析性推理的基础上加以清理。
The philosophy, once vulgarized, needs to be cleared on the basis of analytical reasoning.

"低俗"的意思是"低级庸俗"。英语形容词可以译为 distasteful, coarse；名词可以译为 distastefulness, low taste。例如：

12. 观众中绝大多数人都讨厌这种低俗的幽默。
The majority of the audience hates this kind of distasteful humour.
13. 许多人发现这种笑话低俗。
Many people find this sort of jokes distasteful.

14. 我发现他的黄段子低俗，而且相当庸俗。
I found his dirty jokes coarse and rather vulgar.
15. 家长们不要让他们的孩子看这个电影，因为它包含低俗语言和暴力。
It is advisable for parents to prevent their children from seeing the film as it contains coarse language and violence.
16. 人们不应读低俗的出版物。
People should not read publications of low taste.

"媚俗"或"媚世"的意思是"过分迎合或迁就庸俗或低俗"。英语可以译为 to cater to one's vulgar taste, to pander to one's vulgar taste, to pander to one's base interest, to fish for cheap popularity。例如：

17. 这个女演员正想尽一切可能的方法媚俗，迎合观众。
The actress was trying every possible means to cater to the vulgar taste of the audience.
18. 这部电影媚俗，迎合了部分观众。
The film caters to the vulgar taste of some viewers.
19. 这本时尚杂志因媚俗迎合一些读者而遭到批评。
This fashion magazine was criticized for pandering to the vulgar taste of some readers.
20. 这本书媚俗，迎合一些庸俗的人。
This book panders to the base interest of some vulgar people.

83 撞衫、靠色

汉语关键词：撞衫、靠色、合身、合体、般配、班配

英语关键词：clash, be dressed in the same style and colour, wear the same kind of dress as someone else, be of the same colour, be of the similar colour, fit, be becoming to sb, become sb, match

句子：这位女演员走在红地毯时发现与另一位影星撞衫了。

误译：When this actress was walking on the red carpet, she found her outfit clashed with another film star.

正译：When this actress was walking on the red carpet, she found she happened to wear the same kind of dress with another film star.

解释：

to clash 的意思是 to look ugly when put together，即“放在一起，样子难看”，“不协调”、“不和谐”或“不搭配”。没有“撞衫”的意思。clash 也可以用作名词。例如：

1. 如果你的朋友们穿衣服互不协调，不要介意。
   Don't care if your friends' outfit clashes.
2. 这位女主人的衣服与房间里的家具陈设不协调。
   The hostess' outfit clashes with the furnishings in the room.
3. 如你所知，穿衣服不般配对影星来说是忌讳。
   As you know, outfit clashes are taboo to movie stars.
4. 这位影星的母亲努力避免与其女儿颜色不协调或衣服不搭配。
   The mother of the film star tries to avoid colour or outfit clashes with her daughter.

“撞衫”的意思是“两个明星在出席同一场合时穿了式样和颜色相同的衣服”。英语可以译为 to be dressed in the same style and colour, to wear the same kind of dress as someone else。例如：

5. 在颁奖晚会上，这两位女演员撞衫了。
   At the award-giving party, the two actresses happened to be dressed in the same style and colour.
6. 影星最怕在公众场合撞衫，而观众最爱看影星在公众集会上撞衫。
   Film stars are mostly afraid of wearing the same kind of dress as someone else on a public occasion, while the audience mostly enjoys seeing them dressed in the same style and colour at a public meeting.
7. 这位影星有个形象设计师帮助她避免在晚会上与别的影星撞衫。
   The movie star has an image designer to help her to save her from wearing the same kind of dress as someone else.

“靠色”的意思是“两种事物的颜色相近或相同”。英语可以译为 to be of the same colour, to be of the similar colour。例如：

8. 我发现本小区保安的制服与警服靠色。
   I find the uniform of the security guards in this residential district and the police uniform are of the same colour.
9. 这位老太太的白色新上衣与她的银发靠色。
   This old lady's new white coat is of the similar colour with her silver hair.

“合身”或“合体”的第一个意思是“衣服式样和尺寸适合身材”。英语可以译为 to fit，它的意思是to be the right shape and size for sb，即“式样和尺寸适合身材”。例如：

10. 这件夹克很合身。
    This jacket fits well.
11. 她试穿了这件裙子，但不合身。
    She tried the skirt on but it didn't fit.

“合身”或“合体”的第二个意思是“衣服适合身材，使人显得帅”。英语可以译为 to be becoming to sb，它的意思是 to make sb who wears the clothes look more attractive，即“使穿衣人显得帅”。例如：

12. 她不管穿什么，对她都合身。
    Whatever she wears is becoming to her.
13. 她的衣裙非常新潮，对她很合身。
    Her dress is very stylish, which is becoming to her.
14. 她发现很难买到对她合身的衣服。
    She finds it difficult to buy clothing that is becoming to her.

“般配”或“班配”的第一个意思是“衣着与身份相称”。英语可以译为 to become sb。例如：

15. 这件新的蓝色衣裙对她非常般配。
    The new blue dress becomes her very well.
16. 这件上衣对他很般配。
    The coat becomes him very well.
17. 这身衣着跟你的身份几乎不般配。
    This dress hardly becomes a person in your position.

“般配”或“班配”的第二个意思是“两件衣物颜色、图案或风格匹配，放在一起显得帅”。英语可以译为 to match，它的意思是 to have the same colour, pattern, or style and therefore look attractive。例如：

18. 她身穿一件与她的手套般配的黑色短夹克。
    She wears a short, black jacket which matches with her gloves.
19. 她的靴子与她的衣服不般配。
    Her boots do not match with her outfit.

84 撞墙、撞锁

汉语关键词： 撞墙、碰墙、碰壁、碰钉子、碰一鼻子灰、撞锁、吃闭门羹

英语关键词： go to the wall, butt against, knock against a wall, run into a wall, meet with a setback, suffer a setback, meet with a rebuff, be rebuffed, meet rejection, find the door locked, find that sb is not in，find a locked door, have the door slammed in one’s face, be denied entrance at the door

句子： 他想走后门找工作，但是撞墙了。

误译： He tried to get a job through backdoor dealings, but he went to the wall.

正译： He tried to get a job through backdoor dealings, but he met with a rebuff.

解释：

这句话里的“撞墙”的意思是“遭到拒绝”。而to go to the wall与比赛相关的意思是to lose a conflict, to be defeated，即“失败”、“败北”或“输掉”；与做生意相关的意思是to fail because of lack of money，指一个公司或组织“因缺乏资金而生意失败”。均与“遭到拒绝”没有关系。例如：

1. 尽管他们努力了，但是还是输了。
   In spite of their efforts, they went to the wall.
2. 当这个公司最终生意失败时，没有人感到惊讶。
   No one was surprised when the company finally went to the wall.

“撞墙”的第一个意思是“碰到墙上”，也可以说“碰墙”。英语可以译为to butt against, to knock against a wall, to run into a wall。例如：

3. 他头疼得厉害，直想撞墙。
   His head ached so badly that he wanted to butt against a wall.
4. 我不知道为什么这辆汽车撞墙了。
   I wonder why this car knocked against a wall.
5. 他走到死胡同的尽头，结果撞墙了。
   He walked to the end of a blind alley and ran into a wall.

“撞墙”的第二个意思是“遭遇严重阻碍或挫折”，也可以说“碰壁”。英语可以译为to meet with a setback, to suffer a setback。例如：

6. 即使我撞了墙，我也将努力不丧失信心。
   Even if I meet with a setback, I will try not to lose my confidence

7. 那些不诚实的人可能会成功一时，但他们早晚会碰壁。
Those dishonest people may succeed for a time, but sooner or later, they will suffer a setback.
8. 虽一再撞墙，但他依旧情绪高昂。
Although he has suffered setbacks again and again, he is still in high spirits.

“撞墙”的第三个意思是“遭遇拒绝或斥责”，也可以说“碰钉子”或“碰一鼻子灰”。英语可以译为 to meet with a rebuff, to be rebuffed, to meet rejection。例如：

9. 他没想到会在朋友面前碰钉子。
He didn't expect to meet with a rebuff in front of his friends.
10. 由于这件事不好办，他四处撞墙。
As the matter is difficult to deal with, he has been rebuffed everywhere.
11. 他到一家高科技公司求职，因学历低而碰了一鼻子灰。
He went to look for a job in a high-tech company, but met rejection because of his low qualification.

“撞锁”的意思是“登门找人时，对方的门锁着”。英语可以译为 to find the door locked, to find that sb is not in。例如：

12. 昨天我去拜访我的一位朋友，结果撞锁了。
Yesterday I went to visit a friend of mine only to find the door locked.
13. 我去了他家两趟，都撞锁了。
I have been to his house twice, and found that he was not in.

“吃闭门羹”的意思是“登门找人时，对方的门锁着”，或“被主人拒之门外”。英语可以译为 to find a locked door, to have the door slammed in one' s face, to be denied entrance at the door。例如：

14. 我昨天去拜访你家，可是吃了闭门羹。
Yesterday I went to visit your house only to find a locked door.
15. 他是个挨门挨户的推销员，但是常常吃闭门羹。
He was a door-to-door salesman, but he often had the door slammed in his face.
16. 因为他不是俱乐部会员，而吃了闭门羹。
He was denied entrance at the door because he was not a member of the club.

85 走光、跑光

汉语关键词：走光、跑光、漏光

英语关键词：go away, leave, clear off, wardrobe malfunction, wardrobe mishap, run away, flee away, go flat, run out （of）, be exposed to light

句子：这个影星的走光事件已引起公众关注。

误译：The incident of the film star's accidental exposure has drawn public attention.

正译：The incident of the film star's wardrobe malfunction has drawn public attention.

解释：

这句话的"走光"的意思是"衣服没盖住隐私部位的一种委婉说法"。而 accidental exposure 的意思是"意外暴露",语义太泛,不能表达出"走光"的委婉含义。

"走光"的第一个意思是"全都走开了"，是一个群体的动作。英语可以译为 to go away, to leave, to clear off。例如：

1. 酒席散了，客人都走光了。
   When the feast was over, the guests all went away.
2. 电影散场了，观众很快就走光了。
   When the film show was over, the viewers soon left the cinema.
3. 演出还没有结束，观众就已经走光了。
   The audience had all left before the performance finished.
4. 徒弟们从心底里看不上这门手艺活，最后他们都走光了。
   As the apprentices looked down upon the trade from the bottom of their hearts, they all left their master at last.
5. 住在这个偏远山村的居民因为泥石流都走光了。
   The people living in this remote mountainous village all cleared off because of debris flow.

"走光"的第二个意思是"由于不经意的行为或动作使自己的隐私部位曝光"。英语可以译为 wardrobe malfunction, wardrobe mishap。wardrobe 的意思是"衣柜"，malfunction 的意思是"运转失常"，mishap 的意思是"小事故"。衣柜出现故障或小事故，暗指事先没有发现服装的问题，结果在公众场合走光。例如：

6. "走光"是一个字眼，用来描述由于衣服的一个或若干部件的缺陷而使身体的一个或若干私密部位意外暴露。
   Wardrobe malfunction is a term used to describe the accidental exposure

of an intimate part or parts of the body due to a defect in an article or articles of clothing.

7. “走光”是一个委婉语，用来描述由于某人(特别是艺人)衣服的缺陷或在换衣服时造成的失误引起的过分暴露的意外情况。
Wardrobe malfunction is a euphemism for an accidental instance of indecent exposure caused by a fault in someone's clothing (especially that of a performer) or by an error made while changing costumes.
8. 有些名人走光是意外之事，而另一些名人走光看上去则是纯属故意。
Some celebrity wardrobe malfunctions were accidental while others look to be purely intentional.
9. 对穿衣服缺乏准备的人来说，走光是经常发生的事。
Wardrobe malfunctions happen frequently for people wearing costumes because of lack of preparation.
10. 你应该检查你的衣服，看有没有最终会使你走光的磨平的斑点、拉长的布丝、破洞以及其他问题。
You should check your clothing for worn spots, pulls, holes and other problems that can turn into eventual wardrobe malfunctions.
11. 这位影星在面对几百万观众领大奖时不慎走光而狼狈不堪。
The movie star suffered an embarrassing wardrobe mishap while collecting a big award in front of millions.

“跑光”的第一个意思是“全都跑开了”，是一个群体的动作。英语可以译为 to run away, to flee away。例如：

12. 城管一来，路边的无照小商贩就跑光了。
No sooner when the urban management officers had appeared, than all the small unlicenced traders by the side of the road ran away.
13. 警察来封闭这个赌场之前，赌徒都跑光了。
Before the police came to close down the gambling house, all the gamblers had fled away.
14. 在鬼子进村之前，村民们都跑光了。
Before the Japs arrived at the village, all the villagers had fled away.
15. 一场暴雨冲破了鱼池，结果鳝鱼全部跑光了。
A storm broke down the fish-pond, and as a result, all the eels fled away from it.

“跑光”的第二个意思是“气体或液体全都漏完了”或“燃料全都耗尽了”。英语可以译为 to go flat, to run out (of)。例如：

16. 这个汽车轮胎的气都跑光了。
The tyre of the car has gone flat.

17. 一个充氢气的气球比一个充普通空气的气球更快地气就跑光了。
A hydrogen-filled balloon goes flat more quickly than an ordinary air-filled one.
18. 香槟酒一开瓶，气就跑光了。
Champagne goes flat once opened.
19. 当泡沫挥发了，香槟酒很快气就跑光了。
When the bubbles escape, champagne goes flat fairly quickly.
20. 啤酒受热时，气就跑光了。
Beer goes flat when it gets warm.
21. 如果啤酒气跑光了，就把它扔了吧。
If beer goes flat, just toss it out.
22. 鱼缸破了，水都跑光了。
As the fish bowl was broken, all its water ran out.
23. 在回家路上，我的汽车汽油跑光了。
On my way home, my car ran out of petrol.

"跑光"的第三个意思是"感光材料（如感光纸、胶片）因封闭不严而感光"，也说"漏光"。英语可以译为 to be exposed to light。例如：

24. 由于感光纸已经跑光，现在没有什么用处了。
As the sensitive paper has been exposed to light, it is now useless.
25. 这胶片是照片欠曝、过曝，还是跑光了？
Is the photographic film under-exposed, over-exposed or exposed to light?

86 民间

汉语关键词： 民间、民间资本

英语关键词： folk, private, private capital, of the people, between the people, people-to-people, non-governmental, non-state

句子： 民间资本将可以进入垄断行业。

误译： Folk capital will have access to monopoly industries.

正译： 1) Private capital will have access to monopoly industries.
2) Monopoly industries will be accessible to private capital.

解释：

作为形容词，folk 的第一个意思是 traditional and typical of the ordinary people or a country or community，与普通百姓的传统有关；第二个意思是 based on the beliefs of ordinary people，与普通百姓的信仰有关。这两个意思都与资本无关。其实，“民间资本”与“国有资本”或“公有资本”相对立，就是“私人资本”，应译为 private capital。

“民间”的第一个意思是“人民中间的”、“老百姓的”。英语可以译为 folk, of the people。例如：

1. 这位学者终生献身于研究中国西北的民间文学。
   This scholar devoted his whole life to the study of folk literature in Northwest China.
2. 民间艺术现在正在复兴。
   Folk art is currently enjoying a renaissance.
3. 这是在中国讲给儿童听的一个流行的民间故事。
   This is a popular folk story told to the children in China.
4. 民间故事是源自口头传统的短小故事。
   A folk tale is a short story that comes from the oral tradition.
5. 民间舞蹈是由很少受过或没有受过专业训练的人们在社交典礼上表演的，通常用传统音乐或基于传统音乐的音乐伴奏。
   Folk dances are performed at social functions by people with little or no professional training, often to traditional music or music based on traditional music.
6. 民间音乐是一代一代流传下来的。
   Folk music has been passed down from generation to generation.
7. 一个民间群体集体所做之事就是民间习俗。
   What the members of a folk group do collectively is a folk custom.
8. 每个日本孩子都是听这些民间传说长大的。
   Every Japanese kid grows up listening to these folk legends.
9. 这位民间艺人的内心世界是富有创造性的心灵与一双巧手的完美结合。
   The inner world of this folk artisan is a perfect combination of the creative heart and skillful hands.
10. 托马斯因其用未烧过的泥土塑造雕塑作品而被称作民间艺术家，这些粘土是他从河岸上挖掘而来的。
    Thomas was known as a folk artist for his sculptures made from un-fired clay which he dug out of the banks of the river.
11. 蒜和姜被广泛应用于中国民间医药。
    Garlic and ginger are widely used in Chinese folk medicine.

12. 这个民间验方实用价值极高，并具有方便、简单、廉价和灵验四大特点。
This folk recipe has very high value in practice, featured with convenience, simplicity, cheapness and effectiveness.
13. 我通常使用民间验方加上手边的药草或动物来制药。
I usually make medicine using a folk remedy with herbs or animals nearby.
14. 这种药草常被用作治疗蛇咬伤的民间药物。
This kind of herb is often used as folk medicine to cure snake bite.
15. 民间智慧并不总是像它显现的那样正确。
Folk wisdom is not always right as it seems.
16. 这位影星的粉丝们都把他看作是民间英雄。
The movie star’s fans all see him as a folk hero.
17. 各级政府官员应该关注民间疾苦。
Governmental officials at all levels should show concern for the hardships of the people.

“民间”的第二个意思是“人民之间的”。英语可以译为 between the people, people-to-people。例如：

18. 两国民间一直有定期往来。
There has been regular coming and going between the people of the two countries.
19. 中日两国民间的交往不断增加。
There has been increasing communication between the people of China and Japan.
20. 民间外交是中国整体外交的一个重要部分。
People-to-people diplomacy is an important part of China’s overall diplomacy.
21. 人民调解委员会帮助调解民间纠纷时，不收取任何费用。
When the people’s conciliation board helps to settle a dispute between the people, it will not charge them.

“民间”的第三个意思是“非政府的”。英语可以译为 non-governmental。例如：

22. 这个民间组织不是政府的一部分，因为它独立于政府而运作。
The non-governmental organization is not a part of a government as it operates independently of government.
23. 几天以前，几个民间团体聚在一起向教育部发出一系列公开信，提出他们关于教育改革的建议。
A few days ago, several non-governmental groups came together to send a series of open letters to the Ministry of Education to present their proposals about educational reform.

24. 经过反复谈判，双方签署了一项民间贸易协定。
After repeated negotiations, the two sides finally signed a non-governmental trade agreement.
25. 通过民间协商，双方达成一致协议来解决争端。
Through the consultation on a non-governmental basis, the two sides reached a unanimous agreement to settle the dispute.

“民间”的第四个意思是“非国有的”或“私有的”。英语可以译为 non-state, private。例如：

26. 在中国，民间资本正在影视业起着越来越重要的作用。
In China, non-state capital is playing a more and more important role in movie and television industries.
27. 政府将更加重视民间资本在经济可持续发展中的作用。
The government will attach more importance to the role private capital plays in the sustainable development of economy.

87 跳槽

汉语关键词： 跳槽、不断地跳槽、跳槽者

英语关键词： go to another trough for fodder, abandon one’s job for another, drop onc’s job for a new one, make a job move, job-jump, job-hop, change one’s job, change one’s career, career-hop, job jumping, career jumping, job hopping, career hopping, job change, career shift, jump from job to job, jump from company to company, jump from career to career, skip from job to job, skip from company to company, skip from career to career, job-hopper, career-changer, find a new partner

句子： 在当代社会，跳槽是一件司空见惯的事。

误译： In contemporary society, job hoping is a very common thing.

正译： In contemporary society, job hopping is a very common thing.

解释：

“跳槽”应译为 job hopping。本文 job hoping 的 hoping 是个拼写错误。hop 的意思是“蹦蹦跳跳”，是个闭音节单词，后加 -ing 时要双写末尾字母 p，成为 hopping。而 hope 的意思是“希望”，是个开音节单词，后加 -ing 时要去掉末尾字母 e，成为 hoping。

“跳槽”的第一个意思是“牲口离开原来所在的槽头到别的槽头争食”。英语可以译为 to go to another trough for fodder。例如：

1. 这匹马经常跳槽争食。
The horse often goes to a neighbouring trough for fodder.

“跳槽”的第二个意思是比喻“人离开原来的职业或单位，改变职业或到别的单位”。在当代社会，换工作、换单位和换职业是司空见惯之事，英语表达方法极为丰富。动词可以译为 to abandon one's job for another（换工作），to drop one's job for a new one（换工作），to make a job move（换工作），to job-jump（换工作），to job-hop（换工作），to change one's job（换工作），to change one's career（换职业），to career-hop（换职业）。名词可以译为 job jumping（换工作），career jumping（换职业），job hopping（换工作），career hopping（换职业），job change（换工作），career shift（换职业）。例如：

2. 这个单位的一些研究人员跳槽经商去了。
Some research workers from this unit have abandoned their jobs to go in for business.
3. 他不满意目前的工作，想跳槽。
As he is not content with his current job, he plans to drop it for a new one.
4. 为了多挣一点钱，他打算跳槽。
In order to earn more money, he intended to make a job move.
5. 不管你的理由是什么，彻底权衡利弊再跳槽是很重要的。
Whatever your reason, it's important to weigh the pros and cons thoroughly before you make a job move.
6. 一半以上的美国工人说他们计划形势一好转就跳槽。
More than half of the American workers say they plan to job-jump, as soon as times get better.
7. 雇员们常常因为公司倒闭而不得不跳槽，而且他们不得不在被解雇之前提早一步跳槽。
Employees often have to job-jump because of businesses shutting down, and they also have to job-jump to stay one step ahead of layoffs.
8. 约翰跳槽去了一家著名的计算机公司。
John job-hopped to a famous computer company.
9. 这个年青人想跳槽，但是机会还没有来。
The young man wanted to change his job, but the chance didn't come.
10. 这位专家认为一个平常人一辈子可能跳八次槽。
The expert holds that an average person may change his career eight different times over their lifetime.

11. 这种新思维叫做“策略性跳槽”，它正在取代“沿公司梯子向上爬”以获得晋升的理念。
This new thinking is called strategic job jumping, which is replacing the concept of climbing the Corporate Ladder in order to get promotions.
12. 在有工作的专业人员中间，跳槽已经成为一种司空见惯、而且可以接受的做法。
Career jumping has become a common and acceptable practice among working professionals.
13. 跳槽在高科技界比其他行业更为司空见惯和更被人接受。
Job hopping is more common and accepted in the high-tech world than in other industries.
14. 跳槽对这个年青人来说，曾是一种生活方式。
Career hopping has been a way of life for this young man.
15. 我听说人们谈论他们梦想的工作。我很幸运我在跳槽五年之后找到了我梦想的工作。
I hear people talking about their dream jobs. I am thankful that I have found mine after career hopping for five years.
16. 我问应试者为什么要跳槽。
I asked the interviewee why he was looking for a job change.
17. 突然跳槽常常是痛苦的，而且在经济上是灾难性的。
Sudden career shifts are often painful and financially disastrous.

“不断地跳槽”，英语可以译为 to jump from job to job(不断地换工作), to jump from company to company(不断地换公司), to jump from career to career(不断地换职业), to skip from job to job(不断地换工作), to skip from company to company(不断地换公司), to skip from career to career(不断地换职业)。例如：

18. 不断地跳槽是不容易的，而这也不总是一个好主意。
It isn’t easy to jump from job to job, nor is it always a good idea.
19. 年轻一些的专业人员更容易不断地跳槽来建立职业生涯，而年老一些的专业人员则更可能坚守到底。
The younger professionals are more apt to jump from company to company in an effort to build a career while the older ones are more likely to stay the course.
20. 人们因为不满意和不高兴而不断地跳槽，是司空见惯的事。
It is very common for people to jump from career to career being dissatisfied and unhappy.
21. 这个青年人乐于不断地跳槽，以寻求最高的收益。
The young man is happy to skip from job to job in search of the highest

benefits.

22. 如果你连续不断地跳槽，许多公司可能会不雇用你。
If you keep skipping from job to job, a lot of companies may not hire you.
23. 今天，许多年青人不断地跳槽，而不是一辈子替一个组织工作。
Today, many young people skip from company to company rather than work for one organization for life.
24. 许多人不断地跳槽，而不是呆在一家公司直至退休。
Many people skip from career to career instead of sticking with one company through retirement.

“跳槽者”，英语可以译为 job-hopper, career-changer。例如：

25. 人们会质疑经常跳槽者的诚信和忠诚。
People may question regular job-hoppers' integrity and loyalty.
26. 他一直是个经常跳槽者，大多数工作都不超过一年。
He has been a chronic job-hopper and held most of his jobs for less than one year.
27. 有些跳槽者可能直到他们适应了新的工作才会挣更多的钱。
Some career-changers may earn less until they become accustomed to their new jobs.

“跳槽”的第三个意思是指“在爱情上喜新厌旧，见异而迁”。英语可以译为 to find a new partner。例如：

28. 这对小两口结婚后一吵架，不是男的说想散伙，就是女的说想跳槽。
Whenever the young couple quarreled with each other after their marriage, the husband would say he wanted to get divorced while the wife would say she wanted to find a new partner.

88 走调儿

汉语关键词： 走调儿、跑调儿、不走调儿、音准、调音、调弦、调音师

英语关键词： can't carry a tune, can't carry a tune in a bushel, can't carry a tune in a bucket, can't carry a tune in a paper sack, fail to carry a tune, can carry a tune, sing in tune, go out of tune, be out of tune, stay in tune, be in tune, tune, tune up, check the tuning, key up, tuner

句子： 我五音不全，唱歌爱走调儿。

误译： Being tone-deaf, I tend to go out of tune.

正译： 1) Being tone-deaf, I often fail to carry a tune.

2) As I am tone-deaf, my singing tends to go out of tune.

解释：

“走调儿”具有人唱歌时音不准和乐器音不准两层意思。to go out of tune 的主语为乐器时，指乐器音不准。如果想说人唱歌时音不准，主语不能用人称代词，而要用 one's singing。

“走调儿”的第一个意思是“人唱歌或唱戏不合调子”，也说“跑调儿”。英语可以译为 can't carry a tune, to fail to carry a tune。注意 can't carry a tune 的意思为 to be unable to sing a simple melody，即“连简单旋律都不会唱”，有 can't carry a tune in a bushel, can't carry a tune in a bucket, can't carry a tune in a paper sack 等变体。例如：

1. 他唱个简单曲子都走调儿。
   He cannot carry even a simple tune.
2. 我多么希望我弟弟不要试着唱。他走调儿。
   I wish that my brother wouldn't try to sing. He can't carry a tune.
3. 我不知道为什么玛丽会在唱诗班里。她走调儿。
   I don't know why Mary's in the choir. She can't carry a tune in a bushel.
4. 杰克喜欢淋浴时唱歌，尽管他走调儿。
   Jack likes to sing in the shower, though he can't carry a tune in a bucket.
5. 我来试着给你哼唱这支歌，可是我走调儿。
   I'd try to hum the song for you, but I can't carry a tune in a paper sack.
6. 他五音不全，因此常常走调儿。
   He is so tone-deaf that he often fails to carry a tune.
7. 甚至那些耳朵对音乐敏感的人都可能走调儿。
   Even those people who have a good musical ear may fail to carry a tune properly.
8. 当有几位欠缺音乐天赋的歌手走调儿时，这个过程有点痛苦。
   The process is a little painful when some of the less musically gifted singers fail to carry a tune.

唱歌“不走调儿”，英语可以译为 can carry a tune, to sing in tune。例如：

9. 一项新的研究说百分之九十五的人确实不走调。
   A new study says 90 percent of people can indeed carry a tune.
10. 他们中间没有一个人唱歌不走调儿。
    None of them could sing in tune.

“走调儿”的第二个意思是“乐器的音不准”。英语可以译为 to go out of tune, to be out of tune。例如：

11. 温度变化和潮湿可能使钢琴走调儿。
Changes in temperature and humidity may cause a piano to go out of tune.
12. 在一场音乐会中，吉他可能走调儿好几次。
A guitar can go out of tune several times during a concert.
13. 吉他、特别是便宜一点的吉他，容易很快就走调。
Guitars, particularly cheaper ones, tend to go out of tune quickly.
14. 过一段时间以后，小提琴就会走调儿，而且声音难听。
In time a violin goes out of tune, and sounds awful.
15. 管乐器容易走调，主要是因为乐器里面的空气在演奏时会变暖。
Wind instruments tend to go out of tune mostly because the air inside the instrument gets warm as the instrument is played.
16. 我发现他演奏的每个音符都走调儿，差1/4度音。
I find every note he plays is out of tune by a 1/4 tone.

“音准”的意思是乐器“不走调儿”。英语可以译为 to stay in tune, to be in tune。例如：

17. 钢琴比大多数弦乐乐器音准。
Pianos stay in tune much better than most stringed instruments.
18. 保证做到在你开始演奏以前，小提琴音准。
Make sure the violin is in tune before you start to play it.

“调音”的意思是“把弦乐器调整到合乎规定的恰当音阶”，也称“调弦”。英语可以译为 to tune, to tune up, to check the tuning, to key up。例如：

19. 为钢琴调音需要技巧。
It takes skill to tune a piano.
20. 这架钢琴走调了，需要调音。
The piano has gone out of tune, and it needs tuning.
21. 他正在教我如何给吉他调音。
He is teaching me how to tune a guitar.
22. 管弦乐队正在调音，音乐会马上就要开始。
The orchestra is tuning up and the concert is about to begin.
23. 因为吉他容易很快就走调，你每次演奏时应该调音。
Because guitars tend to go out of tune quickly, you should check the tuning every time you play.
24. 这架钢琴需要调音。
This piano wants keying up.

"调音师"，英语可以译为 tuner 。例如：

25. 这位钢琴调音师正在给钢琴调音。
The piano tuner is tuning the piano.
26. 为钢琴家调音是钢琴调音师的责任。
It is the piano tuner's responsibility to tune the instrument for the pianist.

89

团购

汉语关键词：团购、网络团购、大宗采购

英语关键词：team buying, team purchasing, group buying, group purchasing, group purchase，team buying on the Internet, group buying on the Web，bulk buying

句子：有些人认为团购真的能改变我们购物的方式。

误译：Some people think bulk buying can really change the way we shop.

正译：Some people think team buying can really change the way we shop.

解释：

"团购"需要"众多零散消费者"、"较低价格"和"大批量"等三个因素。bulk buying 具有"大宗采购"的意思，只涉及"较低价格"和"大批量"等两个因素，而不管购物者有多少人，买主可以是个人，也可以是群体。team buying 包含上述三个因素，为"团购"的正确译法。

1. 大宗采购是大批购买产品，比小量购买所需的单件商品价格或单位价格要便宜。
Bulk purchasing is buying products in large quantities at a lower price per item, or unit price, than is available for smaller quantities.
2. 大多数已发生的大宗采购是由个人投资者进行的，他们在寻求巨大的投资机会。
Most of the bulk buying that's been happening is being done by individual investors, who are seeking great investment opportunity.

"团购"的意思是"将具有相同购买意向的零散消费者集合起来，向厂商进行大批量购买的行为"，即"团体购物"。英语可以译为 team buying, team purchasing, group buying, group purchasing, group purchase。例如：

3. 团购描述消费者集合起来向一个零售商购买商品的行为。
Team buying describes the action of consumers grouping together to buy

items from a single retailer.

4. 团购已给中国的网络购物增添了新的内容。
Team buying has added new dimension to China's online shopping.
5. 在中国，人们正在注视团购的蔓延。
In China, people are watching the spread of team buying.
6. 像传统的网络购物一样，团购提供比较便宜的价格，伴随着与具有相似兴趣的人们一起购物的机会。
Like traditional online shopping, team buying offers cheaper prices, along with the chance to shop with people of similar interests.
7. 团购能将消费者集合起来，获得团体折扣。
Team purchasing can bring consumers together and get a group discount.
8. 团购是当今消费行为学中的一个重要现象。
Group buying is now an important new phenomenon in the science of consumption behavior.
9. 团购指的是消费者汇集他们打算购买意向以取得折扣的现象。
Group buying refers to the phenomenon in which consumers aggregate their intended purchases to get a bargain.
10. 团购是由一组独立的消费者集体参与购买产品或服务。
Group purchasing is the collective participation in buying products or services by a group of independent consumers.
11. 团购是网络购物的一种新方式，它在年青人中间变得越来越流行。
Group purchase is a new way to buy things on the Internet, which is becoming more and more popular among young people.

“网络团购”，英语可以译为team buying on the Internet, group buying on the Web。例如：

12. 网络团购现在是团购的主要方式，在国际上通称为B2T(企业对团队)。
Team buying on the Internet is now the main form of team buying, which is internationally known as business-to-team.
13. 近两年来随着电子商务的发展，网络团购在中国网民中流行起来。
With the development of E-commerce over the last two years, team buying on the Internet has become popular among the netizens in China.
14. 尽管网络团购的出现只有两年多时间，却已成为在网民中流行的一种新消费方式。
Although it has been only two years since the emergence of team buying on the Internet, it has become a new way of consumption popular among the netizens.
15. 现在通过网上零售商进行你的网络团购是很容易的。
It is easy now to do your personal team buying on the Internet through

the on-the-Internet retailers.

16. 这位专家指出网络团购其实并不是一个什么新理念。
The expert points out that group buying on the Web is actually not a new concept.

90

偶像

汉语关键词： 偶像、青春偶像、偶像演员、偶像剧、偶像崇拜

英语关键词： idol，icon，teen idol, young idol, youth idol，idol actor, idol actress, matinée idol，idol drama, idol play, idolize

句子： 这个童星作为青春偶像崭露头角。

误译： The child star made his debut as a youth idol.

正译： The child star made his debut as a young idol.

解释：

child star（童星）指 child actor（儿童演员）或 child singer（儿童歌手），属于童年期。youth 指“青年”，比童年期儿童的岁数要大。说 child star 是 youth idol，不太合适。“青春偶像”有不同译法。teen idol 指 13 岁到 19 岁的青少年偶像演员；youth idol 泛指青年偶像演员；young 的意思比较宽泛，指 consisting of young people or young children。young idol 的年龄跨度比较大，包括儿童偶像演员和青年偶像演员。

“偶像”的第一个意思是“用木头、泥土等雕塑的神像”。英语可以译为 idol。例如：

1. 这个人说当他崇拜一个偶像时，他不是在崇拜这个偶像自身，而是崇拜偶像所代表的神力。
The man said when he worships an idol, he is not worshiping the idol itself, but the divine force represented in the idol.
2. 他宁死也不肯跪在泥塑偶像前面。
He would rather die than kneel before an idol of clay.
3. 当地人建造了一尊神的偶像，作为崇拜的对象。
The local people built an idol of god as an object of worship.

“偶像”的第二个意思是比喻“人们盲目崇拜的对象”。英语可以译为 idol。例如：

4. 这个小男孩把老师看作他的偶像。
The little boy considers the teacher as his idol.
5. 这位足球运动员是许多年轻人的偶像。
The football player is the idol of many young people.

“偶像崇拜”，英语可以译为 to idolize。例如：

6. 这个小男孩把父亲当偶像崇拜。
The young boy idolizes his father.
7. 我们不要把伟人当作偶像来崇拜。
We must not idolize great people.

“偶像”的第三个意思是指“人们喜爱的演员、歌手等”。英语可以译为 idol, icon。例如：

8. 那位女演员的粉丝们伸长了脖子来看一眼他们的偶像。
The fans of the actress craned their necks to catch a glimpse of their idol.
9. 披头士乐队是20世纪60年代流行音乐的偶像。
The Beatles were the pop idols of the 1960's.
10. 麦当娜是20世纪80年代流行音乐的偶像。
Madonna was the pop icon of the 1980's.
11. 他是为音像时代设计和造就出来的流行音乐的偶像。
He is a pop icon designed and manufactured for the video generation.

“青春偶像”，英语可以译为 teen idol, young idol, youth idol。例如：

12. 这个男孩的卧室用许多青春偶像的海报装饰着。
The boy's bedroom is decorated with a lot of posters of teen idols.
13. 这个青春偶像歌手已在高中生中间变得非常受欢迎。
This young idol singer has become very popular among high school students.
14. 这些不足12岁的儿童应邀参加了这个青春偶像竞赛。
These kids with an age not over 12 were invited to join the Young Idol Contest.
15. 这个选美比赛造就了许多青春偶像。
The beauty contest produced many popular youth idols.

“偶像演员”，英语可以译为 idol actor, idol actress, matinée idol。例如：

16. 你最喜欢的超级偶像演员是谁？
Who is your favorite super idol actor?
17. “偶像演员”是一个主要用来描述被其粉丝们喜爱到吹捧地步的电影或戏剧明星的名词。

Matinée idol is a term used mainly to describe film or theatre stars who are adored to the point of adulation by their fans.

18. 她说她的最大期望之一是跟她的偶像女演员一道，在一部电影里扮演一个角色。
    She said one of her biggest aspirations is to play a role in a film, alongside her idol actress.
19. 作为一个偶像演员，这位电影明星受到他的粉丝们的大力赞赏。
    As a matinee idol, the movie star is greatly admired by his fans.

“偶像剧”，英语可以译为 idol drama, idol play。例如：

20. 这个美国偶像剧发生在一个宾馆的大堂里。
    This American idol drama took place at the lobby of a hotel.
21. 昨晚，我在首尔去一个剧院观看韩国偶像剧。
    Last night, I went to see the South Korean idol play at a theatre in Souel.

91 底线

汉语关键词： 底线、底限、盈利、底价、端线、内线、卧底

英语关键词： bottom line, end line, back line，base line, backcourt boundary, stooge, planted agent, stool pigeon

句子： 这名足球运动员将球踢出底线。

误译： The footballer kicked the ball out of the bottom line.

正译： The footballer kicked the ball out of the end line.

解释：

在这里不可以将“底线”字对字译为 bottom line，因为 bottom line 与球类运动场地无关。

bottom line 有三个意思。其一是 the last line of a financial statement, used for showing net profit or loss，即“财务账目表上最下面的一行，用来表示盈亏数目”；或 net profit or loss，即“盈利”或“亏损”。例如：

1. The bottom line for 2009 of our company was pre-tax profit of $ 20 million.
   2009年本公司盈利状况是税前利润2,000万美元。
2. Sales last season failed to add to the company’s bottom line.
   上季度的销售额没能够使公司的盈利增加。

3. How will the rise in interest rates affect our bottom line?
利率提高会对我们的盈利产生什么影响？

bottom line 的第二个意思是 the deciding or crucial factor 或 the most important thing that one must consider or accept，即“决定因素或关键因素”或“必须考虑或接受的最重要的事物”，相当于“底限”或“底线”。例如：

4. The bottom line is that we have to increase our sales or we'll take a cut in pay.
底线是我们必须增加销售额，否则我们就要削减工资。
5. The bottom line is that we must get more customers in the next few months, or we'll go out of business.
底线是我们在今后几个月里必须招揽更多的顾客，否则我们就要倒闭。
6. If you don't make a profit, you'll go out of business. That's the bottom line.
如果你不盈利，你就会倒闭。这就是底线。
7. We will do all we can to relieve the symptoms of the patients and reduce fatality. That is the bottom line for us doctors and nurses.
我们将竭尽全力减轻病人的症状和降低死亡率。这就是我们医生和护士的底线。
8. Our hospital's bottom line in treating inpatients is 5,000.
我们医院治疗住院病人的底线是5,000。
9. That there is but only one China in the world is our bottom line.
世界上只有一个中国，这是我们的底线。
10. Diaoyu Islands are China's sacred and inviolable territory. That is our bottom line.
钓鱼岛是中国的神圣不可侵犯的领土。这是我们的底线。

bottom line 的第三个意思是 the lowest price or the lowest acceptable amount of money that you are willing to pay or take for something 或 the least amount of money regarded as acceptable in a business deal，即“底价”。例如：

11. — What's your bottom line for selling the car?
你卖这辆车的底价是多少？
— I can go down to $ 10,000.
我可以最低降到10,000美元。）

“底线”的第一个意思是“足球、篮球、排球、网球、羽毛球等运动场地两端的界线”，又称“端线”。英语可以译为 end line(足球、篮球、排球),back line(排球、网球)，base line(网球、羽毛球)，backcourt boundary(羽毛球)。例如：

12. 如果进攻队员将球踢过底线，防守队员可以在底线任何地方发球门球。
If the offensive team kicks the ball across the end line, the defense gets a goal kick from anywhere on the end line.
13. 这名篮球运动员从底线后的地方将球传给他的一位队友。
The basketball player passed the ball from the place behind the end line to one of his teammates.
14. 在排球比赛中，发球员在发球时可以在底线后面自由移动。
In a volleyball game, the server may move freely behind the end line when serving.
15. 排球发球员的脚不能踩底线或穿越底线。
The volleyball server's foot cannot touch or cross the back line.
16. 这个网球运动员还没来得及救，球就已经落在底线上。
The ball had fallen on the back line before the tennis player could save it.
17. 这名网球发球员站在底线后面，将球抛入空中，斜线击球，使球飞过球网，落入对方发球区。
The tennis server, standing behind the base line, throws the ball into the air and bats it diagonally over the net into his opponent's service court.
18. 这位羽毛球运动员发现他难以在两步之内到达底线。
The badminton player found himself hard in reaching the base line within two steps.
19. 底线用作羽毛球单打的后发球线。
The back boundary line serves as the long service line for the single badminton play.

"底线"的第二个意思是指"最低的条件"或"最低的限度"，也作"底限"。英语可以译为 bottom line, base line。例如：

20. 在谈判中，我们不会低于我们的底线。
We won't go lower than our bottom line in the negotiation.
21. 显然，他在力图试探我们的价位底线。
Obviously, he was trying to test our bottom line for pricing?
22. 谈判底线是谈判策略的组成部分。
The bottom line for negotiation is part of the negotiation strategy.
23. 一个卖家为谈判目的的底线可能是绝密的。
A seller's bottom line for negotiation purposes may be confidential.
24. 公正分配是市场经济的道德底线。。
Fair distribution is the bottom line of morality in market economy.
25. 在我们社会各个领域，诚实是道德的底线。
In every area of our society, honesty is the bottom line of morality.

26. 人们的头像、真实姓名和简介应该放在他们的公开评论旁边，从而确立责任底线。
People's faces, real names and brief biographies should be placed next to their public comments, so as to establish a base line of responsibility.

"底线"的第三个意思是指"暗藏在对方内部刺探情报或进行其他活动的人"，也作"内线"或"卧底"。英语可以译为 stooge, planted agent, stool pigeon。例如：

27. 他在敌人司令部充当底线。
He acted as a planted agent in the enemy's headquarters.
28. 为了获取秘密情报，他在与之竞争的公司里安插了一名底线。
In order to gain secret information, he planted a stooge in his competing business.
29. 这名政客为了个人的政治利益在政府里安插了一个底线。
The politician planted a stooge in the government for personal political interests.
30. 一些历史记录表明这名底线在敌人中间潜伏下来，充当一名政府官员。
Some historical records suggested this stool pigeon hid among his enemies and acted as a government official.

92 人口

汉语关键词：人口、人口普查、群体调查、人口学、人口贩子

英语关键词：population, census, population investigation, demography, number of family members, family size, human trafficker

句子：我国已开始第六次人口普查。

误译：China has started her sixth national population investigation.

正译：China has started her sixth national (population) census.

解释：

population 可以泛指 all the people living in a particular area, city or country，即"地区、城市或国家人口"，也可以特指 a particular group of people，即"特定群体"。population investigation 多指"群体调查"，与流行病有关，没有"人口普查"的含义。

1. 这个小组在三个地区进行了群体调查，发现那里存在细菌感染的疾病的风险。
   The team has made a population investigation in three districts and found there a risk of illness for bacterial infection.

census 的意思是the process of officially counting sth, especially a country' s population, and recording various facts,具有“人口普查”的含义。不一定要说 population census。

“人口”的第一个意思是“居住在一定地区内的人的总数”。英语可以译为 population。例如：

2. 这个城市有将近三百万的人口。
   This city has a population of nearly three million.
3. 这个地区人口稠密。
   This area has a dense population.
4. 与其面积相比，加拿大人口稀少。
   For its size, Canada has a small population.

“人口”的第二个意思是“生活在一定社会生产方式、时间和地域，实现其生命活动并构成社会生活主体，具有一定数量和质量的人所组成的社会群体”。英语可以译为 population。例如：

5. 中国每10年举行一次人口普查。
   China holds its national population census every 10 years.
6. 一个国家人力资源的质量取决于它的人口构成。
   The quality of human resources in a country depends upon its population composition.
7. 说到人口因素，重要的是人口规模、密度、出生率和年龄分布。
   Speaking of demographic factors, the important ones are population size and its density, birth rate and distribution of ages.
8. 世界人口地图提供世界各地人口密度的概况。
   World population map gives an overview about the population density in various parts of the world.
9. 提高人口素质是一个国家可持续经济发展战略的优先考虑的问题。
   The improvement of population quality is a top priority of a country's sustainable economic development strategy.
10. 高出生率和低死亡率的结合已导致全世界许多国家人口爆炸。
    The combination of high birth rates and low death rates has led to the population explosion in many countries throughout the world.

11. 这位科学家正在研究人口压力对自然资源的影响。
The scientist is studying the impacts of population pressure on natural resources.
12. 在这本书里，作者论述了出生率、死亡率和人口自然增长率。
In this book, the author deals with birth rate, death rate and natural growth rate of population.
13. 人口老龄化意味着流动减少、而依赖性、慢性病及医疗消费增加。
Ageing of population implies decrease in mobility, and increase in dependence, chronic diseases, and medication consumption.
14. 人口增长包括自然增长和移民增长。
Population growth includes natural growth and immigration growth.
15. 一些国家正在经历人口负增长，尤其是在欧洲。
Some countries are experiencing negative population growth, especially in Europe.
16. 我们已目睹人口过剩对生物多样化的毁灭性后果。
We've already witnessed the devastating effects of overpopulation on biodiversity.

"人口学"，英语可以译为demography。例如：

17. 这位学者从事人口学研究。
The scholar is engaged in the study of demography.

"人口"的第三个意思是"一户人家的人的总数"或"家庭规模"。英语可以译为number of family members, family size。例如：

18. 这个地区每户人口平均4人。
The average number of family members in this area is four.
19. 他家人口少，他负担不重。
As his family size is small, his burden is not heavy.

"人口"的第四个意思是"人"或"人的"。英语可以译为human。例如：

20. 这位老奶奶说她们家快添人口了。
The old woman said they would soon have a new born baby.
21. 贩卖人口是严重的社会问题。
Human trafficking is a serious social problem.
22. 贩卖人口是以商业性的性剥削或强迫劳动为目的的买卖人口的非法交易。
Human trafficking is the illegal trade in human beings for the purposes of commercial sexual exploitation or forced labour.

23. 人口出生率取决于营养、性行为、文化、天性、内分泌、时间选择、经济状况、生活方式和情感。
    Human fertility depends on factors of nutrition, sexual behavior, culture, instinct, endocrinology, timing, economics, way of life, and emotions.
24. 这项研究描述了天气对这个国家许多地方人口死亡率的影响。
    This study describes the impact of weather on human mortality at numerous locations in this country.

"人口贩子"，英语可以译为 human trafficker。例如：

25. 这些人口贩子真是可恨。
    These human traffickers are really detestable.
26. 警方正加大力度打击人口贩子。
    The police are intensifying their efforts to crack down on the human traffickers.

"人口"的第五个意思是泛指"众人的嘴"，实指"口碑"。英语字面可以译为 mouth, lips。例如：

27. 莎士比亚的十四行诗脍炙人口。
    Shakespeare's sonnets are in everyone's mouth.
28. 李白的诗歌脍炙人口。
    Li Bai's poems are on everyone's lips.
29. 迈克尔·杰克逊的所有歌曲都是脍炙人口的。
    All of Michael Jackson's songs have won universal praise.
30. 佳名不离人口。
    A person's good fame is much talked about.

93 拐点

汉语关键词： 拐点、刘易斯拐点、转折点

英语关键词： inflection point, turning point, turn, Louise inflection point, Louise turning point, Lewis inflection point, Lewis turning point

句子： 有些经济学家将拐点的数学概念应用于经济学。

误译： Some economists applied the mathematical concept of the turning point to economics.

正译： Some economists applied the mathematical concept of the inflection point to economics.

解释：

turning point 具有“转折点”的意思，不可用作数学术语取代 inflection point，作“拐点”解。

“拐点”的第一个意思是“曲线上凸与下凹的分界点”或“凸曲线与凹曲线的连接点”，为高等数学术语。英语可以译为 inflection point。例如：

1. 在微分学里，拐点是曲线上曲率变换图像的那个点。
   In differential calculus, an inflection point is a point on a curve at which the curvature changes sign.
2. 拐点是曲线凹面由上向下或由下向上变化的那个点。
   An inflection point is a point at which a curve changes from concave up to concave down, or vice-versa.
3. 在这本书里，作者描述了拐点的数学概念，并将其用于商业策略。
   In this book, the author describes the mathematical concept of the inflection point and applies it to business strategy.

“拐点”第二个意思是“某种数值持续向高后转低或者持续向低后转高的转折点”，为经济学术语。英语可以译为 inflection point 。例如：

4. 这位经济学家指出世界在经济方面很可能正在接近拐点。
   The economists points out that the world is probably getting close to the inflection point in the economy soon.
5. 这位经济学教授认为全球工业生产已经达到拐点。
   The professor of economics holds that global industrial production has reached inflection point.

“刘易斯拐点”，指“劳动力过剩向短缺的转折点”。英语可以译为 Louise inflection point, Louise turning point, Lewis inflection point, Lewis turning point。例如：

6. 当农村的剩余劳动力被工业部门吸取殆尽，就会出现“刘易斯拐点”。
   When the rural surplus labour force is totally absorbed by the industry sector, there will appear the Louise inflection point.
7. 在中国经济学家中间，有一场关于中国是否已到达“路易斯拐点”的热烈辩论。
   Among the Chinese economists, there is a heated debate as to whether China has arrived at the Louise inflection point.
8. 有些学者认为由于中国人口红利将近用完，“路易斯拐点”已经临近。
   Some scholars hold that as the Chinese population dividend is nearly

exhausted, the Louise turning point is imminent.

9. 这些经济学家深信虽然我们可能正接近“刘易斯拐点”，但是尚未处于这个拐点。
These economists believe that we are not at the Lewis inflection point yet, although we may be closing to the point.
10. 这位学者认为中国已经达到“刘易斯拐点”。
This scholar argues that China has reached the Lewis turning point.
11. 现在我们听说有一种越来越普遍的论点，说中国正在临近“路易斯拐点”。
Now we hear that there's a growing argument that China is approaching its Lewis turning point.

“拐点”第三个意思是“市场运行中由高价位开始下跌或由低价位开始上升的转折”，为经济学术语。英语可以译为 inflection point。例如：

12. 风险投资人总是在市场寻找拐点，即能使市场大涨或大跌的项目。
Venture capitalists are always looking for inflection points in a market — events that turn a market up or down dramatically.
13. 有些学者认为楼市拐点即将来临。
Some scholars believe that the inflection point is imminent in the real estate market.

“拐点”第四个意思是“事物发展过程中运行趋势或运行速率的变化”。英语可以译为 turn。例如：

14. 企业负债增加是信贷周期走向拐点的第一步。
An increase in corporate indebtedness is the first step towards a turn in the credit cycle.
15. 企业越来越担忧信贷市场将会出现拐点。
Enterprises have shown growing concerns about a turn in the credit markets.

“拐点”第五个意思是“转折点”。英语可以译为 turning point。例如：

16. 我在18岁考入北京大学，这是我人生的拐点。
I was admitted to Peking University at the age of 18, which was a turning point in my life.
17. 自从他跳槽到一家计算机公司，他的职业生涯得到非常顺利的发展。看来这次跳槽是他人生的拐点。
Since he job-hopped to a computer company, his career has had a very smooth development. It seems that this job-hopping is a turning point in his life.

94 恶性

汉语关键词： 恶性、恶性竞争、良性、良性竞争、恶性通货膨胀、超级通货膨胀

英语关键词： malignant, benign, vicious, virtuous, pernicious, grave, cutthroat, galloping inflation, runaway inflation, rampant inflation, malignant inflation, vicious inflation, virulent inflation, boiling inflation, hyperinflation

句子： 最近，这两家公司一直在搞恶性竞争，而不是良性竞争。

误译： Recently, the two companies have been carrying on a malignant competition, instead of a virtuous one.

正译： 1) Recently, the two companies have been carrying on a malignant competition, instead of a benign one.

2) Recently, the two companies have been carrying on a vicious competition, instead of a virtuous one.

解释：

使用反义词时，要注意对应。malignant 的反义词是 benign，如“恶性肿瘤”是 malignant tumour，而“良性肿瘤”是 benign tumour。vicious 的反义词是 virtuous，如“恶性循环”是 vicious circle，而“良性循环”是 virtuous circle。表示“恶性竞争”和“良性竞争”时，要用 malignant competition 和 benign competition，或 vicious competition 和 virtuous competition，不可混淆。

“恶性”的意思是“能产生严重或危险后果的”。英语可以译为 vicious, malignant, pernicious, grave, cutthroat。例如：

1. 圈地的后果是将贫穷农民陷入贫困的恶性循环。
   The effect of the land enclosure was to leave the poor peasants in a vicious circle of poverty.
2. 警方已对这个恶性刑事案件进行调查，其中受害者的性命仍处在危险之中。
   The police have investigated this vicious criminal case, in which the victim's life is still in danger.
3. 这个恶性刑事案件已对受害者家庭造成极大痛苦。
   This case of vicious crime has inflicted great pains on the family of the victim.
4. 由于一些工业部门恶性竞争正在增长，专家已经警告说存在可能恶化的商业氛围。
   Experts have warned of a possibly worsening business environment as

vicious competition is increasing in some industrial sectors.

5. 恶性竞争将不仅伤害企业，而且伤害整个工业和顾客。
Vicious competition will not only hurt enterprises, but also the whole industry and customers.
6. 现在存在着恶性竞争，它正在摧毁我们的经济。
There is now vicious competition that is devastating our economy.
7. 中药治疗恶性肿瘤有其独特的优势。
The treatment of malignant tumour with traditional Chinese medicine has its unique advantage.
8. 医生对女病人说她的肿瘤不是恶性的。
The doctor said to the woman patient that her tumour was not malignant.
9. 如果红血球形状异常，可能是恶性贫血所致。
If the red blood cells have a strange shape, it may be due to pernicious anaemia.
10. 那场恶性交通事故发生在冬季的一个寒冷刺骨的早晨。
The grave traffic accident occurred on a piercing chilly winter morning.
11. 大学生毕业后面临着恶性竞争。
University students are confronted with cutthroat competition after graduation.

“恶性通货膨胀”，又称“超级通货膨胀”，是“发展迅速的，性质严重的通货膨胀”，英语有许多方法表示，可以译为 galloping inflation, runaway inflation, rampant inflation, malignant inflation, vicious inflation, virulent inflation, boiling inflation, hyperinflation。例如：

12. 政府已采取有效措施遏制恶性通货膨胀。
1) The government has taken effective measures to curb the galloping inflation.
2) The government has taken effective measures to check the runaway inflation.
3) The government has adopted effective measures to halt the rampant inflation.
4) The government has adopted effective measures to curtail the malignant inflation.
13. 根据作者看法，中国经济不太可能发生恶性通货膨胀。
According to the author, the Chinese economy is unlikely to see galloping inflation.
14. 由于恶性通货膨胀，那个亚洲国家的货币大大贬值了。
Owing to runaway inflation, that Asian country’s currency has greatly depreciated.

15. 那个南美国家的恶性通货膨胀是由于货币供应量大大超过市场需求而引发的。
The rampant inflation in that South American country was triggered because the currency supply volume had greatly exceeded market demand.
16. 这次加息的目的是为了防止恶性通货膨胀。
The increase in interest rates this time is for the purpose of preventing malignant inflation.
17. 这位专家担心当衰退真的结束时，有产生另一轮恶性通货膨胀的严重危险。
This expert worries that when the recession is truly over, there is a serious danger of another round of vicious inflation.
18. 这位美国经济学家认为他们即将经历那种重新构建整个经济体系的恶性通货膨胀。
This American economist thinks they’re about to experience the kind of virulent inflation that will remake entire economies.
19. 恶性通货膨胀能大大削弱低收入家庭的购买力。
Boiling inflation can greatly erode the purchasing power of the families with lower income.
20. 这位经济学家认为没有什么良方能制止超级通货膨胀。
The economist holds that there are no remedies to bring the hyperinflation to a halt.

95

给力

汉语关键词： 给力、不给力

英语关键词： great, cool, fabulous, awesome, fantastic, wonderful, gorgeous, marvelous, exciting, encouraging, disappointing, discouraging, give strength, give a support

句子： 江苏给力“文化强省”。

误译： They have given a strength to Jiangsu for a culturally powerful province.

正译： They have given strength to Jiangsu for a culturally powerful province.

解释：

strength 作“力量”解时，是不可数名词，前面不能加不定冠词。如果 strength 前面加不定冠词，就变成可数名词，具有 advantage, strong point 的意思，即“优点”或“长处”，是 weakness, weak point（弱点、短处）的反义词。例如：

1. Plato says,"Good actions give strength to ourselves and inspire good actions in others."
   柏拉图说："善行给我们自己力量，也激励他人行善。"
2. In an interview, it is very important for you to give a strength that can compensate for your weakness.
   在面试中给出能弥补你的短处的一个长处，对你至关重要。

"给力"的第一个意思是"很牛"、"很棒"、"很酷"或"很精彩"，用作形容词，是对良好事物的客观赞扬。英语可以译为 great, cool, fabulous, awesome, fantastic, wonderful, gorgeous, marvelous。例如：

3. 许多网民称赞广州亚运会的开幕式很给力。
   Many netizens praised the opening ceremony of the Guangzhou Asian Games as very great.
4. 他刚买的苹果iPad平板电脑有许多新功能，太给力了。
   The Apple iPad that he has just bought has many new functions. It's really cool!
5. 我从来没有见过这样美丽的图画，太给力了。
   I have never seen such a beautiful picture. That's fabulous!
6. 你的谈话信息量大，而且富有启发性，真给力啊！
   Your talk is very informative and enlightening. It's really awesome!
7. 西班牙队又进一球，太给力了。
   The Spanish team has scored another goal. It is really fantastic!
8. 她唱歌那样有激情，那样专心，太给力了！
   She sings with such passion and devotion. That's wonderful!
9. 她跳舞非常优美，人们都赞誉她，真是给力！
   She dances very gracefully and people all praise her. It's really gorgeous!
10. 这些外国客人都喜欢这个幼儿园孩子们的表演。我想这太给力了。
    The foreign visitors all enjoy the performance given by the children in the kindergarten. I think it's marvelous.

"给力"的第二个意思是"带劲"、"令人振奋"、"令人鼓舞"，用作形容词，多与个人利益相关，是主观情感的流露。英语可以译为 exciting, encouraging。例如：

11. 老板又给员工加薪了，真给力。
    The boss has given his employees a pay rise. It is very exciting!
12. 我居然在上海世博会巧遇我三十多年没见的老同学。对我们俩来说，简直是太给力了。
    At the Shanghai Expo, I accidentally met one of my old classmates whom I hadn't seen for over 30 years. It's just exciting for both of us.

13. 我们工作的影响在增长，太给力了。
    It is encouraging that the influence of our work is on the rise.
14. 这名学生获得大学领导颁发的大奖。简直是太给力了。
    The student won a great award issued from the university authorities. That's simply encouraging!

"不给力"的意思是"令人失望"、"令人沮丧"。英语可以译为 disappointing, discouraging。例如：

15. 这堂课上得好枯燥，不给力呀!
    The class is very tedious. That is really disappointing.
16. 他不肯帮忙，真不给力。
    He has refused to give a helping hand. That is really discouraging!

"给力"的第三个意思是"给予力量"、"给予支持"，用作动词。英语可以译为 to give strength, to give a support。例如：

17. 我们的计划已经制订好了。大家要给力啊!
    Since our plan has been worked out, every of us should give a support.

96 贬值

汉语关键词： 贬值、货币贬值、通货贬值、跌价、掉价

英语关键词： devalue, depreciate, devaluation, depreciation, currency devaluation, currency depreciation, decrease in value, lose value

句子： 20国集团领导人同意避免竞争性货币贬值。

误译： The G20 leaders agreed to refrain from competitive devaluation of currency.

正译： The G20 leaders agreed to refrain from competitive devaluation of currencies.

解释：

如果说一种货币贬值，译成 currency devaluation 或 devaluation of currency，都是可以的。但是在这句话里，"20 国"和"竞争性"决定了不是一种货币，而是多种货币的问题，因此 devaluation of 后面要用复数 currencies，而不能用单数 currency。当然，将"竞争性货币贬值"译成 competitive currency devaluation，其中 currency 用作 devaluation 的定语，还是可以的。

"贬值"的第一个意思是"币值下跌"、"货币购买力下降"。英语可以译为 to devalue, to depreciate。例如：

1. 在1997年亚洲金融危机中，一些东南亚国家货币急剧贬值。
During the Asian financial crisis in 1997, the currencies of some Southeast Asian countries sharply devalued.
2. 随着1997年晚些时候的金融危机，许多东亚国家货币急速贬值。
Many East Asian currencies rapidly devalued following the financial crisis in late 1997.
3. 在拉丁美洲，货币贬值持续到2002年。
In Latin America, currencies depreciated until 2002.
4. 今年，这个拉丁美洲国家的货币一再贬值。
This year, the currency of this Latin American country has been depreciated time and again.

"货币贬值"，又称"通货贬值"，英语可以译为 currency devaluation, currency depreciation。例如：

5. 货币贬值可能引起贸易战。
Currency devaluation may lead to trade wars.
6. 货币贬值的第一个意思是通货膨胀或一种货币在一段时间里价值的下跌，而它的第二个意思是一种货币对另一种货币价值的下跌。
The first meaning of currency depreciation is inflation or the loss of value of a currency over a period of time while its second meaning is the loss of value of one currency against another.

"贬值"的第二个意思是"降低货币对黄金的含金量"或"降低本国货币对外币的比价"。英语动词可以译为 to devalue, to depreciate。名词可以译为 devaluation, depreciation。例如：

7. 上周，日元对美元贬值了。
Last week, the Japanese yen devalued against the U.S. dollars.
8. 在过去几周里，美元对欧元贬值了。
The U.S. dollars devalued against the Euro in the last few weeks.
9. 今年，所有的货币对黄金和白银贬值了。
All currencies have depreciated against gold and silver this year.
10. 比索对外国货币贬值使得移民工人的家庭能够改善他们的生活。
The peso's depreciation against foreign currencies has allowed families of migrant workers to improve their lives.

"贬值"的第三个意思是泛指"价值降低"，又称"跌价"或"掉价"。英语动词可以译为 to devalue, to depreciate, to decrease in value, to lose value。名词可以译为 devaluation, depreciation。例如：

11. 最近，过时商品跌价了。
Outdated goods have been devalued recently.
12. 新汽车一开上路就开始掉价了。
New cars start to depreciate as soon as they are on the road.
13. 年纪大一点的人们总是感到传统正在失去光彩，而他们积累的学问和知识也已经贬值。
Older people are always feeling that tradition is being dishonored and their accumulated lore and knowledge have depreciated.
14. 这名大学生说考试现在变得太容易，文凭也贬值了。
The university student said that the exams had now become too easy and the qualification devalued.
15. 既然我家房子跌价了，我的财产税也应该下降了。
Since my home decreased in value, my property taxes should also go down.
16. 铁路轨道或飞机场附近的房产容易跌价。
Property in the vicinity of railway tracks or airports is likely to decrease in value.
17. 从你开车离开卖家的那一分钟算起，汽车就掉价了。
The car loses value the minute you drive it out of the dealership.
18. 贬值现象正向经济领域以外延伸和扩展。
Devaluation phenomena are extending and expanding beyond the economic sector.

97 揭秘、解密、泄密

汉语关键词： 揭秘、解密、解密高手、加密、泄密

英语关键词： declassify, decode, decipher, cypherpunk, encrypt, encryption, decrypt, decryption, reveal a secret, leak a secret, disclose a secret, divulge a secret

句子： "维基揭秘"最近揭秘了大量的美国政府关于伊拉克和阿富汗战争的加密文件。

误译： WikiLeaks has recently declassified large amounts of classified US government documents concerning the wars in Iraq and Afghanistan.

正译： WikiLeaks has recently revealed large amounts of classified US government documents concerning the wars in Iraq and Afghanistan.

解释：

国内媒体对WikiLeaks有三种译法：维基解密、维基揭秘和维基泄密。“解密”是政府公开保密文件；“揭秘”是民间或非官方组织或个人揭露秘密；“泄密”是当事人或知情人泄露秘密。笔者认为将WikiLeaks译为“维基揭秘”比较合适。“解密”应译为to declassify，其意思是to state officially that secret government information is no longer secret。

“解密”的第一个意思是“政府解除对文件、档案等的保密措施，允许对外公布”。英语可以译为 to declassify。例如：

1. 这些外交文件现在已经解密。
   These diplomatic documents have now been declassified.
2. 国防科技成果解密的目的是为了加速成果转移，促进技术进步。
   The scientific and technological achievements for national defence are declassified for the purpose of accelerating achievement transfer and promoting technological progress.
3. 有关肯尼迪遭暗杀的档案尚待解密。
   The files on the Kennedy assassination have yet to be declassified.
4. 我不理解这些加密记录为什么已被解密了。
   I don't understand why these classified records have been declassified.

“解密”的第二个意思是“给加密的信息除去密码，使其还原为加密前的状态，以便获取信息”。英语可以译为 to decode, to decipher。例如：

5. 军方利用计算机来加密和解密信息。
   The military uses computers to encode and decode messages.
6. 这个程序可以用来安全地加密和解密信息。
   The programme can be used to encode and decode messages securely.
7. 我曾千方百计试图解密这些信息。
   I have tried every means to decipher these messages.

“解密高手”，英语可以译为 cypherpunk。例如：

8. 许多加密高手十分精通技术；他们非常了解密码，会写软件。
   Many cypherpunks are technically quite sophisticated; they do understand ciphers and are capable of writing software.
9. 他不愧是一名解密高手。
   He is worthy of being called a cypherpunk.
10. 这些文字很难懂，难倒了众多解密高手。
    These words are so difficult to understand that they have baffled many cypherpunks.

“解密”的第三个意思与“加密”相对应。“加密”是“在信息传输或存储中，采用密码技术对需要保密的信息进行处理，使得处理后的信息不能被非受权者（含非法者）读懂或解读”，动词可以译为 to encrypt，名词可以译为 encryption。“解密”是“处理保密的信息，使受权者能读懂或解读”，动词可以译为 to decrypt，名词可以译为 decryption，例如：

11. 加密锁软件用于加密和解密，以保护软件系统程序。
    Lock encryption software is used for encryption and decryption to protect software system procedures.
12. 加密允许交流双方通过他们独有的密钥对发送给对方的信息进行编码，而解密允许交流双方通过他们独有的密钥对对方发送的信息进行解码。
    Encryption allows two communicating parties to scramble information they send to each other via special keys only they possess, while decryption allows two communicating parties to unscramble information they send to each other via special keys only they possess.
13. 他要分割、合并、加密和解密这些文档。
    He wants to split, merge, encrypt and decrypt these files.

“揭秘”，即“揭露秘密”，应译为 to reveal a secret 或 to leak a secret。例如：

14. 这个线人许诺向警察局揭秘。
    The informer promised to reveal the secret to the police.
15. 这个网站最近揭秘了各种各样的原先保密的文件。
    The website has recently leaked a variety of formerly secret documents.

“泄密”，即“泄露秘密”，应译为 to disclose a secret, to divulge a secret 或 to leak a secret。例如：

16. 他从来没有泄密他的所见所闻。
    He never disclosed the secret what he had seen and heard.
17. 最近，这个委员会主席向一名报社记者泄了密。
    The chairman of the committee has lately divulged the secret to a newspaper reporter.
18. 这位外交官在一个鸡尾酒会上泄了密。
    The diplomat leaked the secret at a cocktail party.

98 收回

汉语关键词：收回、恢复行使主权

英语关键词：get back, take back, recall, recover, retrieve, repossess, recoup, reclaim, regain sovereignty over, withdraw, rescind, countermand, retract, revoke, tighten

句子：央行将上调准备金率，意在收回市场上过多的流动性。

误译：The central bank would raise the banks' reserve requirement ratio for the purpose of regaining excessive liquidity in the market.

正译：The central bank would raise the banks' reserve requirement ratio for the purpose of tightening excessive liquidity in the market.

解释：

"收回过多的流动性"的意思是"收紧过多的流动性"。在这里，"收回"没有"拿回来"的含义，不能译作 to regain。英语没有 to regain excessive liquidity 的搭配，应译为 to tighten excessive liquidity。

"收回"与"物归原主"或"物归原处"有关。"收回"的第一个意思是"拿回或重获发出去或借出去的东西，及借出去或用出去的钱"。英语可以译为 to get back, to take back, to recall, to recover, to retrieve, to repossess, to recoup, to reclaim。例如：

1. 借出去的书，你应该收回了。
   You should get back the books that have been lent out.
2. 他所有的钱都借出去了。眼下他还收不回来。
   All his money has been loaned out. He can't get it back for the moment.
3. 天开始下雨了，我急忙出去收回晾晒的衣服。
   As it was starting to rain, I hurried out to get back my drying clothes.
4. 我们收回了属于我们的东西。
   We took back what was ours.
5. 她收回了她的同班同学借她的自行车。
   She took back the bike that her classmate had borrowed from her.
6. 放款人在到期之前收回了贷款。
   The moneylender recalled a loan before the due date.
7. 秘书收回了已发出的文件。
   The secretary recalled the documents which had been issued.
8. 这些银行贷款将在接下来的十年里陆续收回。
   These bank loans will be recovered in succession over the next ten years.
9. 这位钻石公司经理想要收回一笔贷款，就向律师寻求帮助。

The manager of a diamond company wanted to retrieve a loan and turned to the lawyer for help.

10. 这所房子拖欠贷款，银行将会收回。
The house is in default and the bank will repossess it.
11. 我们希望头一年就能收回前期投资。
We hope to recoup our initial investment in the first year.
12. 如果你拖欠贷款，银行可以卖掉你的车，收回其余的钱。
If you default on your loan, the bank can sell your car and recoup the rest of its money.
13. 市政府将要收回这个城市的闲置土地和其他非法获得的地块。
The municipal government will reclaim the idle land and repossess other illegally acquired plots in the city.
14. 银行可以一经通知收回这些贷款。
The bank can reclaim these loans on demand.
15. 多余的差旅费必须全额收回。
The full amount of excess travelling expenses must be reclaimed.

“收回”的第二个意思是“拿回或重获失去的主权或领土”。但是“收回领土”是个敏感的话题。汉语表述要注意准确，英语翻译也要注意分寸。以“香港回归”为例。英国是归还领土的一方，而中国是收回领土的一方，亦即恢复行使领土主权的一方。外国媒体有如下的表述：

16. Britain returned Hong Kong to China on July 1st, 1997.
英国于1997年7月1日向中国归还香港。
17. China took back Hong Kong from Britain on July 1st, 1997.
中国于1997年7月1日从英国收回香港。
18. Britain handed over Hong Kong to China on July 1st, 1997.
英国于1997年7月1日正式将香港交给中国。
19. China took over Hong Kong from Britain on July 1st, 1997.
中国于1997年7月1日从英国接管香港。

我国不采用上述说法，而说“恢复行使主权”，英语译为 to regain sovereignty over。例如：

20. 中国于1997年7月1日恢复对香港行使主权。
China regained sovereignty over Hong Kong on July 1st, 1997.

再以“塔吉克归还领土”为例。外国媒体有如下说法：

21. Under the agreements already signed, China took back about 1,000 square kilometers of territory from Tajikistan.
根据已签署的协议，中国从塔吉克斯坦收回大约1,000平方公里领土。

我国不采用上述说法，而从另外一个角度叙述：

22. 根据已签署的协议，塔吉克斯坦将大约1,000平方公里领土归还中国。
Under the agreements already signed, Tajikistan returned about 1,000 square kilometers of territory to China.

“收回”的第三个意思是“撤回、撤销或取消意见、命令、承诺或说过的话”。英语可以译为 to take back, to withdraw, to rescind, to countermand, to retract, to revoke。例如：

23. 我可以收回我对她所做的评论，表示道歉，并让她确信我的善意。
I can take back the comment I made about her, offer an apology, and assure her of my good will.
24. 她丈夫收回了他关于要个孩子的事所说的话。
Her husband took back what he said about having a baby.
25. 这种旧硬币已经收回不再流通了。
The old coins have been withdrawn from circulation.
26. 我将收回我在早些时候答复时所说的话。
I'll withdraw what I said in my earlier reply.
27. 我坚持你必须立即收回你的那些冒犯人的话。
I insist that you withdraw your offensive remarks immediately.
28. 这些反对党下院议员强迫这位部长收回他的声明。
These Opposition Members of Parliament forced the minister to withdraw his statement.
29. 我敦促他收回他的建议。
I urged him to withdraw his proposal.
30. 这位法官收回了他签署的一个传票。
The judge rescinded an order he had signed.
31. 这个商人收回了购货的订单。
The merchant countermanded an order for goods.
32. 他作了假供词，后来又收回了。
He made a false confession which he later retracted.
33. 他们试图说服我收回我的话。
They tried to persuade me to retract my words.
34. 据《圣经》讲，上帝收回了对诺亚做出的不再水淹整个世界的承诺。
According to the Bible, God retracted his promise to Noah not to drown the entire world again.
35. 他没有收回他所说的关于她的隐私的话。
He retracted nothing that he had said about her privacy.
36. 经过卖主允许，你可以收回投标。

You can retract a bid with the seller's permission.

“收回”的第四个意思是“收紧流动的东西”。英语可以译为 to tighten。例如：

37. 这个渔夫开始收回渔网。
The fisherman began to tighten the fishing net.
38. 政府已采取一些有效措施收回市场上过多的流动性，防止通胀。
The government has taken some effective measures to tighten excess liquidity in the market and prevent inflation.

“收回”的第五个意思是“收缩到靠近主体的位置”。英语可以译为 to retract。例如：

39. 这只猫很快地把爪子收回。
The cat retracted its claws quickly.
40. 这只豚鼠收回爪子约两毫米。
The guinea pig retracted its paw by about two millimetres.
41. 这只鹰立即收回爪子，靠近身体，但再也一动不动。
The hawk immediately retracted its foot, pulling it in close to its body, but made no further move.
42. 这只狗把腿收回，放在身体下面。
The dog retracted its leg underneath its body.
43. 飞机起飞后，轮子收回。
The wheels retract after the aircraft takes off.
44. 轻型飞机飞行时起落架并非总是收回。
The undercarriage on light aircraft does not always retract during flight.
45. 起落架已完全收回。
The undercarriage has been fully retracted.

99 过去

汉语关键词：过去、从前、以前、以往、曾经、昔日、往日、旧日、旧时、老物件、应付、对付、过世

英语关键词：past, bygones, last, former, previous, old, old thing, old object, in the past, formerly, previously, pass, lapse, tick away, wear off, go over，walk over, pass by, go further, manage to cope with, pass away

句子：他在整理祖父的老宅时，发现了许多过去的东西。

误译：When he tidied up his grandfather’s old house, he found many former things.

正译：When he tidied up his grandfather’s old house, he found many old things.

解释：

former 用来修饰事情，不修饰具体的实物。former things 指“过去的事情”。而“过去的东西”就是“老物件”，要译为 old things 或 old objects。例如：

1. 这个青年学生问了我许多过去的事情。
   The young student asked me many former things.
2. 他的谈话使人回忆起许多过去的事情。
   His talk brought many former things fresh to remembrance.
3. 在这个博物馆里，能够看到许多过去的东西。
   1) We can see many old things in this museum.
   2) There are many old objects on show in this museum.
4. 这位正在中国拍电影的外国导演说在中国很难找到过去的东西。
   1) The foreign director who was making a film in China said that it was difficult to find old things in this country.
   2) The foreign director who was making a film in China said that old objects were difficult to get in this country.

“过去”的第一个意思是“说话时或某一特定时刻以前的时间，有别于现在和将来”，表示时间概念。汉语有“从前”、“以前”、“以往”、“曾经”、“昔日”、“往日”、“旧日”、“旧时”等同义词。名词可以译为 past, bygones。形容词可以译为 past, last, former, previous, old。副词可以译为 in the past, formerly, previously。例如：

5. 你显然对我的过去有一些了解。
   You clearly have some idea about my past.
6. 过去的事不是要美化的,也不是要怀念的或感伤的，因为过去的事已经过去。
   The past isn’t something to be glamorized, to be nostalgic about, or to be sentimental about, because the past is gone.
7. 他说他要让过去的事成为过去。
   He said he wanted to leave the past in the past.
8. 忘记过去就意味着背叛。
   Forgetting the past implies betrayal.
9. 这个失足青年下定决心与过去决裂。
   The juvenile delinquent made up his mind to break with his past.

10. 让过去的事成为过去吧。
Let bygones be bygones.
11. 在过去的几年里，我们城市的房价已急剧增长。
1) In our city, housing prices have risen sharply in the past few years.
2) In our city, housing prices have increased sharply over the last few years.
12. 他过去的邻居都搬到这个新建小区了。
1) His old neighbours have all moved to this newly-built residential area.
2) His past neighbours have all moved to this newly-built residential area.
3) His former neighbours have all moved to this newly-built residential area.
4) His previous neighbours have all moved to this newly-built residential area.
13. 当接到一个过去的同班同学的电话时，她非常高兴。
1) She was very happy when she received a phone call from one of her old classmates.
2) She was very happy when she received a phone call from one of her past classmates.
3) She was very happy when she received a phone call from one of her former classmates.
4) She was very happy when she received a phone call from one of her previous classmates.
14. 过去，这个地区经常发生地震。
In the past, earthquakes often occurred in this area.
15. 我们现在享用这些我们过去仅仅听说的舒适设施。
We now enjoy these comforts of which we formerly only heard.
16. 这家公司过去属于一个国际银行集团。
The company previously belonged to an international banking group.

“过去”的第二个意思是“时间流逝”（强调过程）或“时间消逝”（强调结果）。英语可以译为 to pass, to lapse, to tick away。例如：

17. 自从我们上次见面，五年已经过去了。
1) Five years have passed since we last saw each other.
2) Five years have lapsed since we last saw each other.
18. 他在童年过去以后就不再玩泥巴了。
He stopped playing with clay after his childhood lapsed.
19. 我必须在十点钟之前到达飞机场，而时间在一分钟一分钟地过去。
I had to get to the airport at ten and the minutes were ticking away.

20. 当他挚友生命的最后时刻在一秒钟一秒钟地过去的时候，他恐惧地注视着。
He watched in horror as the final seconds of his best friend's life ticked away.
21. 他在病房里的生活一个小时一个小时地过去。
The last hours of his life in the medical ward ticked away.

“过去”的第三个意思是“反应或作用逐渐消失”。英语可以译为 to wear off。例如：

22. 他一动不动地躺在床上，直到药物的作用过去。
He lay in bed motionless, until the effects of the drug wore off.
23. 她用冷水洗了洗脸，困劲儿顿时就过去了。
She washed her face with cold water, and her sleepiness wore off instantly.

“过去”的第四个意思是指“离开或经过说话人或被叙述对象的所在地，向另一个地点去”。表示空间概念。英语可以译为 to go over, to walk over, to pass by, to go further。例如：

24. 你在这里等着，我过去看看。
You just wait here, and I'll go over to have a look.
25. 妈妈轻轻地过去叫醒儿子。
Mother walked lightly over to wake up her son.
26. 一辆汽车刚从大门口过去。
A car has just passed by the gate.
27. 再过去是一个大池塘。
When you go further, you'll see a large pond.

“过去”的第五个意思是“应付”或“对付”。英语可以译为 to manage to cope with。例如：

28. 你不要太较真，只要能过去就过去了。
You don't need to take it too seriously. If you can manage to cope with it, you just do it.

“过去”的第六个意思是“过世”，是委婉语。英语可以译为 to pass away。例如：

29. 昨天夜里他祖父过去了。
Last night his grandfather passed away.

100 达人

汉语关键词： 达人、高人、高手、能手、专家、美丽达人、美容专家、情感达人、恋爱达人、爱情专家、管理达人、管理专家、历史达人、英语达人、音乐达人、数字达人、个性达人、魅力达人、网络达人、游戏达人

英语关键词： expert, talent, geek，beauty expert, beautiful expert, relations expert, expert of love, management expert, expert of history, expert of English, music talent, digital talent, talent with personality, talent with charm and charisma, Internet geek, game geek, wise man, open-minded person, successful person

句子： 她就如何护肤请教了一位美丽达人。

误译： She consulted a beautiful expert about skin care.

正译： She consulted a beauty expert about skin care.

解释：

“达人”指某方面比较擅长的专家。beautiful expert 的意思是 expert who is beautiful，即“相貌美丽的专家”。而“美丽达人”指美容专家，不是指自身相貌美丽的专家。“美丽达人”应译为 beauty expert，其意思是 expert who gives advice to people about how to make them beautiful。例如：

1. 这位美丽达人在护肤、护发、健康、时装潮流、整容、服装、化妆、化妆品和肢体语言等方面提供咨询。
   The beauty expert provides advice on skin care, hair care, health, fashion trends, plastic surgery, wardrobe, makeup, cosmetic products, and body language.

“达人”的第一意思是“在某一领域非常专业、出类拔萃的人”。或“在某方面很精通的人”。亦称“高人”、“高手”、“能人”或“专家”。英语可以译为 expert, talent, geek。“情感达人”，英语可以译为 relations expert。例如：

2. 最近我心里很纠结，想请一位情感达人来帮忙。
   As I have been entangled in my mind recently, I'd like to ask a relations expert for help.

“恋爱达人”，即“爱情专家”，英语可以译为 expert of love。例如：

3. 她被朋友们描述成为一个“恋爱达人”。
   She was described as an expert of love by her friends.

“管理达人”，即“管理专家”，英语可以译为 management expert。例如：

4. 如果你想要成为管理达人，你必须精通管理学。
If you want to become a management expert, you must have a good mastery of management science.

“历史达人”，英语可以译为 expert of history。例如：

5. 我不是历史达人，也不想自称是历史达人。我只是个在世界历史之中找到刺激的历史迷。
I am not an expert of history, nor do I claim to be. I am simply a history buff who finds thrill in world history.

“英语达人”，英语可以译为 expert of English。例如：

6. 你能在一夜之间变成英语达人，简直是太可笑了。
It is simply ridiculous that you can become an expert of English overnight.

“音乐达人”，英语可以译为 music talent。例如：

7. 作为一个音乐达人，他喜爱、关注、了解和精通音乐。
As a music talent, he has a love for, shows concern for, and has a good knowledge and mastery of music.

“数字达人”，英语可以译为 digital talent。例如：

8. 我们正在寻找一名兼职的或全职的数字达人，加入我们的数字生产团队。
We are looking for a digital talent, part-time or full-time, to join our digital production team.

“个性达人”，英语可以译为 talent with personality。例如：

9. 在和谐社会，个性达人可以有更多的发展和提高的机会。
In a harmonious society, a talent with personality may have more opportunities for development and advancement.

“魅力达人”，英语可以译为 talent with charm and charisma。例如：

10. 魅力达人能以自信和真诚控制舞台。
A talent with charm and charisma can hold the stage with confidence and truth.

“网络达人”，英语可以译为 Internet geek。例如：

11. 我发现到处都有网络达人。
I find there are Internet geeks everywhere.

“游戏达人”，英语可以译为 game geek。例如：

12. 他已经玩网络游戏多年，自夸是游戏达人。
He has been playing network games for many years and boasts of himself as a game geek.

“达人”的第二个意思是“通达事理的人”。英语可以译为 wise man。例如：

13. 达人知命。
1) A wise man is aware that all things depend upon the will of Heavens.
2) A wise man understands the will of Providence.

“达人”的第三个意思是“豁达豪放的人”。英语可以译为 open-minded person。例如：

14. 这位达人总是什么事情都想得开。
1) This open-minded person is always looking on the bright side of things.
2) This open-minded person is always looking at things from the bright side.

“达人”的第四个意思是“事业成功，并有一定财富的人”。英语可以译为 successful person。例如：

15. 这位达人不仅事业有成，而且拥有许多财富。
This successful person has not only made achievements in his career, but also owns a great deal of wealth.

附 录

附录1 汉语关键词索引（Index for Chinese Key Words）

雷人
达人

附录2 英语关键词索引（Index for English Key Words）